A Book of Puzzlements

Other Books by Herbert Kohl

The Age of Complexity
36 Children
The Open Classroom
Golden Boy as Anthony Cool
Reading, How To
Half the House
On Teaching
Math, Writing and Games
Growing With Your Children

With Judith Kohl
The View From the Oak

HERBERT KOHL

A Book of
Puzzlements

Play and Invention with Language

Schocken Books

NEW YORK

First published by Schocken Books 1981
10 9 8 7 6 5 4 3 2 1   81 82 83 84

Library of Congress Cataloging in Publication Data
Kohl, Herbert R.
A book of puzzlements.
Includes index.
1. Word games. I. Title.
GV1507.W8K63   793.73   81–40410
AACR2

Designed by Jackie Schuman

Manufactured in the United States of America
ISBN 0–8052–3786–0

A state of puzzlement is good for the young as it leads to a spirit of enquiry.

—*Lewis Carroll*

Acknowledgments

I would like to thank all of those people who have indulged and encouraged my obsession with language play. Special thanks to my children and their friends who always made time to try out a new game or answer a riddle, and to my typist Lorna Cordy who patiently and meticulously checked and rechecked all the games in the book. A final note of thanks to my wife, Judy, who has lived through the boring games, flat jokes, inadequate riddles, and all those other attempts at play that didn't work and won't be published.

Contents

Introduction

One day my family was at the beach. It was the time of year when the whales were migrating south to Baja California, and we were talking about the possibility that gray whales might become extinct. My son Josh, who was six at the time, picked up a long, sharp piece of driftwood and started throwing it at a log. I asked him if he was hunting whales and he replied that, no, he was hunting the hunters with his poonharp. My immediate impulse was to correct him and I told him it was a harpoon, not a poonharp. He insisted it was a poonharp and explained that a harpoon went from hunters to whales and a poonharp went from whales to hunters. He was right, it was a poonharp.

Josh has referred to that incident a lot. He thinks it's delightful that he invented a word that fit so well with what he meant. The experience for him consisted of that combination of play and seriousness which is an essential component of most creative work. However, what Josh did wasn't unique, the product of a special gift. Language is flexible and full of possibility. This is apparent in children's word play, but also in adult language, in punning, comedy, poetry, and other forms of experimentation with language. However, most play with language is neither random nor arbitrary. For example, just the other day a nine-year-old girl in my writing class began a story with these sentences: "Once there was a man who was a worrywart. He had a wife who was a hurrywart." Rachel's invention, like Josh's, was appropriate to her thoughts and structurally sensible. Josh reversed components of his word: harpoon became poonharp. Rachel used the same construction for her new word as its original form, only changing a part, echoing worrywart with hurrywart and opening the possibility of there being all kinds of other -wart words. What's interesting in these examples and many more I've seen of invented words is that the new words play with standard structures using reversals, substitutions, oppositions, ambiguities, sound similarities, rhymes. The work of comedians such as Richard Pryor, Robin Williams, and Lily Tomlin also uses the same techniques of invention.

Most of word play has this element of playing with standard structures about it. For example, there are times when the standard rules of speech are broken or when meaning is dissolved into nonsense while the inflection of speech is preserved. Many nursery and street rhymes have these characteristics. One I remember begins:

> Kiss your acker, your backer,
> Your big fat soda cracker
> Your GTO
> Your mama, your daddy
> Your big fat granny
> Got a hole in her panty
> Go beep beep down Filmore Street

The children who taught me the rhyme had no idea what an acker, backer, or GTO were, although perhaps these words did have meaning to the originators of the verse. Incidentally, I learned that street rhyme four years ago in Berkeley, California. Three weeks ago I heard it from a twelve-year-old boy in Point Arena, California, which is 150 miles north of Berkeley. His version went:

> Kiss my acker, my packa,
> My big fat soda cracker
> My BPO
> My mama, my daddy
> My big fat granny
> Got holes in her pantry
> Go beep beep beep down the street

The vitality and persistence of street rhymes is an indication of how much informal teaching and learning goes on among children, as are the secret codes they create to conceal messages and the word games they teach each other. Play and invention are central ways of acquiring power over speech, of learning to command one's language and use it in the service of one's thoughts. This is as true for adults as it is for children.

Throughout the world people play word games, invent or repeat riddles and jokes, solve puzzles, sing and chant, try to outdo each other in inventing praises and insults, and play games that involve rhymes and challenges and ritual recitations. Through this play with words, as well as through poetry and stories, people discover themselves as speakers and learn to develop their own personal voices. They also learn that speech can be used in many ways—that it can trick, persuade, question, ridicule, insult, praise, delight, inform, etc.—and therefore that it has great power. Play with words is one way to practice using different modes of speech and to experiment with controlling situations through the use of words.

Just recently I found myself the victim of such good-natured verbal manipulations. I walked into our kitchen, where my son Josh, my daughter Erica, and two of their friends were sitting at the table having a snack. They ignored me and I began to fix dinner. Then, in a whiny voice that she knew I didn't like, Erica said, "Heerb." I turned and said "What!" to which she replied, "You have five minutes to get rid of that word." I responded in the same way again and Josh said, "You have five minutes to get rid of that word." I burst out with "What word?" to which they all answered "That word." I turned to the stove exasperated and they smiled, very pleased with themselves. It took a few minutes for me to figure out what they were up to. The word I had to get rid of was "what." In my most commanding voice I said, "Erica!" and she answered "What?" to which the others, catching on that I had entered the game, said to her, "You have five minutes to get rid of that word."

There are many ways to play with language. Some people are inveterate punsters; others are obsessed with language challenges like crossword puzzles, acrostics, and Scrabble. Few people are so precise, literal, and humorless that they can't appreciate a deliberate and clever inversion of words, a striking image, or a joke that depends on verbal nuance. In this book I've brought together many of the different forms that have developed through play and invention with language. They range from simple anagrams and word chains through code and cipher systems, play songs and poetry, puns, fables, and proverbs, to games involving metaphor and other figures of speech. Some of the games, exercises, and puzzles are extremely simple; others are complex. There are many challenges for the reader to tackle.

Some involve the manipulation of letters; others, the creation of poems, images, even writing systems. A number of the exercises demand word play that seems easier for children than for adults. Making up riddles or fables, creating new symbol systems, developing insult and praise games seem to provide no problem to children, although many adults become awkward and embarrassed to try these exercises.

Recently I suggested to a group of friends that we sit around and make up and tell riddles. I felt silly asking them although everyone agreed. For the first few minutes all we could think of were "chicken crossing the road" and "moron throwing the clock out of the window" riddles that we dragged up from our childhood. After a while (and a few glasses of wine) we overcame our shyness with language and began to create riddles of our own. Some were silly, some actually quite ingenious. It turned out to be wonderful for us to be able to play with language, to let ourselves be silly, and to try to surprise each other with our riddles.

In addition to providing many puzzles and challenges, this book has another main emphasis—the creation of new puzzles and games. Throughout the text there are strategies for the development of new puzzlements as well as for variations on old ones. There are also suggestions about how to develop game and puzzle themes and how to go about inventing and solving puzzles with other people. For these reasons the book should be useful to teachers, although it should also be of interest to anyone concerned with language as a living and changing source of pleasure.

The book is organized around certain aspects of language. The first chapter deals with play involving letters and words, and ranges from simple word games through comic alphabets and more complex word combinations and transformations. The next chapter deals with the parts of speech and illustrates ways in which the nature of verbs, adverbs, adjectives, nouns, etc., can be explored through play. It also discusses the creation of new words.

Chapter 3 considers phrase and sentence variations, and Chapter 4 moves from the level of structure to the level of meaning, dealing with sense and nonsense. Many of the activities and challenges in that chapter deal with the distortion of meaning and the limits of language. The fifth chapter deals with images and figures of speech, while the sixth deals with proverbs, riddles, and fables, all of which are basically complex images.

The seventh chapter is an interlude of songs and poems that involve movement and dance. Chapter 8 deals with codes, ciphers, and other forms of concealing messages, and the last chapter deals with a variety of writing systems that use pictograms.

From this outline it can be seen that the book begins with simple elements—words and letters—proceeds through semantics and poetics, and ends with a consideration of whole writing systems. The chapters are independent of each other but there is a general flow from simple aspects of language to more complex and systematic ones. However, within each chapter there are puzzlements of differing levels of complexity. Some of the word challenges in Chapter 1 are as difficult as any in the last sections of the book. Since the emphasis of the book is on the development and testing of word puzzlements, I urge the reader to play and invent, and not worry about making mistakes. Also, corner friends and have them try out your creations. Hopefully, through some of the activities in this book, language will seem as alive and full of wonder to adults and schoolchildren as it does to infants playing with their first words and just discovering the wonders of language.

Note: At the back of the book are teaching suggestions related to the material in the body of the text. An asterisk (*) indicates that suggestions related to specific games or game techniques are to be found in this final section.

A Book of Puzzlements

* At the back of the book are teaching suggestions related to the material in the body of the text. An asterisk (*) indicates that suggestions related to specific games or game techniques are to be found in this final section.

Warm-Up Games*

Go masters in Japan warm up by playing Dozo, a game that is much simpler than Go, takes a short time to play, and yet presents a challenge. Similarly, here are some warm-up problems that involve combinations of letters. In their simplest forms they take only a few minutes to solve. However, the addition of a few new conditions turns them into complex puzzles. I've found it useful to warm up with simple language challenges before tackling complex problems. Warming up seems to loosen my hold on everyday language and put me in the mood to think about language in a playful manner. It's not very different from warming up in baseball or basketball or soccer, and it's a relaxing way to get ready to play more seriously.

A-to-Z Words

Make up a list of words which contain all the letters of the alphabet. This is a simple challenge which could be met by going through a dictionary and picking a word at random under each letter listing. However, the resulting list of twenty-six words is cumbersome. Here's a list of seven words which contain all the letters in the alphabet:

command	yak	jazz
exhibit		squaw
flip		verge

Are there any shorter lists? What is the shortest list of words that contain all the letters of the alphabet (given a certain dictionary that determines acceptable words). These last questions turn the original challenge into complex problems that could best be solved with computer assistance. That seems to be the case with most simple word challenges—change the terms and conditions a bit and the complexity increases geometrically rather than arithmetically.

A-to-M and
N-to-Z Words

Make up words that use only the letters of the first half of the alphabet, i.e., A B C D E F G H I J K L M. Then make up sentences using those words. Try to take the exercise a bit further and make up a story. Then try the same things with words made out of the letters of the second half of the alphabet: N O P Q R S T U V W X Y Z.

A bit of practice makes it clear that the first half of the alphabet, with A, E, and I, is easier to work with than the second half. It also helps highlight the role vowels play in our language and writing system. Here are some A-to-M words and some N-to-Z words:

> A–M   ham, deed, flake, male, female
> N–Z   zoo, not, strum, prow, stun

What is the longest A-to-M word you can find? N-to-Z word? How did you go about finding it? Are there any systematic ways to find A-to-M and N-to-Z words? Here's a partial strategy. Begin with a vowel and build on it, adding letters from the half of the alphabet that it belongs to. For example,

A   U
AD   PUT
FAD   PUTT
FADE PUTTS

OO–EEE

List words like "s*oo*n" with two of the same letter. List words like "m*e*l*ee*" with three of the same letter. List words like "ind*e*p*e*nd*e*nc*e*" with four of the same letter.

Are there any words with five or more of the same letter? What is the greatest number of times a letter appears in a word (given a particular dictionary, of course)? Again, the simple challenge can easily be made complex.

NOSPACE

Write a number of words together with no spacing in between them. Then ask someone to pick out as many words as he can in a certain time (30 seconds or a minute or two). A sample run of words:

MEWASHOWTOHOMEGOHE

Another way to deal with the same run of words is to ask who can separate the words and recombine some of them into a sentence. One sentence that can be teased out of the sample above is "How was he to go home?" Is there another one?

Carefully designed runs can be developed so that all the words can make a sentence. The simplest way to do this is to write a sentence first and then scramble it.

G GRID IS D S

Start with the alphabet and pick any ten letters you choose. Then build a Scrabble-like grid and see if you can use up all ten letters (words can only be read from right to left and from top to bottom). For example, starting with A, E, M, N, P, S, I, B, T, and O, here's a grid using all ten:

B
MEN
A
TIPS
O

Now try with twelve, fifteen, twenty, and twenty-six letters if you want to make the exercise more complex. I haven't been able to make a continuous grid with the whole alphabet using each letter only once, and I wonder whether it's possible. It would also be interesting to explore the question of how many (and which) letters have to be used several times to make the smallest possible continuous grid.

Building Words

The combination PRE begins many English words. Can you make a list of PRE-words that start with four letters and increase a step at a time up to ten-letter words without using a dictionary?

PRE
PRE_
PRE_ _
PRE_ _ _
PRE_ _ _ _
PRE_ _ _ _ _
PRE_ _ _ _ _ _
PRE_ _ _ _ _ _ _

Here's one list:

   pre/ prep/ preen/ pretty/ prevent/ precious/ premature/ precocious

Try the same thing with words beginning with

BAR-, TO-, NO-, PRO-

Then vary the exercise and try to build lists with endings such as

_ER   _ON   _IST

Another variation could consist of building out from the center of a word:

_ E_
_ _ E_ _
_ _ _ E_ _ _
etc.

For example: met, steam, streams.

Word Tic-Tac-Toe

Start by drawing a three-by-three grid (which is actually the same as a Tic-Tac-Toe grid):

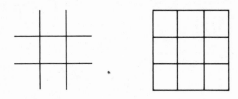

Then players take turns adding letters to the grid, scoring one point for each letter of each word they make until no more words can be made. Words can be made horizontally, vertically, and diagonally from bottom to top and top to bottom. Here's a sample game:

		H	E
	I	I	I
	S	S	S

	Points			
Player 1	1		3	
Player 2		2		2

S	H	E		S	H	E		S	H	E		S	H	E
	I				I	E		P	I	E		P	I	E
	S				S				S			P	S	L

Totals

	Points				
Player 1	3		3	3	13
Player 2		0		3	7

Sometimes there are multiple scores in this game. For example, in this situation two words can be made and the player gets a score for each word:

+	0	+		+	0	+
		0	→	N	0		score 4

There is a solitaire version of this game. The goal is to try to get a maximum score by making words that read in the following ways:

Another version can have any number of players. All draw their own grids and, within a certain time limit, fill in the grids trying to get the maximum number of words (and therefore points).

In order to make all of these versions somewhat more complex, a principle can be borrowed from Scrabble and the letters can be given weighted scores. One way of doing this is:

1 point: a, d, e, i, m, o, p
2 points: b, c, g, j, l, n, r, s, t, u
3 points: f, h, k, v, w
4 points: q, x, y, z

Then the word ZIP would be worth six points and TIP would be worth four. Of course there are many other weighting systems and it's fun for a group to make up several systems and experiment to discover which one makes the game most challenging.

There are other restrictions that can be tried. For example, here are three: (1) all repetitions of letters can be eliminated; (2) each player must choose ten letters before the game starts and neither player can show the other the letters chosen; (3) words can be made from top to bottom and right to left as well as diagonally. Thus words can be formed in the following ways:

(4) Finally, the board can be enlarged and the game played on a grid of any size (four by four, five by five, etc.).

Guess the Word

Here is a simple version of one of the most interesting word-guessing games I've come upon, as well as a description of some of its more complex variations. The game was shown to me by a friend, Reed Hamilton, who said that his grandmother learned it from her grandmother a hundred years ago in western Pennsylvania.

The game is for two players. One player writes a word down on a slip of paper. Before each play, the number of letters in the word is agreed upon. It is up to the second player to guess the word. On a separate piece of paper the second player writes down his or her first guess. Then the first player gives the following information about the guess: (1) whether the word has been guessed or not; (2) how many right letters in the right position have been guessed; and (3) how many right letters but in the wrong position have been guessed.

The second player keeps on guessing until the initial word is guessed correctly. A simple way to score the game is to give each player one point per guess. Then after five or ten turns each, the player with the *lowest* score (i.e., the fewest total number of guesses) wins.

Here is a sample game with three-letter words (✔ means a correct letter in the correct place, "X" means a correct letter in the wrong place, "0" means nothing correct):

Target word: POT

Guess	Feedback
1. HAT	✔
2. TOY	✔ X
3. HOT	✔ ✔
4. POT	✔ ✔ ✔

Score 4

Using five-letter words creates a much more complex game. Here's an example with the target word "grump."

Target word: GRUMP

Guess	Feedback
1. FOUND	✔
2. BOUND	✔

At this point the player guessing can be sure that F and B are not in the target word and that one of the letters O U N D is correct and in the correct place.

It is useful when playing a complex version of this game to write the alphabet on a sheet of paper and cross out letters you've eliminated and circle those you're sure about. At this stage the alphabet would look like this:

A B̸ C D E F̸ G H I J K L M N O P Q R S T U V W X Y Z

Guess	Feedback
1. FOUND	✔
2. BOUND	✔
3. ROUND	✔ X

R is now a letter that one can be sure is in the word, but it has to be moved about.

A B̸ C D E F̸ G H I J K L M N O P Q Ⓡ S T U V W X Y Z

4. FRUMP ✔ ✔ ✔ ✔

A lucky close guess. Usually the game goes on much longer than this.

5. GRUMP ✔ ✔ ✔ ✔ ✔
Score: 5

For young children the following versions of the basic game seem effective:

1. Begin with a three-letter word with the ending known, e.g., _ AT (initial word CAT).
2. Begin with a three-letter word with the middle vowel known, e.g., _ O_ (initial word POP).
3. Use three-letter words.
4. Play a silent E game, using words of the form _ _ _ E, for example (initial word LIKE).

There are also versions in other languages. Here are some simple Spanish versions:

1. Begin with four-letter words where the last two letters are known, e.g., _ _ SA (initial word CASA).
2. Beginning with four-letter words where the first two letters are known, e.g., ME_ _ (initial word MESA).
3. Begin with four-letter words with only the last letter given, e.g., _ _ _ A (initial word HADA).

Of course the game can be played with words of any length. The longer the words, the more the information you gather has to be sorted and the more complex the game becomes.

It is possible to make a wooden board to use for simple versions of this guessing game. Cut out a rectangular piece of wood eight by sixteen inches. Then coat one side of the wood with blackboard paint. After the paint dries, cut a groove across the board about four inches from the end:

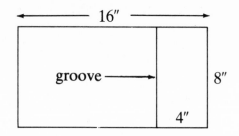

Cut out a piece of cardboard eight inches long and four inches high. Then, using chalk, you can play the game by hiding the target word behind the cardboard barrier:

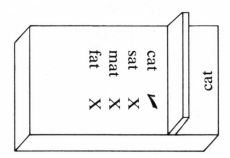

Dan Peletz, who teaches fifth grade at Longfellow School in Berkeley, showed me a complex version of the basic word-guessing game.

1. The first player writes down a five-letter target word.
2. The second player then writes down any five-letter word and asks the first player if the target word and the first guess word have any letters in common. The answer is either yes or no.
3. The second player keeps on putting down five-letter words until he or she is ready to guess at the target word.
4. The game continues until the target word is guessed. Each of the guesses counts as one point. The players switch roles when a word is guessed correctly. After several turns, the points are added up and the player with the lowest number of points is the winner. The reason this game is more complex than the others is that less information is given after guesses, leaving more possibilities open. If you find this game easy, try it with eight-letter words.

Finally, there is a different version of Dan Peletz's guessing game called Jotto. It is usually played by two people, although any number can play. Each player puts down a five-letter target word on a piece of paper. The players then take turns guessing at each other's target words. After each guess the player guessing is told how many letters the guessed word has in common with the target word. The first player who guesses the other's word wins. Here's a short game of Jotto:

Player 1	*Player 2*
target word: TIMER	target word: SMOKE
guess 1: STOVE	response 1: 3
response 1: 2	guess 1: GRAPE
guess 2: SLOPE	response 2: 3
response 2: 2	guess 2: TABLE
guess 3: SMOKE (wins!)	

SMOKE was a good guess, but the word could have been POKES, which would have been harder to figure out.

Some target words are more difficult than others. Words with repeated letters, for example, can be a problem for there is no simple way of knowing in Jotto whether letters are the same or different. One of the readers of this manuscript came up with two difficult Jotto words: KHAKI and USURY. Can you think of others of equal difficulty?

Letter and Word Puzzlements

Some Comic Alphabets
Combinations
Transformations

Some Comic Alphabets*

Here is one of the first comic alphabets. It was brought out by Thomas Nelson, a Scottish publisher, in 1876:

A is an ARCHER alarmed, for his arrow,
Aimed at an antelope, stuck in a sparrow.
B is a BUTCHER, both burly and bluff;
Bob, his big bull-dog, is ugly enough.
C is a CAPTAIN, commanding a corps,
Courageous as Cromwell's companions of yore.
D is a DAMSEL, dashingly dressed,
Delighted in pleasing, and doing her best.
E, an ESQUIRE, of course nothing less;
Elegant both in his manners and dress.
F is a FARMER, ploughing his field;
For if he neglects it, no crop will it yield.
G is a GAMBLER, throwing the dice.
Gambling, young folks, is a terrible vice.
H is a HUNTER, pointing his gun;
His aim is so bad, the deer think he's in fun!
I, an INNKEEPER, intent on his gain,
Imbibing malt liquor, and muddling his brain.
J is a JOINER, large-headed and lank,
Just now he is busy in sawing a plank.
K is a KING, of ancient renown,
Keeping his sword up to fight for his crown.
L is a LADY: how graceful her airs!
Lace cap, and lace trimmings, and bugles she wears.
M is a MISER: he sits in the cold.
Minding his bank-notes, and silver, and gold.
N is a NOBLEMAN, Numskull his name,
No one has ever yet heard of his fame.
O is an OYSTER-GIRL, healthy and strong;
Oysters from market she carries along.
P is a PIPER, a pibroch he'll play;
Please don't forget the poor piper to pay.
Q is a QUACK, empty-headed and vain,
Quick to take money, unskilled to ease pain.
R is a ROBBER, now forcing a door;
Right glad shall we be to see robbers no more.
S is a SAILOR, the pride of the crew—
See how he laughs!—Is he laughing at you?
T is a TINKER, an active young man,
Tin kettles and saucepans he mends when he can.
U is a USURER, nothing he lends

Unless to his *interest* greatly it tends.
V is a VETERAN, never yet famed;
Victory left him in poverty, maimed.
W is a WAITER, when gentlemen dine,
With bowing and scraping he brings them the wine.
X, XENOPHON, fought in a battle; and then
Xenophon wrote about many great men.
Y is a YEOMAN, his weapons are bright;
Yet he hopes he may never be called upon to fight.
Z is a ZANY, in motley array;
Zanies, in plain dress, are seen ev'ry day.

It's fun to make up rhyming comic alphabets. I've found it is best done by a group of people together. There are a number of ways to go about developing the rhymes. One person can do the first (letter) line and the next complete the rhyme. Each letter line can begin

A is for _____

or   A is a _____

or   A woke one day _____

or   A met a _____
                    etc.

Here are some examples of couplets generated by two people:

1. A is for an apple, big as could be.
2. It grew so large, it toppled the tree.

1. B is a big barn
2. Full of purple yarn.

1. C awoke one day and found his cat
2. Running away from a giant rat.

1. D met death one day
2. And quick as he could, turned away.

Another way to develop a rhyming alphabet is have people take alternate lines and give each letter only one line. Thus:

1. A is for an ant on a rug.
2. B is for a baby to hug.
1. C is for a car that moves fast.
2. D is for the devil at last.

A third type of comic alphabet tells a story rather than listing twenty-six separate entries. Here's an old story alphabet that's included in Iona and Peter Opie's *The Oxford Nursery Rhyme Book* (London: Oxford, 1955):

A was an Apple-pie;

B bit it;	M mourned for it;
C cut it;	N nodded at it;
D dealt it;	O opened it;
E eat it;	P peeped in it;
F fought for it;	Q quartered it;
G got it;	R ran for it;
H had it;	S stole it;
I inspected it;	T took it;
J joined for it;	U upset it;
K kept it;	V viewed it;
L longed for it;	W wanted it;

X, Y, Z, and Ampersand,
All wish'd for a piece in hand.

There are many ways to begin a story alphabet. Here are some you could use:

A bought a _____
A took a walk
A fell down
A got kissed
    etc.

One alphabet I did with my children began

A got kissed
B got missed
C cried and
D died
E decided to start again so
F got kissed and
G got hissed
    etc.

This was not as sophisticated as the example; we forgot to use verbs beginning with the appropriate letters.

Here's a second effort which sticks to the original alphabet:

A was asked
B balked and
C cried
D decided but
E made no effort so
F forfeited and
G gave up.

In creating story alphabets it has been useful to end lines with words like "but," "and," or "so" in order to bring the story along. When done by a lot of people those words set a challenge and a direction to the next player.

There is one other type of comic alphabet that is much more difficult to create. It depends on puns, word plays, and sound equivalents, and could be called a literary phonetic comic alphabet although some of its humor can be pretty low. The first such alphabet was devised by Jonathan Swift somewhere between 1710 and 1724. Swift called it his Guinea alphabet and used the Greek alphabet. It began:

> half a Guinea   (alpha Guinea)
> bet a Guinea   (beta)
> game a Guinea (gamma)
> dealt a Guinea (delta)

In English phonetic alphabets, common puns are:

> A (hay) is for horses
> A for gardener (Ava Gardner)
> A for disiac (aphrodisiac)
> B for dinner (beef for dinner)
> B for honey (a honeybee)
> C for yourself
> D for ential (differential)
> D for nition (definition)

Each pun begins with a letter and the word "for" (e.g., A for _____, M for _____). Here is a list of other common phonetic puns:

E

E for or (<u>either</u>).
E for you do or you don't.

F

F for T (effort).
F for yours ("ever yours").

G

G for creepers (popular song: "Jeepers Creepers").

H

H for himself (<u>each for</u> himself; also: "H for all," with clue "Each for all, and all for each").

I

I for get, or got (<u>I</u> <u>forget</u> or <u>forgot</u>).

J

J for E (Jeffery).

K

K for a drink ("care for a drink?").
K for teria (cafeteria).

L

L for Bet (alphabet, pronounced "elferbet").

M

M for sis (emphasis).
M for size and M for tick (emphasize).

N

N for red rays (infrared rays).
N for mation (information).

O

O for board (overboard).

R

R for the doctor (say ah for him).

S

S for you (as for you).

T

T for two (this comes from the song "Tea for Two").
T for golf or golf ball (tee).

U

U for mism (euphemism).
U for mystic (euphemistic).

X

X for breakfast (eggs).

Developing phonetic alphabets is more difficult than spinning out other comic alphabets. I've found it easiest to work with a group of people a letter at a time and produce a common product. We begin with the form:

_____ for _____

For example:

> A for ism (aphorism)
> B for the ball is over
> C for birds over there on the fence
> D for payments
>   etc.

Combinations*

Letter and word combinations are ways of deriving new words from given words without adding new letters. A simple combination exercise consists of combining the letters of a given word to make other words. Thus the letters of PART can be combined to yield: PAT, TAP, RAT, TAR, ART, RAP, A, AT, TARP.

Here are some more complex challenges and versions of the *words-in-a-word* game and other examples of combinations:

Bad Mixers

Can you think of words of three or more letters which yield no new words however the letters are combined? (These words can be called bad mixers.) Two-letter words are simple: TO only yields T, O, and OT, none of which is a word (at least in my dictionary), and OX yields O, X, and XO, which are not words (in English at least; should the challenge allow words in other languages?).

With three-letter words it gets more complex. Let's try TRY, a likely candidate. Here are the possibilities:

TRY:			
RYT	TR	T
YTR	TY	R
YRT	RT	Y
TYR	YT	
RTY	RY	
	YR	

The only likely candidate is TYR, which is not listed as a word in the *Shorter Oxford English Dictionary,* so we have one example. Can you come up with others? What about four- and five-letter words?

I've been unable to come up with any common words with more than three letters that do not yield other words, although trying has left me in awe of the power and scope of combinations of a small number of sounds and letters.

Two-Letter Words

How many two letter words are listed in most dictionaries? Here is a list of two-letter words:

AD	AX	HA	IF	ME	ON	SO
AM	BE	HE	IN	MY	OR	TO
AN	BY	HI	IS	NO	OW	US
AT	DO	HO	IT	OF	OX	WE
AS	GO	ID	MA	OH	PA	

How many new words can one make by adding just one letter to these new words? For example, from the word AD you can get:

AND	MAD	HAD	(etc.)
SAD	PAD	FAD	

Using the list, there are other interesting problems. For example, how many words can be generated by combining two or more words on the list. GO and AT make GOAT, ME and OW make MEOW, SO and ME produce SOME. How many others are there?

It's interesting that in making these combinations sometimes the sounds of the letters change. The O in ON and A in AT produce the OA combination in GOAT.

Here's another challenge. What is the longest word one can make out of the letters in the list? Can you set any other problems for yourself using the list?

Buried Words and Word Interlocks

Some words have other words buried within them. For example *meat* has *eat* within it, and *robot* has *rot* (*ro*b*ot*). A buried word can either have letters that are consecutive in the original word (like *eat* in *meat*), or can be found by skipping over some letters although retaining the original order in the main word like (*rot* in *robot*). Here are some other examples of buried words:

Buried in *captain:* cat, cap, tin, pin, tan, in, pain
Buried in *outside:* out, side, tide, tie, outs, ide, id, I
Buried in *mother:* moth, other, her, the

One way to develop buried-word challenges is to make a list of words and see how many buried words the list generates. For example, here's a list to try:

> information
> understanding
> forgotten
> withdrawal
> foundation

Another way of posing a buried-word problem is to give a list of words and then find as many as you can of the words they are buried in. For example: *the* is buried in *mother, father, thrower, betrothed.*

Are there words that bury the following words in such a way that all the letters in the buried word *do not* appear consecutively:

net (consecutive)
wait
hour
smell
fiend

Here are a few words that are buried in this strong sense of one word's being buried in another word:

cad is buried in command
pay is buried in psychiatry

There is an even stronger imbedding or burial of words in each other called *word interlocks*. I came upon this imbedding in an article by Ross Eckler in *Games and Puzzles* magazine. Word interlocks are two (or more) words which are buried in another word and which between them use all the letters in the burying word in the order of their appearance. Trivial examples of word interlocks are compound words. "Understand," for example, consists of *under* and *stand*. Nontrivial examples are:

(d) r (a) w i (n) g s consists of *dawn* and *rigs*

(a)(c) h i (e) v e s consists of *ace* and *hives*

Can you break down the following words into their interlocking parts?

birdseed	(reed, bids)
schooled	(hoe, scold)
bracelet	(race, belt)
magnetic	(magic, net)

One way to discover more interlocks is to make a list of words and examine them systematically. Another way is to start with one or two small words and see if they somehow could be interlocked. For example, start with a word like "net," and write it down with the letters spread apart so that interlocking letters could be added:

n   e   t

The addition of an *s* keeps a word and seems to be a good beginning

n   e   s   t

In fact, by just adding an *ing* a word interlock results:

(n)(e) s (t) i n g   consists of *net* and *sing*

Another word one might start with is

r   a   t

An *e* would produce

r   a   t   e

and then *i* at the beginning would produce (i)(r) a t (e), which is an interlocking product of *ire* and *at*.

Of course constructing word interlocks is not as easy as it might seem from these successful examples. In addition to *rat* and *net*, I played around with *red, bed, bit, sad, mat,* and *pit* without any success. (That doesn't mean that they can't be used to construct interlocks, just that I didn't come up with any that time. One of the readers of the manuscript came up with two: *breeding = being + red;* and *breaded = read + bed.*)

Palindromes and Semordnilaps*

There are some words that have interesting combinatorial characteristics. For example, there are certain words (or sentences) that read the same backward and forward. They are called *palindromes*. An old joke claims that Adam's first words to Eve were in the form of a palindrome. He was supposed to have said "Madam, I'm Adam."

The word "eve" is another palindrome. It's not difficult to think of three-letter palindromes. Here are a few:

tot	mom	sis	pep
pop	Nan	eye	

Here are five four-letter palindromes:

toot	poop	peep
boob		noon

Moving on to five letters we find words such as: *level, rotor, radar,* and *stats* (which is admittedly an abbreviation for statistics); but as the words get longer, it gets harder to find palindromes. It is a challenge to find any that are five letters or longer. Here are a few:

kayak	madam	shahs
sexes	rotor	civic
solos	tenet	redder
refer		reviver

Whole-sentence palindromes are hard to come by, although simple ones can be made out of words that are palindromes. A few made out of some of the palindromes listed above are:

mom eye mom
tot eye tot
peep, sis, peep
toot, pop, toot
sis, level sis

Going beyond this Dick and Jane simplicity, here are a few classical palindromes:

STEP ON NO PETS.
WAS IT A RAT I SAW?
LIVE NOT ON EVIL.
A MAN, A PLAN, A CANAL—PANAMA!
NO LEMONS, NO MELON.
NO EVIL, LIVE ON!

Lewis Carroll created his own version of palindromes; words that spell other words in reverse. His favorite example was DOG. Carroll called a word with this characteristic a *semordnilap* (why?). Here are a few:

no   deliver   pin   not
evil   repaid   top

Try to discover others and even to put them together to make sentences which are also semordnilaps. Here is one:

NO EVIL REPAID.

A dictionary comes in handy here. Take any page at random and try to spell every word on the page backward and see if any palindromes or semordnilaps result. I know this might sound a little farfetched, but word play can become obsessive and one never knows what can be discovered on a random page of a dictionary.

Anagrams

Anagrams are scrambles of particular words or phrases. The word "anagram" comes from the Greek *ana* meaning anew and *gram* meaning something written, and means making some new written form out of another one. Here are two anagrams of "anagram": NAG A RAM and RAM A NAG.

The simplest way to create anagram puzzles is to scramble the letters in some words and ask people to discover the word (or words) that can be made from these letters. Simple three-letter anagrams can be fun for young children to unscramble:

TPO *leads to* TOP *and* POT
ATC *leads to* CAT *and* TAC
TMA *leads to* MAT

Here are some more three-letter scrambles:

TFA PLA IST ORT

A slightly more complex way of presenting anagrams is to scramble three-, four-, and five-letter words that have a common theme which gives focus to the process of unscrambling. Here are a few examples:

Theme: the weather
Words to unscramble:

NWOS	(snow)	ANIR	(rain)
UYNNS	(sunny)	THO	(hot)
ODLC	(cold)	GFO	(fog)

Theme: animals
Words to unscramble:

NIOL
ITREG
GDO
SHFI
ANLSI

Another way to play with anagrams is to turn one word into another using all and only the letters of the first word. This is easy to do with a lot of three-letter words like POT (TOP), RAT (TAR), PIT (TIP), etc. Four-letter words present more of a challenge:

LAME	to	MALE
COAT	to	TACO
SLID	to	LIDS
TIME	to	MITE

Try some of these:

MEAN	to	?
SANG	to	?
MADE	to	?
PART	to	?

Try one with five letters:

BRUSH   to   ?

As the number of letters increases a lot more play with letters and combinations of letters is involved to transform one word into another. Here are some to try:

ADMIRER	(MARRIED)
ANGERED	(ENRAGED)
ASTRONOMERS	(MOONSTARERS)
CIPHERS	(SPHERIC)
DETOUR	(ROUTED)

The above five anagrams were gotten from Howard Bergerson's book *Palindromes and Anagrams* (New York: Dover, #20664–5), in which he lists 1169 anagrams which have the interesting property of relating the meaning of the starting word or phrase to the one it gives rise to. He does not restrict himself simply to word anagrams, but gives examples of words and phrases transformed into other phrases as well as words. Here are some examples:

THE ANSWER	to	WASN'T HERE
THE ACCIDENTAL	to	CHANCE DEALT IT
THE BAYONETS	to	THEY STAB ONE
BURYING THE HATCHET	to	(a) BUTCHERING THY HATE
		(b) THEY CURB THE HATING
BELLIGERENTS	to	REBELLING SET
CONSIDERATE	to	CARE IS NOTED
CONSTRAINT	to	CANNOT STIR

Anagrams with related meaning are more difficult to uncover than simple word transformations. It might make sense to begin simply by trying to create any phrase from a word first. Just pick a long word, say, CONSTITUTION, and play with it. I find it easier to write each letter on a little slip of paper and move them around on a tabletop than to try to write out each variation. I came up with the three words—CUTS, IT, and NOTION—and combined them into the somewhat awkward phrase NOTION IT CUTS, not at all comparable with the ones Bergerson has collected, but a beginning.

Lewis Carroll, who was an ingenious inventor of games and puzzles as well as an author, composed anagrams on names of famous people. One of his best is:

FLORENCE NIGHTINGALE to FLIT ON, CHEERING ANGEL

I showed this to some young people and they suggested that we try our hands at constructing an anagram of THE ROLLING STONES. We wrote down the name and started playing with ROLL ON THE, leaving the letters ING and STES. A number of words were possible with these letters: STING, SING, SINGS, and STINGS, which would have given us ROLL ON THE STINGS, but left an E. That, added to ON, gave the four words ONE STINGS ROLL THE. We played with combinations of these words:

THE ONE ROLL STINGS
ONE STINGS THE ROLL
THE STINGS ROLL ONE

and finally

ROLL THE STINGS ONE

We printed this up as part of an anagram puzzle of names of rock groups:

hint	*anagram of*
1. English group	ROLL THE STINGS ONE

Because the word "roll" was in the anagram many students got the answer quickly. In order to get more of a mix of letters and make the anagram more remote from the original spelling, another group took a crack at THE ROLLING STONES. I suggested that they begin by writing down the letters in a random way so that they wouldn't be so tempted to use words like "roll" which gave away the group. They put down the letters in ROLLING STONES, dropping the "the"

IL   LSST   O   OR   N   NGE

Then they picked out the word TROLLS, given that the Stones are a little wicked. After that they constructed SING and so had SING TROLLS, leaving the letters O, N, and E. Everything fell into place and the final anagram was

SING ONE, TROLLS

It's fun to have two groups of people make up lists of anagrams of pop groups, book titles, singers, or historical characters, and then try to solve each other's list. It makes sense to ask that the anagram refer in some way, however remote, to the original.

As a final challenge at the end of this section on anagrams, here are a number of the phrases from Dmitri Borgmann's book *Language on Vacation* (New York: Scribner's, 1965). See if you can transform them into what he calls their *antigrams*, i.e., a phrase with the opposite meaning. Here's an example:

united   to   untied

Try these:

1. nice love   to   ?
2. Satan   to   ?
3. real fun   to   ?
4. ill fed   to   ?
5. Is it legal? No!   to   ?

The answers: 1. violence; 2. Santa; 3. funeral; 4. filled; 5. legislation.

Simple Word and Letter Grids*

Many interesting games and puzzles depending on combining and re-combining letters have developed using grids of intersecting lines. As an introduction, see how many words you can make by filling in the empty squares in these diagrams:

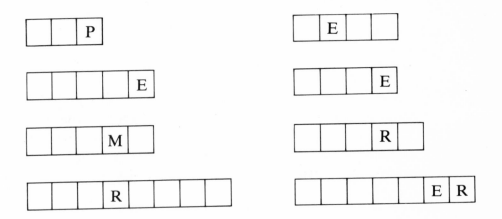

Here's a hard one:

| | A | | E | | I | O | U | | | Y |

Answer: facetiously.

One can develop dozens of versions of this. For example, how many ways can you find to fill in the empty squares to make words both horizontally and vertically?

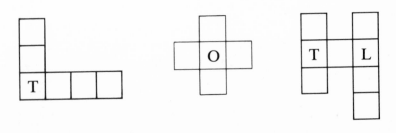

Here are some other challenges. Make a word by filling in each of these grids:

| T | | | (THAT)

| | T | | | (STOP)

| | | T | | (WITH)

| | | | T | (SPOT)

Fill in this grid so that there are words that read horizontally and vertically:

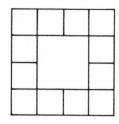

Here is another grid to fill in:

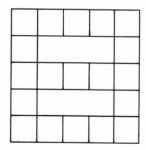

Word Squares

A slightly different grid game consists of drawing a three-by-three grid, filling it in with letters, and then seeing how many words can be made using the grid. For example, how many words can you make using all and only the letters in this grid?

X	W	L
M	A	E
R	T	I

How many words could possibly be made using the letters in a three-by-three grid? The answer takes a while to compute. [This was calculated using the standard formula $N_s = n(n-1)(n-2) \ldots (n-s+1)$, where n is the size of the population, s is the size of the sample, and N_s the number of possible ordered samples of size s.] There are:

$$
\begin{array}{rl}
9 & \text{possible 1-letter words} \\
72 & \text{possible 2-letter words} \\
504 & \text{possible 3-letter words} \\
3{,}024 & \text{possible 4-letter words} \\
15{,}120 & \text{possible 5-letter words} \\
60{,}480 & \text{possible 6-letter words} \\
181{,}440 & \text{possible 7-letter words} \\
362{,}880 & \text{possible 8-letter words} \\
362{,}880 & \text{possible 9-letter words}
\end{array}
$$

986,409 total possible words

Thus a simple three-by-three grid could possibly generate almost a million words (if there were no repetition of letters in the grid), a staggering example of how powerful a simple alphabetic code can be.

Given this possibility, how close can one actually get to the possible in terms of generating words in our language? Try to find an optimum grid—that is, one that produces as close an approximation to the maximum number possible given the allowable combinations in English. Try other square configurations: four by four, five by five, etc.

An extension of using the letters in a three-by-three grid to make words is to set up rules for moving from one letter in the square to another in order to generate words. For example, start with a three-by-three grid and fill in the squares with any letters you please, making sure, however, to use two or three vowels. For example:

B	C	I
E	F	D
P	A	R

Now how many words can you make up by starting at any letter in the square and moving in a continuous circuit horizontally, vertically, or diagonally (i.e., permitted moves are up, down, to the left or right, and diagonally in these four ways from any given square)?

Here are a few words:

B	C	I
E	F	D
P	A	R

BEAR

B	C	I
E	F	D
P	A	R

PAR

B	C	I
E	F	D
P	A	R

RAP

Using a five-by-five square and omitting Q, one can fit the whole alphabet into a square:

A	B	C	D	E
F	G	H	I	J
K	L	M	N	O
P	R	S	T	U
V	W	X	Y	Z

How many words can you find in that array? It's fun to work in teams trying to find words, or to make finding words into a group game so that the group with the longest list wins.

There are other ways to fit the alphabet (minus Q) into a five-by-five square. Do any of them produce more words than others? How many different ways are there to fit the alphabet into the square? Is there a way to arrange the letters so that only a few words can be made? Is there a way to arrange them so that no words other than I and A can be made? What if you start by jamming up the vowels in a corner of the square?

		A	E	Y
		I	O	U

Or if you try to isolate them in different corners?

A	V			
Z	P			

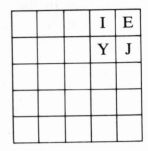

Another way to produce a square that yields a small number of words might be to cram consonants together in the middle of the square:

	M	N	R
	T	S	V
	B	L	X

An exploration of these and other questions can help gain an understanding of the way combinations of letters function in our alphabet as well as the central role some clusters of letters play in our written system.

Magic Word Squares

Probably the most studied word grids are magic word squares. Word squares are square grid arrangements with letters filling in the squares. The simplest word square is ☐ and can be filled in with an A or I to make a word (A or I). The next word square is two by two,

and it can be filled in a number of ways so that it reads the same horizontally and vertically. Here are two ways to fill it in. Are there others?

I	T
T	O

N	O
O	N

Word squares such as these which have the same words in the columns as in the rows are called magic word squares. Here's a three-by-three magic word square with the words ATE, TAG, and EGG:

A	T	E
T	A	G
E	G	G

Here are three partially completed three-by-three word squares to finish:

	N	
N	E	W
	W	

	L	
L	E	E
	E	

	H	
H	A	L
	L	

Here are two four-by-four word squares and one five-by-five square:

K	I	N	G
I	D	E	A
N	E	X	T
G	A	T	E

L	A	N	E
A	R	E	A
N	E	A	R
E	A	R	S

W	A	S	T	E
A	C	T	O	R
S	T	O	N	E
T	O	N	I	C
E	R	E	C	T

Here is a five-by-five Christmas word square to solve:

		S		
		A		
S	A	N	T	A
		T		
		A		

One way to go about solving this square would be to list five-letter words with S, A, and T as third letters

```
__ __ S __ __
__ __ A __ __
__ __ T __ __
```

S	A	T
NASTY	TEARS	AFTER
HASTE	BRAIN	ENTER
PASTE	PLANE	ANTES
UPSET	BLAME	

Then one can begin to look for words that meet the conditions of the puzzle. For example, a word whose middle letter is S must have a last letter which is the same as the first letter of a word with A in the middle. On the list above the only words that fit the condition are UPSET and TEARS, which can then be tried in the puzzle:

U	P	S	E	T
P		A		E
S	A	N	T	A
E		T		R
T	E	A	R	S

Once we have gotten this far the rest of this puzzle is simple, for now we really only have to solve the simpler grid (which is worth drawing as you work on the problem):

	P		E	
P		A		E
	A		T	
E		T		R
	E		R	

One solution to this is:

```
      P   E
  P L A N E
      A   T
  E N T E R
      E   R
```

So the final grid would be:

```
U P S E T
P L A N E
S A N T A
E N T E R
T E A R S
```

Of course, I've described a lucky shot because often a lot more trial and error goes into solving a magic square.

It's easy to turn a magic word square you've figured out into a puzzle. Simply make up definitions of the words in the square and write them on a sheet of paper along with a blank grid. For example, the simple square

```
A T E
T A G
E G G
```

can be turned into this puzzle:

```
    1 2 3
1 [ ][ ][ ]
2 [ ][ ][ ]
3 [ ][ ][ ]
```

1. I finished my food

2. You're it

3. Which came first?

Here's another example:

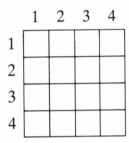

can be turned into this puzzle:

	1	2	3	4
1				
2				
3				
4				

1. I rule the land
2. At last I have an _____
3. After me
4. Close the _____ after you come in

A Digression on Word Squares and Mazes

Word squares are like mazes. You have to work your way through and about them in order to construct words. At this point a diversion on mazes and how to develop them makes sense. Making up games is as much a form of play as is playing games.

The English word "maze" comes from the Old Norwegian *masast*, which means to lose one's senses! Mazes are structures that one can get lost in. There are many types of mazes. Some are large and made out of walls and bushes. Others which can be written down are called paper-and-pencil mazes. Here are a number of different types of paper-and-pencil mazes:

Space Mazes. In these mazes you have to find your way through a series of lines without crossing any of the lines. Here is a simple space maze. Find your way out.

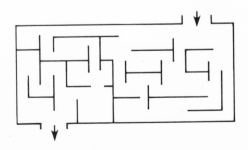

Here is a more complex space maze:

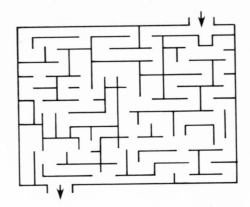

Symbol Mazes. In these mazes you have to move from one symbol to another according to a key of moves. Here is a key to use with these five symbols:

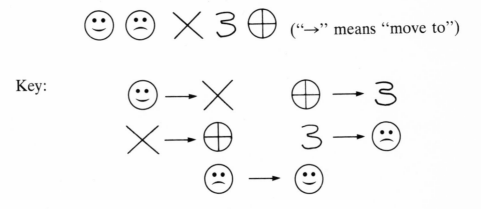

("→" means "move to")

Key:

Try to find your way out of this maze. Moves can only be horizontal or vertical:

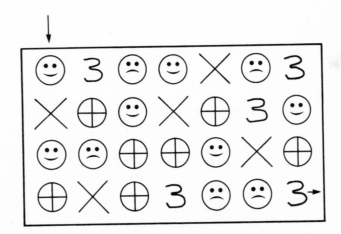

Number Mazes. The mazes use adding, subtracting, multiplying, and dividing to define moves through the maze. Simple number mazes use only adding and subtracting. Here is a simple number maze where you begin at 1 and have to end at 10. Moves can be made by adding 2 or 4, or subtracting 2 or 3.

Key: +2, −2
+4, −3

in →	1	3	8	6	4	
	6	7	5	3	5	
	4	2	4	7	9	
	6	5	1	4	8	
	1	9	3	7	10 → out	

Here is a more difficult number maze:

Key: ÷2, ×3
+1, −4

in →	1	3	4	2	7	4	
	4	6	2	5	3	9	
	2	8	6	2	3	4	
	7	5	6	18	6	2	
	4	1	3	9	7	6	
	2	5	9	10	5	1 → out	

Letter Mazes. Here is a letter puzzle that could be called an AM puzzle. The goal is to go from A to M using the following key, which tells you how many letters in the alphabet you can move forward or back:

Key: +2 letters;   −2 letters
+4 letters;   −3 letters

in →	A	E	C	F	
	C	D	G	E	
	O	P	R	I	
	S	E	B	M → out	

Here are some suggestions on how to make up mazes:

1. Determine the kind of maze you want to make. Let's start with a number maze. (It would be the same if we had started with a symbol, letter, or space maze.)

2. Determine a beginning, an end, and a grid to use. The puzzle constructed here goes from 1 to 100 and is on a five-by-five grid.

1				
			100	

3. Decide on the rules for moving. Here one can multiply, add, subtract, or divide by 2 and 5. The key would look like this:

1 to 100 mazes
Rules:

×	2	5
+	2	5
−	2	5
÷	2	5

4. Then decide on a path through the maze and figure out how to make it work.

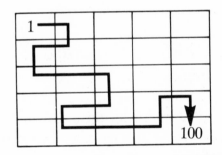

1	5			
12	10			
6	8	10		
	7	5	22	20
	14	12	24	100

Figure out how this path works using the rules in the key.

5. Then fill in the empty spaces with other numbers and you have a maze with at least one solution. There may be others generated by the numbers you added to the diagram, and that makes it more interesting.

1	5	12	10	11
12	10	4	16	12
6	8	10	9	4
9	7	5	22	20
11	14	12	24	100

Here are two mazes you can reproduce to practice on:

A			
			Z

A to Z
maze

Rules:

◯				
				△

◯ to △
maze

Rules:

◯	
▢	
△	
⏢	

Transformations*

A transformation is a change in form or shape. There are mythological transformations: King Midas transforms things into gold and Medusa transforms men to stone. There are biological transformations such as that of a caterpillar into a butterfly and of a polywog into a frog. There are also mathematical transformations such as +, which transforms two numbers into their sum, and −, which transforms two numbers into their difference. In all these cases some coherent form is changed into another coherent form. On the level of words, changing PIT to SIT could also be considered a transformation.

For the sake of this chapter, word transformations will consist of systematic changes of a word or group of words into other words or groups of words.

There are four simple forms of word transformations: *substitutions, additions, deletions,* and *transpositions.* In *substitutions* one or more letters is substituted in a word to yield another word. Some substitutions would be:

MEAT → MEAL   by substituting L for T
SELL → TELL   by substituting T for S

In *additions,* one or more letters is added to a word in order to yield another word. For example, A → AN → AND → SAND → STAND →

Letter and Word Puzzlements

STRAND, by adding one letter at each step. This process can also be written as a word pyramid:

A
AN
AND
SAND
STAND
STRAND

Deletions are the inverse of additions, subtracting one or more letters from a given word and yielding new words as in: SPLICE → SLICE → LICE → ICE.

Finally, *transpositions* consist of rearranging the letters of one word to yield another word. Most of the word combinations in this section are transpositions. Some simple transpositions are the following anagrams:

TEAM → MEAT
NOT → TON
DOLE → LODE

There can also be combinations of these different transformations so that a given word can be changed through a combination of substitutions, deletions, and transpositions, or transpositions and additions, etc.

The first time I tried to explain these different word transformations to a group of people they became confused and someone asked me if there wasn't a simpler way to write down the transformations.

It occurred to me that a simple way to do this could be modeled on mathematical notation. Moreover, it would have the advantage of showing why notation systems are invented. I suggested the following notation:

transformation	T
substitution	S
addition	+
deletion	−
transposition	C (for "change position")

$T(S, +, -, C)$, which is like functional notation in mathematics, stands for: a transformation having (x substitutions, y additions, z deletions, and w transpositions). Thus $T(1,0,0,0)$ means a substitution of one letter, and $T(1,1,0,2)$ means a substitution of one letter, an addition of one letter, and a transposition of two letters.

As we tried out the notations, we came upon some problems. Does $T(1,1,0,2)$ mean that each time you change a word you have to have a substitution, an addition of one letter, and a transposition of two letters?

Or does it mean that you can choose which of those transformations to use? The notation doesn't indicate that, so we had to modify it to include the strong case, where all transformations apply, and the weak case, where any combination can be chosen. Thus:

T $\wedge$ (S,+,−,C) means all operations used
T $\vee$ (S,+,−,C) means any one or more can be used at each step.

(The reason $\wedge$ and $\vee$ were chosen is that $\wedge$ is used in symbolic logic as the symbol for "and" and $\vee$ is the symbolic logic symbol for "or.")

There was another problem: T(0,0,0,1) didn't make sense since a letter has to be transposed with another letter. We eliminated that as a possibility much in the way that division by zero is eliminated in ordinary arithmetic as a notion meaningless within the system.

Another interesting aspect of word transformations was discussed by someone who was playing around with substitutions. A substitution of one letter is represented T(1,0,0,0). The transformation of a particular word, say "mean," can be represented in equation form (with the arrow → meaning "is transformed into"):

$$T\wedge(1,0,0,0) \text{ (MEAN)} \rightarrow \text{LEAN}$$

Now someone noticed that LEAN wasn't the only solution to the equation. In fact:

and others. As opposed to most ordinary arithmetical transformations where there is only one answer, word transformations can have many solutions. They are, in mathematical terms, one-to-many transformations instead of one-to-one or many-to-one transformations.

It isn't necessary to use these mathematical analogies to play the games in this chapter. I've found the notation useful to classify the games, and interesting to use because it gives people an opportunity to see how systems and notations evolve and how they condense description and clarify relationships. Here are some transformations. See how many solutions you can come up with (*n* means "any number of"):

T$\wedge$(2,1,0,3)   (INDEPENDENCE) ⟶ ?
T$\wedge$(1,0,1,0)   (ANY WORDS) ⟹
T$\wedge$(0,1,0,*n*)   (SLEEP) ⟶ ?

T(n,0,0,0) —Substitution Games and Puzzles

The simplest substitutions can be played by beginning readers. These games and puzzles could be called *Word Ladders*. Begin with a list of words. Then have each person pick a word and see how far he or she can go by changing one letter at a time. In a game, you can get one point for each new word made. As a puzzle, one can see how many words can be generated from the whole. For example, starting with this list of simple words, the following word ladders can be generated:

List: POT, SIT, LIKE, MINE, SAVE

Ladders:	POT	SIT	LIKE	MINE	SAVE
	TOT	SIP	PIKE	PINE	SANE
	TOP	NIP	PILE	PILE	MANE
	TIP	NAP	POLE	PILL	MINE
	LIP	CAP	SOLE	BILL	MIND
	LAG	CAT	SOLD	BALL	BIND
	LEG	FAT	COLD	BALD	BOND

After some practice with some open-ended word changes, it's easy to use the lists to make up puzzles. For example, using the list above, the following puzzles could result:

1. Start with a POT and put on a TOP
2. Is it possible to SAVE the MINE

Answers:

2. SAVE, SANE, MANE, MINE.
1. POT, TOT, TOP;

There are a number of ways to complicate the word ladders. First one can start with a longer word. Generally it's harder to transform a long word into another word by a single letter substitution. Because of this, it's possible to set up a puzzle challenging people to discover how many words on a list can be transformed through a single substitution. For example, how many of these words can be transformed into other words through the substitution of a single letter?

word
single
through
letter
these

these	→	those
word	→	ward
single	→	tingle
letter	→	better

What about "through"? Is there any way to transform it into another word with a single letter substitution? I haven't been able to do it.

Moving from a T(1,0,0,0), we can try a two-letter substitution T(2,0,0,0). For example, starting with the following words, substituting two letters at a time, you get the following ladders:

MOVE   FLING

hole   sting

cold   STONE

COAL

(This could be called   ("flinging the stone"?)

"moving the coal")

These ladders could go on longer. What is the longest ladder you could build out of a word of a certain length making one, two, three, n substitutions? (Of course, where n is the same as the number of letters in the original word, the game is trivial.) These challenges can be ongoing, with the current longest lists being posted somewhere.

A Simple Substitution Game. A simple substitution game can use the idea of substituting any number of letters, but one letter at a time. First, pick any word from a dictionary at random. The goal of the game is to transform that word to any other word using the minimum number of single-letter substitutions. Each player gets, as a score, the number of letters he or she used, and the *lowest* score wins! Here's a sample round:

Word:	certain		
	Player 1	*Player 2*	*Player 3*
	curtain	curtail	corsair
Number of substitutions:	1	2	3

For some people the scoring system might not be satisfactory. Going from "certain" to "corsair" is more interesting than going from "certain" to "curtain." Scoring systems are not sacred and it's possible to change them to suit the goals you have in playing the game.

Word ladders generated by T(1,0,0,0) were first set forth as puzzles by Lewis Carroll, who called them *doublets*. In a letter to the editor of *Vanity Fair* written in 1879 (published in *The Magic of Lewis Carroll*, edited by John Fisher [New York: Simon & Schuster, 1973], p. 131), he describes how he came to develop doublets:

Dear Vanity,

Just a year ago last Christmas, two young ladies . . . besought me to send them "some riddles." But riddles I had none at hand, and therefore set myself to devise some other form of verbal torture which should serve the same purpose. The result of my meditations was a new kind of puzzle. . . .

The rules of the Puzzle are simple enough. Two words are proposed, of the same length; and the puzzle consists in linking these together by interposing other words, each of which shall differ from the next word by one letter only. . . . I call the two given words "a Doublet," the interposed words "Links," and the entire series "a Chain" of which I here append an example:

HEAD
heal
teal
tell
tall
TAIL

It is, perhaps, needless to state that it is de rigueur that the links should be English words, such as might be used in good society.

Here are some of Carroll's challenges to try:

1. Drive PIG to STY
2. Raise FOUR to FIVE
3. Evolve MAN from APE
4. HOOK FISH
5. Put ROUGE on CHEEK
6. Put LOAF into OVEN
7. Turn WITCH to FAIRY
8. REST on SOFA

Answers:

8. REST → lest → lost → loft → soft → SOFA
tills → tills → fills → falls → fails → fairs →FAIRY
7. WITCH → winch → wench → tench → tenth → tents → tints →
OVEN → even →
6. LOAF → leaf → deaf → dear → deer → dyer → dyes →eyes → eves
cheap → cheep → CHEEK
boats → brats → brass → crass → cress → crest → chest →cheat →
5. ROUGE → rough → sough → south → sooth → booth → boots →
4. HOOK → hoot → host → hist → fist → FISH
3. APE → are → ere → err → ear → mar → MAN
2. FOUR → foul → fool → foot → fort → fore →fire → FIVE
1. PIG → wig → wag → way → say → STY

Rhyme Substitution. A further extension of the substitution principles can go beyond letter substitution to rhyme substitution. For example, it is possible to extend the idea of transforming words by changing one letter at a time to include replacing a word by another word with the same number of letters that rhyme with it, sounds the same as it does, has the same meaning, or is an anagram of it (i.e., is composed of the same letters in a different order: TOP is an anagram of POT). Thus the following transformations are possible:

from MIND to BODY

MIND	
MINE	(replace letter)
LINE	(replace letter)
LONE	(replace letter)
LOAN	(rhyme or sound the same)
LOAD	(replace letter)
LODE	(rhyme or sound the same)
BODE	(replace letter)
BODY	(replace letter)

Here's another very simple one:

from SEE to APE

SEE	
PEA	(rhyme)
APE	(anagram)

T(0,*n*,*n*,0) —Additions and Deletions

The simplest letter additions consist of beginning with a single letter and then, through the successive addition of one more letter, building up a word triangle like these:

```
      I                    A
      I T                  A M
      S I T                H A M
      S I T E              S H A M
      S P I T E            S H A M E
      S P I T E S          S H A M E N


      T                    P
      T O                  U P
      T O N                P U P
      T O N E              P U M P
      S T O N E            S T U M P
                           S T U M P S
```

There are a number of interesting questions that can be explored with respect to these simple additions.

1. Can a Word Triangle Be Built out of Every Letter? Basically this means: Can a two-letter word be formed for every letter in the alphabet?

A – at	H – hi	N – no	T – to
B – be	I – it	O – oh	U – up
C –	J –	P – up	V –
D – do	K – ok	Q – IQ	W – ow
E – he	L – lo	R – or	X – ox
F – if	M – me	S – so	Y – yo
G – go			Z – oz

C provides a problem. However CB (as in CB radio) should do. For J, the *Oxford English Dictionary* lists JO as "joy" or pleasure in sixteenth-century English. It's a matter of judgment whether to accept such an esoteric usage or not. DJ (as in disc jockey) might be more acceptable although that is usually spelled "deejay." V is also a problem, but by stretching a point we could use A-V, an abbreviation of audio-visual.

Given this list, another challenge would be to see how many of these one-step additions could be built onto with new additions. What is the longest chain that can be built using these two-letter words? Here are a few attempts:

G	N	O
G O	N O	O R
A G O	N O W	O R E
A G O N	S N O W	S O R E
A G O N Y	S N O W Y	S P O R E
		S P O R E S

2. Another Question Is: How Many Different Lists Could One Letter Generate? For example, I can begin the following triangles:

i i i i i i i i i
pi is ie it hi id iq if in

Taking it a step further, which of these I beginnings can generate the longest additive triangle? And how many different routes can a given two-letter word take. For example, A → AT can proceed in these directions:

A	A	A	A	(etc.)
A T	A T	A T	A T	
S A T	A T E	F A T	T A T	
S A L T	L A T E	F L A T	S T A T	
	S L A T E	F L O A T	S T A T E	

If more than one letter can be added, the possibilities increase. For example, adding one or two letters, the following triangles develop:

```
        A                    U
       A T                  U P
      P A T                P U P
     P L A T E            P U P I L
                         P U P I L S
```

If only two letters are added the challenge becomes a bit greater:

```
        I
      S I T
     S P I T E
    D E S P I T E
```

It is easier to build a word triangle from a given letter than to delete letters and create an inverse triangle from words picked at random. Obviously every additive word triangle, when stood on its head, produces a subtractive or deletion triangle. For example:

```
    S C A T              A
      C A T            A T
        A T          C A T
          A        S C A T
```

are simply the inverse of each other. However:

```
    P L E A S E
      L E A S E
        E A S E
```

doesn't reduce any further, and therefore isn't the inverse of any additive triangle beginning with a single letter.

Beheading Words. Dmitri Borgmann, whose *Language on Vacation* was described in the last section, has studied several different kinds of word deletions. He calls deletions *word surgery* and gives examples of one particular form he calls *decollation* or *beheading*. Here are some beheadings:

```
    T H I S
      H I S
        I S
          I
```

```
S L A U G H T E R
L A U G H T E R

A S P I R A T E
S P I R A T E
P I R A T E
I R A T E
R A T E
A T E
```

Borgmann then gives an example of a dazzling series of decapitations which turns several sentences into others. By decapitating all the words in (1) you get (2):

1. Show this bold Prussian that praises slaughter, slaughter brings rout. Teach this slaughter-lover his fall nears.
2. How his old Russian hat raises laughter, laughter rings out! Each, his laughter over, is all ears.

Using this idea it's possible to make a list of decapitable words and try to see how many decapitable sentences you can make. (A decapitable sentence is one which yields another grammatical sentence when all its words are decapitated.) Here's a list of a few decapitable words to begin with:

can – an	teach – each
mother – other	roar – oar
when – hen	plane – lane
hear – ear	flower – lower
this – his	stool – tool
code – ode	box – ox
ran – an	hit – it

Borgmann gives an example of another form of surgery, *internal surgery,* where letters are successively deleted from within a word:

```
S P A R K L I N G S
S P A R K I N G S
S P A R I N G S
S P R I N G S
S P R I G S
S P I G S
S I G S
S I S
S S
```

(Of course, in this example there are some esoteric words which one would need a dictionary to verify.)

Here is one exercise to try. Take a list of words chosen at random from a dictionary and discover:

1. How many are decapitable
2. How many can be reduced to other words through internal word surgery
3. How many can be reduced by removing two, or three, or more letters at a time.

T(0,0,0,*n*)— Transpositions

A transposition is a shift of letters within a word. A word is transposable if it can be changed into another word by rearranging its letters. Thus ON is transposable to NO, and CAME is transposable to MACE. Try to make lists of transposable words of two, three, four, five, six, seven, etc., letters. Also, pick any word and try to figure out whether it is transposable. For example, is the word "word" transposable? Is the word "transposable" transposable?

Letter transpositions in combination with letter substitutions give rise to an interesting series of word puzzles which are an extension of Lewis Carroll's doublets that were presented in the section on word substitutions. These puzzles could be described in the notation developed in this section as a T (1,0,0,*n*) transformation, where *n* can be any number from zero to the number of letters in the word. Thus an allowable extended doublet would be:

MEAL
TEAM   (substitution and transposition)
MEET   (substitution and transposition)
FEET   (substitution)
FEAT   (substitution)
HEAT   (substitution)

To make your own extended-doublets puzzles, begin with a pair of related words which have the same number of letters. Then, using one substitution and any number of letter transpositions, see if you can get from one to the other. Try, for example, WORK and PLAY:

WORK
WORD   (substitution)
DOOR   (substitution and transposition)
ROAD   (substitution and transposition)
LOAD   (substitution)
DALE   (substitution and transposition)

PALE   (substitution)
PLAY   (substitution and transposition)

Now that you have the solution, you can define the puzzle for others in a number of different ways:

1. Can you get from WORK to PLAY?
2. Turn PLAY into WORK.
3. Turn PLAY into WORK in eight or fewer steps.
4. Use seven steps to turn WORK into PLAY.

Finally, a combination of word additions (or deletions) and transpositions expands the possibilities of word transformations enormously. Consider this triangle I found in Selma and Jack Orleans's *Pencil Puzzles* (New York: Grosset & Dunlap, 1975), which was constructed by adding one letter and then transposing results:

I
I T
T I E
S I T E
T I N E S
I N S E R T
S T A I N E R
G R A N I T E S
A S S E R T I N G
S I G N A T U R E S

Many of the possibilities of combining substitutions, additions, deletions, and transpositions are still to be explored. These forms of word transformations provide an open field for the creation of new puzzles.

Playing with the Parts of Speech

Some Simple Constructions*

Three-by-five index cards and a pencil are all you need to play a number of simple games that generate complex and often funny sentences. It seems best to begin (for the benefit of those who don't know or have forgotten the parts of speech as defined in traditional grammar) with a chart in this form:

The ant	Article noun
The ant walked	Article noun verb
The greedy ant walked	Article adjective noun verb
The greedy ant walked gingerly	Article adjective noun verb adverb

These four examples are enough as a beginning, even though they don't contain prepositions or pronouns. To start a bit of word play, make five piles of blank index cards labeled as follows:

article   adjective   noun   verb   adverb

The first pile is completed by filling in two cards,

the   and   a

The other piles are completed by having players (from two to about twelve can play) write down adjectives, nouns, verbs (in past tense), and adverbs, and put their words in the appropriate piles without letting the other players see what they've written. There should be at least a dozen cards in each of the four piles. (If only two people are playing, that means each player should fill out six adjective, six noun, etc., cards). After shuffling the cards, players take turns picking out one card from each pile and reading the resulting sentence. This game can turn out dull or delightful depending on how creative people are in picking their words. I've found that the key to generating amusing and interesting sentences is in picking striking nouns and verbs. A good starting list would contain words like:

adjectives: boring, smart, curious, energetic
nouns: slug, dictator, poet, politician
verbs: awoke, spoke, attacked, retreated
adverbs: weakly, inconsiderately, warmly, hostilely

I know a number of people who find it hard to play a game like this. There are no points or winners and losers. The interest is in the created sentence, not in some final outcome of the game. The pleasure such games can provide derives from some unexpected juxtaposition of words and from the selection of words that make interesting combinations. It's a slow game, one children play easily and one which is worth trying if only to help slow down things a bit and play with others without competing with them.

After playing a few times, a fifth pile of cards can be added with connecting words like "then," "meanwhile," "when," "while," "nevertheless," "and." This pile should be placed to the left of the article pile and a card drawn from it after the completion of each sentence. In that way a continuous story, or at least a loosely connected narrative, can develop. Here are a few sentences using the above words:

> The boring dictator spoke curiously,
> Nevertheless the slug attacked inconsiderately,
> While the energetic politician retreated warmly.

Mad Libs

Filling in Mad Libs is a favorite pastime of my children and their friends. There are dozens of *Mad Lib* pads created by Roger Price and Leonard Stein (Price/Stein/Sloan Publishers, Los Angeles) that can be found in toy stores, airports, bus terminals, and bookstores. In general, Mad Libs are stories with words left out. One player reads the paragraph silently, and then goes through the story and calls on the other players to give him or her words to fill the blanks. Under each blank the part of speech needed to keep the sentence grammatical is indicated. Thus in the following sentence,

> The old _____ ran off with a _____ man.
>   noun   adjective

the reader would call out "noun," and one player would pick a noun, any noun. The next player would pick an adjective. The reader fills in the blanks and at the end reads the whole paragraph back. The parts of speech used are nouns, adjectives, and adverbs. Also, place names, numbers, and exclamations (like "ow!" "ha!" "ouch!") are indicated under some blanks.

Here's a Mad Lib from *Mad Libs #1* with the words my children filled in:

ADVICE TO PROSPECTIVE PARENTS

Congratulations to all of you ___RED___ Mothers and ___BUMPY___
                                   adjective   adjective

Fathers. You are about to give birth to a (an) ___CHAIR___. Remember,
                                                  noun

a happy child comes from a happy ___DISH___. Undoubtedly the
                                        noun

___NOISY___ arrival will cause many ___TERRIBLE___ changes in your life.
adjective   adjective

You'll have to get up at four a.m. to give the little ___CHAIR___ its bottle
                                                noun

of ___PURPLE___ milk. Later when he's ___500___ years old he'll learn
adjective   number

to walk and you'll hear the patter of little ___CRASHES___ around the
                                          pl. noun

house. And in no time he'll be talking ___WEIRDLY___ and calling you his
                                        adverb

___SPOON___ and ___FORK___. It's no wonder they are called little
noun   noun

bundles of ___PEANUT BUTTER___.
                  noun

Any number of people can play Mad Libs, and so long as one person in the group can read, people of just about any age can play together. The Mad Lib above was done when my children were five, seven, and nine. My oldest daughter was the reader and Judy and I played with the children. At first Josh didn't know what the parts of speech were, but he learned them quickly as part of the rules of the game. In fact, a few days of Mad Libs and almost anyone will learn to identify nouns, adjectives, and adverbs.

In addition to purchasing *Mad Libs* (which are all cleverly written and set up humorous situations) it's possible to make up your own. Here's one I made up with the help of my son and his friends at his eighth birthday party:

One day I went to a _____ game. It was for the championship of
                           adjective

_____. The teams that were playing were the _____
place   adjective

_____ and the _____ _____. At the end of the
pl. noun   adjective   pl. noun

game the score was _____ to _____. The crowd was so
                      number   number

excited that they _____ when the game ended.
                 verb

Compounding Words

Compound words are words that are constructed by combining two other words. There are two general kinds of compounding of words. In one case the words are joined together by a hyphen. Examples of this kind of word are "old-fashioned" and "peace-loving." Other compounds eliminate the hyphen. Some of these are "underground," "overdo," "blueberry." Maxley Brooke analyzed compound words in *Word Ways,* which is a journal of recreational linguistics (see resource section for more information about the journal), and found that nouns, adjectives, adverbs, and verbs can be joined in different combinations to create compound words. For example, compound words can consist of:

1. noun-noun combinations where the first noun qualifies the second —aircraft, bookcase, cardboard, tabletop
2. noun-noun combinations where the second noun is a verb with *er* added on—dressmaker, roadrunner, groundskeeper, beekeeper
3. verb-noun combinations like daredevil and cut-throat
4. adjective-noun combinations like software, hardware, and bluebird
5. noun-verb combinations where the verb is a present participle —peace-loving, tough-talking, rough-riding
6. adjective-verb combinations where the verb is a past participle —hard-bitten, low-slung
7. adjective-adjective combinations—blue-black, true-blue.

Brooke even took this analysis a step further and created a chart of compound words using all the parts of speech. Pronouns and nouns were joined into one category, as were adverbs and prepositions, since these pairs function in the same way in compound words. Here's the chart with examples filled in:

	Pronoun-noun	Adjective	Adverb-preposition	Verb
Pronoun-noun	he-man chalkboard	seaworthy winedark	southwesterly	toothpick
Adjective	blueberry	blue-violet true-blue	blackout	coldcut
Adverb-preposition	onlooker inside	blackout turnout	forevermore without	nearsighted
Verb	playboy turncoat	high-flying	cut-up walk-on	panic-stricken

There are many ways to use this chart to experiment with new words, classify familiar ones, and develop games and verbal contests. While doing this it's possible to develop an ease with different parts of speech and move from one to the other. Certainly playing with compound words does not provide a systematic study of the ways words function in English, but it is a useful supplement to that study. Here are some ways to play with compound words.

Developing Your Own Compounds

Make a list of five pronoun-nouns, five verbs, five adverb-prepositions, and five adjectives. The list can be picked randomly from a dictionary or thesaurus, or come from your mind or a book you skim, or from your friends. Here's a list I did with my eight-year-old son:

Pronouns and nouns	Adjectives	Adverb-prepositions	Verbs
dog	bumpy	quickly	run
pepper	gray	in	skip
salt	smooth	out	hit
song	soft	happily	grip
hand	hard	slowly	limp

One thing to do with the list is to see if any of the words are already compound words or common two-word combinations that are close to compound words. On this list there are a few:

dog run   handgrip   hit song

There are combinations that are close to existing compound words and could probably be used without problem in descriptive writing:

a grayout   similar to a blackout
a hardhand   similar to a hardhat
a doglimp }
or a dogskip }   similar to a dog run

Finally, there are those combinations for which meanings can be imagined. It might be fun, for example, to create a *Dictionary of Words That Almost Exist* and try to give definitions for the following words:

a limpsong   _____
happilyin   _____
happilyout   _____
a softhit   _____
a hardhit   _____
a saltout   _____   etc.

Battles of Praise and Insult

Another way to use compound words could be a bit like the medieval Verbal Battles of Praise and Insult that have their modern forms in the dozens. The battles consist of people taking turns trying to produce the most ingenious and unexpected ways of insulting or praising a person, idea, place, or thing. The ability to coin new compound words makes it possible to elaborate on this form of contest, even for people whose culture does not practice the form. Here's an example of a verbal praising contest between two people. In each case one compound word is added to the praise each time, after repeating all the past praises:

Contest 1. To praise your opponent more than he or she praises you
    Person 1: You seaworthy giant
    Person 2: You insightful wizard
    Person 1: You high-flying, seaworthy giant
    Person 2: You creative-minded, insightful wizard
    Person 1: You world-stomping, high-flying, seaworthy giant
    Person 2: You depth-sounding, creative-minded, insightful wizard
                              (etc.)

Contest 2. To insult your opponent more than he or she insults you
    1. You low-lying slug
    2. You rock-headed sardine
    1. You belly-clutching, low-lying slug
    2. You grease-sweating, rock-headed sardine
                              (etc.)

Contest 3. To have any number of people try to outdo each other in praising themselves, or insulting someone else about the way they do something—perhaps how they write, play ball, look, dress, etc. For example, a football player might say about himself:

> I'm high-flying, low-riding, tough-talking, knee-breaking, arm-bending, world-shaking.

Contest 4. To praise or insult a city or institution, a public figure, a notable event.

In all of these contests the intent is humor and ingenuity. They are public displays, not acts of arrogance or anger. There are a number of ways to judge the winners (and there don't have to be winners—in a good contest all the participants are applauded for their play with words):

    1. Anyone who successfully completes ten turns without forgetting the whole sequence is a winner. In this case, everyone who finishes wins.
    2. The group can vote on a winner.

3. The insults or praises can be written down and judged on the way they go together. In the first example of praise a giant was chosen as the object for comparison by one contestant and a wizard by the other. All ten praises can then be looked at to see if they qualify the giant or wizard chosen as central image.

Collecting Compounds

A final thing that I enjoy doing is going through the dictionary at random, selecting a page, and writing down all the compound words. I'm collecting a list of as many compounds as possible and I add to the list every once in a while. This could be considered an example of recreational linguistics —of playing with words and their relations for pleasure and to broaden my knowledge of the scope of language. Here's a list that appears on page 1998 of *The Shorter Oxford Dictionary of the English Language* (the list includes words used in the definitions as well as words defined):

topsail	pikemen	wildfowl
panic-stricken	without	watchman
stopping-place	card-playing	open-air
standing-place	tiptoe	football
after-damp	fellowship	onset
standstill	water-tight	oneself
sportsman	weather-proof	stand-patter
race-meeting	upright	godfather
	quarter-rails	

Lipograms

A lipogram is a composition from which all words that contain a certain letter or letters are omitted. A. Ross Eckler, who is the editor of *Word Ways*, recreated "Mary Had a Little Lamb" six times, excluding the letters S, H, T, A, and E. In the last version, he used only half the alphabet: E, T, A, Y, N, C, D, L, M, H, R, I, and P.

The Original Verse
Mary had a little lamb,
    Its fleece was white as snow,
And everywhere that Mary went
    The lamb was sure to go;
He followed her to school one day,
    That was against the rule;
It made the children laugh and play
    To see a lamb in school.

The verse without H

Mary owned a little lamb,
  Its fleece was pale as snow,
And every place its mistress went
  It certainly would go;
It followed Mary to class one day
  It broke a rigid law;
It made some students giggle aloud,
  A lamb in class all saw.

The verse without T

Mary had a pygmy lamb,
  His fleece was pale as snow,
And every place where Mary walked
  Her lamb did also go;
He came inside her classroom once,
  Which broke a rigid rule;
How children all did laugh and play
  On seeing a lamb in school!

The verse without E

Mary had a tiny lamb,
  Its wool was pallid as snow,
And any spot that Mary did walk
  This lamb would always go;
This lamb did follow Mary to school,
  Although against a law;
How girls and boys did laugh and play,
  That lamb in class all saw.

The verse without S

Mary had a little lamb,
  With fleece a pale white hue,
And everywhere that Mary went
  The lamb kept her in view;
To academe he went with her,
  Illegal, and quite rare;
It made the children laugh and play
  To view a lamb in there.

The verse without A

Polly owned one little sheep,
  Its fleece shone white like snow,
Every region where Polly went,
  The sheep did surely go;
He followed her to school one time,
  Which broke the rigid rule;
The children frolicked in their room
  To see the sheep in school.

The verse without half the letters of the alphabet

Maria had a little sheep,
  As pale as rime its hair,
And all the places Maria came
  The sheep did tail her there;
In Maria's class it came at last,
  A sheep can't enter there;
It made the children clap their hands,
  A sheep in class, that's rare.

Certainly lipograms are not directly related to learning the different parts of speech. However, I've found that trying my hand at rewriting a sentence or nursery rhyme without using certain letters or in studying Eckler's reworkings, I had to search for appropriate verbs, prepositions, nouns, adjectives, etc. It helped develop a sense of the weight of different adjectives or adverbs, say, and therefore provided the opportunity to hone my sense of the various parts of speech. For example, in going over Eckler's version of "Mary Had a Little Lamb," the second line provides an interesting study in the way parts of speech can be used:

1. Its fleece was white as snow

adjective change   2. Its fleece was pale as snow
verb and pronoun elimination,
preposition added, noun replacement   3. With fleece a pale white hue

pronoun and adjective
replacement
verb replacement
noun replacement

4. His fleece was pale as snow

5. Its fleece shone white like snow

6. Its wool was pallid as snow

etc.

Here are some exercises involving the principles of lipograms to try yourself or with other people:

1. Write a short story without using some vowel, for example, without E:

John's mom told him to go to visit his dad. John did, but couldn't find him. It took days for John to find out that his dad was sick. John finally did visit his dad who was happy to talk to John.

2. Write a story and then rewrite it dropping a vowel, much the way Ross Eckler rewrote "Mary Had a Little Lamb." Here's a version of the story in exercise 1, dropping all the As and allowing E:

John's mom told him to go visit his pop. John did, but couldn't find him. It took weeks for John to find out his pop took sick. In time John did visit his pop, who delighted to converse with John.

3. It's also possible to write a simple sentence, remove all the vowels, and ask people to try to reconstruct the original sentence. Here's an example:

It is fun to make up games

TSFNTMKPGMS

Sometimes the run of consonants left seems impossible to decipher. In that case, dashes can be included to indicate where the vowels would go. The above sentence would then be written:

_ T_ SF_ NT_ M_ K_ _ PG_ M_ S

4. There's another way to restrict the use of letters. For example, try to write sentences, or even stories, where all the words begin with the same letter. Here's one attempt at using A:

An alluring ant ambled along.

Now going on with B:

But before bug became bold, brother bear banged.

It's getting a bit awkward, but I'll try to go on with C:

Can company come calling?

To D:

Darn door doesn't divert.

And finally with E:

Elsewhere Elsie elf enlivened everybody.

Rop He Irst Etter

An oral game akin to lipograms, although consisting of dropping first letters instead of restricting their use, was sent to me by Joan McCreary, an elementary school student. Here's her letter:

I have a word game that you might like. . . . Here's how it goes: you take the first letter from a word and say the word without the first letter. I started out saying, (J)eff sure is trong. Then the whole family at supper started making up new words with the first letter off. Like (p)ass the roccoli please and there's a poon in the owl. I sure hope you put it in the game book.

Creating New Words*

There are actions, objects, and qualities that have not been named yet, and there are many words that have just recently been added to our vocabulary. Think, for example, of black holes in the universe, of quarks and neutrinos, herstories and bionic people, of Black with a capital B and ICBMs. It is an interesting exercise to create words for aspects of experience that do not yet have words to describe them. There are two ways one can go about doing this.

Think of a Combination of Letters That Is Not a Word in English

Decide on whether it is to name a person, place, or thing (i.e., is a noun), or to describe an action (a verb) or a quality (an adjective or adverb). Then say the combination a few times and try to write down a definition of it, or draw a picture of what it represents. I chose to experiment with an *ing* and a *nrg*. After repeating them a few times it became clear that an ing was a creature or a story that went on and on without end like an infinitely long snake or a shaggy-dog tale that had no conclusion. A nrg, on the other hand, was an energetic but nervous creature made of antimatter. Everytime a nrg collided with a grn, they negated each other and vanished, leaving free-floating nervous energy in the world.

There are many other letter combinations that set off similar silly speculation. One way to turn this play into a game is have two players or two groups each make up a list of new words and definitions. Then they exchange words but not definitions, and make up second definitions for the words. Then at the conclusion they compare definitions, and if it seems appropriate to take the game further, they decide on a best definition and write a story containing all the new words used in their proper senses.

One time I played the game the following definitions resulted:

a pstotol: 1. an exotic cloth with magical powers, found only in Peru
2. the seed of a rare mustard plant that induces dreams of power

to rmdoat: 1. to stay on the edge of things, to avoid contact with people and act docile
2. to ram things down people's throats

Start with the Definitions

Another way to create new words is to start with the definitions and the parts of speech, and then come up with a combination of sounds that seems to fit the definition. Here are some definitions in search of words:

nouns: 1. a person who refuses to do anything sitting down
2. a place where everything that isn't good for you becomes turned into something that's okay
3. an object used to hold collections of junk

verbs: 1. to hold your breath until you turn blue
2. to go from one place to another without leaving a trace of yourself behind, including other people's memories of you

qualities (adjectives and adverbs):
1. the quality of being able to change one's smell at will
2. the quality of being ugly and beautiful at the same time

Here are some more ideas in search of a word:

A person who always promises to call you and never does

Someone who's always late and yet gets upset when other people are late

Someone who drives a car with one hand, talking all the time and looking at you more than at the road

The sound made by an amorous moth

The smell of sawdust or of paint or of onions cooking

A messy bedroom

Name a Group

Another word-inventing game consists of inventing names for groups. There are herds of cattle, prides of lions, bevies of doves, schools of fish, gaggles of geese, and a whole swarm of less familiar group names like:

a sloth of bears	a rag of colts
a drift of hogs	a husk of jack rabbits
a stud of mares	a down of hares
a haras of horses	a nest of cottontails
a shrewdness of apes	a barren of mules
a crash of rhinoceros	a spring of teal
a sedge of herons	a fall of woodcock
a walk of snipe	a murmuration of starlings
a eule of turtledoves	an ascension or exaltation of larks
a watch of nightingales	(and finally) a host of angels

Not all groups have a name yet. What could one call a group of judges? a roomful of lovers? an auto graveyard? Answers I've gotten are a sentence of judges, a trance of lovers, and a jumble of cars. How about naming these groups and other collectives you can dream up?

people with colds
people caught in a traffic jam
children playing in a sandbox
all of the pets in a house
all of the objects in a person's pocket or purse

There are also other group names. For example, have you ever noticed the types of names musical groups give themselves. Some names try to glorify the group. In this category are names like:

The Supremes
The Sensations
The Magnificent 4
The Glorious Seven

Other names like the Dynamites, the Wailers, and Tower of Power try to convey strength and energy. Then there are mystical names such as the Searchers and the Mysterians, as well as names with a religious overtone like the Righteous Brothers and the Saints. There are even demonic or threatening names like the Punks and Satan's Six. A lot of hard-rock groups take names to be absurd and try to surprise or shock by the contrasts they use. Consider, for example, the Grateful Dead, the Iron Butterfly, and Pink Floyd.

It's fun to make up names for imaginary groups and write press releases describing the members of the group and the kind of music it plays. For example, what kind of music could the following groups play? What might the musicians look like?

The Tower of Babel
Jacob and the Snakes
Thunderbird
The Tire Irons
Flat Tire
Dirty Socks
Bitter Lemon
Peaches and Pairs
The Quintuplets

There are other naming exercises. For example, you can think up names for companies and products. Absurd products and work can lead to absurd and interesting word play. Here are some descriptions to start fooling around with:

1. What could be the name of a product that claimed it helped breathing and was simply a fancy box full of air?
2. What about a soap guaranteed not to clean? A cigarette that offers your money back if you don't get cancer? A car that is pollution free because it has no motor but looks beautiful if you park it in front of your house?
3. And how about a company that guarantees to make water wet or one which repairs keyholes and other empty spaces, or one that guarantees to cure you of all ills even if it kills you?

Super Titles

Sometimes names are given to activities or roles people play in order to make them sound more important than they are. Temple Porter calls such names "Super Titles," and wrote a short essay about them in volume 1, no. 2, of *Word Ways*, which is a journal of "recreational linguistics" (a super title for word play) that is a must for word freaks. The essay, which I'll quote in full, has dozens of super titles:

Super Titles

If someone were to tell you that he was in the REFUSED METAL PRODUCTS INDUSTRY, it would probably take you a while to figure out that he was a *junk dealer*. "Super titles" are becoming increasingly prevalent as the lust for a burnished image dominates any interest in the substance it obscures.

Sometimes, super-titling is simple euphemism, wherein the distasteful becomes acceptable, as in UNDERFASHIONS for *underwear* (itself a euphemism). In this way, *sexual intercourse* emerges as CONJUGAL RELATIONS. We can soften the harshest realities, such as *nuclear missiles*, simply by calling them FACTORS OF PEACE (for the good guys) or INSTRUMENTS OF AGGRESSION (for the bad guys). The super title may be totally unrecognizable without its referent by its side, as when we call a *bar of soap* a BEAUTY CAKE. "Euphemism," quoth H. W. Fowler, "is more demoralizing than coarseness."

In a recent issue of *The New Yorker* there was a story about a man hired by an oil company to take complaints over the telephone. On his first day, he jotted down a customer's complaint about an oil burner that had exploded. It was his boss who then exploded: "You won't get far in this business until you learn that we do *not* have explosions. We have PUFFBACKS." It is this sort of mentality that gives us MEMORIAL GARDEN for *graveyard*, HOME ENTERTAINMENT CENTER for *radio-phonograph combination*, and PRESENTATION SESSION for *class*.

The death industry is especially replete with super titles. MORTICIANS place LOVED ONES in CASKETS for INTERMENT [Translation: *Undertakers* place *dead persons* in *coffins* for *burial*]. (Incidentally, and quite beside the point, there is an Indianapolis undertaker who advertises that his coffins come with a "lifetime guarantee"!)

People, in the hands of bureaucrats, become PERSONNEL, who don't *live* anywhere, but are DOMICILED. *Old people* have become SENIOR CITIZENS, and the *poor,* when they are mentioned at all, are merely UNDERPRIVILEGED. We are no longer *fired* from our jobs; we are TERMINATED.

Perhaps you managed to hold on to your marbles through the TV meetings of the UN during the MIDDLE EAST CONFLICT [*Arab-Israeli War*]. Did you notice the all-time record number of polite synonyms for *lie* and and *liar*? It was a marvel of semantic gymnastics. Some members groped and stammered for minutes at a time, searching for new ways in which to call their ESTEEMED COLLEAGUES [*fellow members*] liars. Here are some of the astounding results: UTTERANCE WITHOUT FOUNDATION IN FACT; UNFOUNDED STATEMENT; MISREPRESENTATION OF THE TRUE FACTS (and we hadn't even suspected the existence of *untrue* facts!); COMPLETE FABRICATION; WOVEN FROM WHOLE CLOTH (Ambassador Goldberg's favorite); and UTTERLY WITHOUT RELATION TO REALITY. In all fairness, we must mention that Lord Caradon alone used the words *lie* and *liar* when characterizing the statements and speakers with which and with whom he disagreed. GODFREY DANIEL! (as W. C. Fields often said in order to circumvent the movie censor's ruling against profanity).

Just as the *undertaker* elevates himself to a MORTICIAN, so does the *gardener* become a LANDSCAPE TECHNICIAN, the *tax collector* a REVENUE AGENT, the *plumber* a WATER SYSTEMS SPECIALIST, and the *film projectionist* a MULTI-MEDIA SYSTEMS TECHNICIAN. We no longer have *janitors;* we now employ SANITATION MAINTENANCE SUPERINTENDENTS. If a limb of one of your trees is sagging, don't bother to look in the Yellow Pages for a tree trimmer; look rather under HORTICULTURAL SURGEONS. Remember when Art Carney used to get a laugh on the Jackie Gleason Show by describing himself as a SUBTERRANEAN SANITATION TECHNICIAN? It's no laughing matter any more; just call City Hall some time and ask for the help of a *sewer worker*—they won't know what you're talking about.

While you're on the line to City Hall, you might ask about the *dog catcher:* you'll learn that he's now the CANINE CONTROL OFFICER. And did you know that policemen no longer carry *clubs*? No sirreebob! That long, wooden, blunt instrument is a NIGHT BATON! Joining the *dog catcher* in oblivion is the *barber;* in his place we now have a HAIR STYLIST. Should your stomach start to turn on your next plane trip, don't bother looking for the old *vomit bag,* because you won't find it; in its stead is something called an AIR SICKNESS CONTAINER. While on the subject of containers, we must mention the fact that there are many localities in which milk no longer comes in *bottles,* but in OPENIZED CARTONS, delivered with what is emblazoned on the truck's side as PERSONALIZED SERVICE. Oh, yes—the next time you are in the market for a *used car,* be careful. Some newspapers are advertising PRE-OWNED VEHICLES.

NASA's rocket fuel workers at Cape Kennedy recently wondered why they couldn't find the *portable field showers* at the supply depot with which to wash the rocket fuel from themselves. It was probably due to the fact that the Quartermaster had redesignated them as ROCKET PROPELLANT PERSONNEL NEUTRALIZERS.

It is all a sad, even frightening, spectacle. We cannot close more appropriately than by quoting a line from G. M. Young: "Really there are times when I feel that civilization will come to an end because no one will understand what anybody else is saying."

It is interesting to look around and find examples of what Temple Porter calls super titles. It is also a good exercise in demystifying this use of language to give false status to simple ideas or actions by making up your own super titles. For example, here are some things in school to give super titles to:

> the bathroom pass
> the teacher's desk
> the principal's office
> the detention room
> a late slip
> punishment
> grades

Here's one: a report card in modern dress is a "performance evaluation document." How about the following other possibilities for super titles:

1. Super titles for excuses, e.g., You can't come to a party because of stress-related hyperanxiety you are currently undergoing (that is, you don't feel like going)
2. Super titles for asking people for favors
3. Super titles for ways of borrowing money, evading an issue, expressing affection, describing something you like or something you can't stand
4. Super titles for ordinary activities, e.g., washing the dishes (cleansing the culinary functionals?), sweeping the floor, driving to work, reading the newspaper.

3

Phrase and Sentence Variations

Crossword Puzzles and Thematic Word Squares
How Do I Love You?
Catchy Combinations
Sentence Grids and Magic Sentence Grids
Good News/Bad News

Crossword Puzzles and Thematic Word Squares*

According to the *Oxford English Dictionary* a "phrase" is a small group of words expressing a single notion, or entering with some degree of unity into the structure of a sentence. In grammatical terms a phrase is a group of words equivalent to a noun, adjective, or adverb that does not have a finite verb of its own. While searching for games and puzzles with phrases, I happened to glance at some crossword-puzzle books. It struck me that many crossword-puzzle definitions are phrases, and they are often elegant condensations of meaning. It occurred to me that one way of playing with phrases could be to create crossword puzzles.

After some research on crosswords, I discovered that the first crossword puzzle was made up by Arthur Wynne, who edited the puzzle page of the Sunday *New York World*. It was published on December 21, 1913, in the Fun Section of the *World* and almost immediately began the crossword-puzzle craze which still hasn't abated. Here's that first published crossword puzzle:

2–3   what bargain hunters enjoy
4–5   a written acknowledgment
6–7   such and nothing more
10–11 a bird
14–15 opposed to less
18–19 what this puzzle is
22–23 an animal of prey
26–27 the close of day
28–29 to elude
30–31 the plural of is
8–9   to cultivate
12–13 a bar of wood or iron
16–17 what artists learn to do
20–21 fastened
24–25 found on the seashore
10–18 the fiber of the gomuti palm
6–22 what we all should be
4–26 a day dream
2–11 a talon
19–28 a pigeon
F–7   part of your head
23–30 a river in Russia
1–32 to govern
33–34 an aromatic plant
N–8   a fist
24–31 to agree with
3–12 part of a ship
20–29 one
5–27 exchanging
9–25 to sink in mud
13–21 a boy

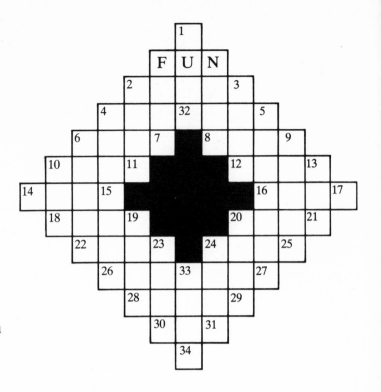

The Solution:

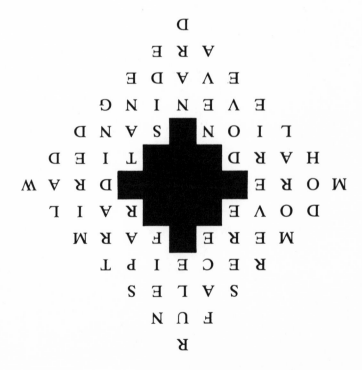

Most people have tried their hand at solving crossword puzzles at one time or another. It's also fun to try your hand at making up puzzles for others to solve. It's best to start simple and make up a thematic word square. Pick a theme or subject, preferably one you are familiar with. Here are some: fish, dogs, cats, superheroes, clothes, games. Next, make a list of some of the words that fit the theme. For example, with fish here's one list:

carp   swordfish
catfish   goldfish
guppy   shark
flounder   trout
perch   bass

Then take an empty five-by-five grid of squares and try to fit in as many of the words as you can. The words can be fit in so long as the letters are adjacent to each other. Thus the words can be read horizontally, vertically, or diagonally. Here's an example using the fish list:

After you've squeezed in as many words as you can, you'll end up with a thematic word puzzle. Here's one called *Fish Fry*. Start in any square and move to any adjacent square in any direction. Move one square at a time. Keep on going until you spell out the name of a fish. How many fish can you find?

C	T	P	K	O
T	A	R	G	T
H	F	L	O	U
S	I	D	N	P
W	O	R	E	Y

After creating a few thematic word puzzles, try a crossword puzzle. It's useful to have reference books available to help you find words to squeeze into awkward places on your puzzle grid. A good dictionary, a thesaurus, and an etymological dictionary (like Eric Partridge's *Origins*) are adequate. I've also found crossword-puzzle dictionaries to be useful. A good one is the *Barnes and Noble Crossword Dictionary*. Crossword-puzzle dictionaries differ from ordinary dictionaries in that:

1. they list synonyms instead of definitions; an entry might be:
   small: tiny, miniscule, diminutive, bitsy
2. they give some phrases that can be used as crossword definitions:
   car race   –rally
   created creature –golem

Crossword puzzles can be generated just like thematic word puzzles. Begin with a theme and make a list of words associated with the theme. Then look up the word in your reference books and see if they add any words to your list. The first puzzle I developed was on the theme of pollution. Here's the list of pollution-related words I began with:

pollution	oil
smog	ecology
cough	Nader
dirty	environment
air	breathe
cars	earth
factory	protect
control	EPA
exhaust	work
clean	money

The longest word on this preliminary list, "environment," has eleven letters, and the shortest ones, "air," "oil," and "EPA," have three letters. That means that if we want to include "environment" the puzzle will have to be at least eleven by eleven squares. Let's draw a grid and try to fit in as many of the words on the list as possible, remembering that they can be entered either horizontally or vertically.

Here's a start. Put "environment" somewhere in the middle of the grid and begin to add to that word, remembering that all the vertical and horizontal combinations of letters have to make sense.

Adding "earth," "smog," and "breathe" is easy. However, if the *g* in "smog" is used to add "cough," a square has to be blocked in since "cough ■ e" can't produce a word.

										B
										R
										E
							S			A
E	N	V	I	R	O	N	M	E	N	T
A							O			H
R				C	O	U	G	H	█	E
T										
H										

Now let's try to add some more words to the grid, blacking in another square whenever two words would otherwise run together and become meaningless. This rough method squeezes ten of the words into the grid. Other approximations might even be able to get more in.

P	O	L	L	U	T	I	O	N	█	
							I			B
N	A	D	E	R			L			R
							█			E
		A					S			A
E	N	V	I	R	O	N	M	E	N	T
A		R					O			H
R				C	O	U	G	H	█	E
T										
H										
		E	C	O	L	O	G	Y		

Now it's time for stretching out and playing a bit. For example, the P in "pollution" has an empty space beneath it followed by the N in "Nader." A three-letter word like "pan" would fit nicely, and to relate "pan" to "pollution" one can use an oft-repreated phrase used when referring to ecological problems like "out of it into the fire." However, to preserve "earth" two squares would have to be blacked in.

P	O	L	L	U	T	I	O	N	■	■
A	■	O				I			■	B
N	A	D	E	R			L			R
■		E					■			E
■		A		M		S				A
E	N	V	I	R	O	N	M	E	N	T
A			R		R		O			H
R	O	T	■	C	O	U	G	H	■	E
T		I			N					
H		M								
		E	C	O	L	O	G	Y		

A few other words vaguely related to pollution have been added and the squares needed to protect them have been blacked in. They are: rot, time, lode, moron. Now there are fifteen words in the puzzle and still a lot of empty places. At this point it's possible to begin all over again, expand the word list, and move things around. A puzzle freak would certainly do that, noting that there aren't any nicely nestling word combinations like:

```
        H
    N A T
H O P E
        P S Y C H E
    P E T
    N
```

where words like "hope," "nat," and "no" can be this close on the grid:

	N	A	T
H	O	P	E

because of the way the letters are used to complete other words.

However, for nonfreaks the puzzle we have is a good approximation. One thing is to note how many two- or three-letter words or abbreviations could be added to fill up the grid. It looks like the places marked with a circle could be filled in, possibly making some complex combinations.

Here is one possible way to fill in the circles that is as consistent with the theme as possible. All the squares that are left over have been filled in, as have those squares marked with circles that we couldn't fit into the whole (one principle we used, and one that is used in most crossword puzzles, is that no word is used more than once).

Crossword Puzzles and Thematic Word Squares

When the words are removed, the puzzle looks a bit more imposing:

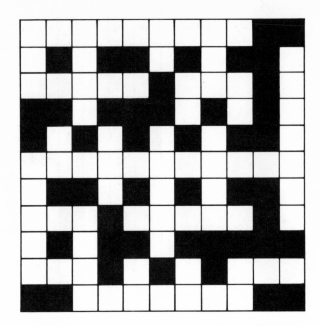

That looks a lot more like a crossword puzzle. All that's missing are the numbers and the definitions, which are easy and fun to do. One way to approach these problems is by listing and numbering the words, starting with the horizontal from top to bottom and left to right.

Horizontal Words:

1. pollution   4. environment   7. him
2. Nader   5. rot   8. buy
3. ale   6. cough   9. ecology

Then enter the numbers on the horizontal to reference these words.

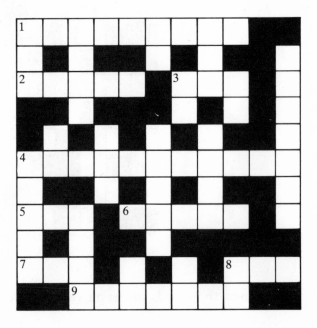

Next, make a list of the words that are entered in the grid vertically going from left to right and top to bottom:

pan	ax	earth
lode	eg	time
ta	on	po
oil	air	lo
breathe	moron	by
	smog	

Any of the words on this new list whose first letter is in a square that has a number in it should be listed under that number:

1. pan
3. ax
4. earth
8. lo

Then the rest of the vertical words can be numbered (again starting from top to bottom and moving from left to right) beginning with the number after the last one used in the horizontal numbering sequence. In this puzzle the last number used to reference horizontal words was 9, so the first new number used for vertical words would be 10.

Thus the key to the puzzle would read at this stage:

Across

1. pollution
2. Nader
3. ale
4. environment
5. rot
6. cough
7. him
8. buy
9. ecology

Down

1. pan
3. ax
4. earth
8. lo
10. lode
11. ta
12. oil
13. breathe
14. eg

15. on
16. air
17. moron
18. time
19. po
20. by

Now the fun begins. Replace all the words by some phrase or definition or hint. These clues should not be too obscure or too simple. Often it takes a lot of play with phrases, sayings, and proverbs to come up with a level of complexity in the clues that makes the puzzle challenging and do-able at the same time. Here's one list of clues which completes the pollution puzzle:

Across

1. it fouls up the earth
2. he tries to undo 1 across
3. can cause internal disorder
4. the world around us
5. decay
6. an effect of 1 across
7. referring to a man or boy
8. we do too much of this
9. care of the earth household

Down

1. out of this into the fire
3. can be used to cut
4. what we cannot live without
8. _____ and behold
10. a vein of minerals
11. a way of relating to yourself and others (abbreviation)
12. liquid gold
13. if we are not careful people, we'll no longer be able to do this
14. for example (abbreviation)
15. inversion of no
16. it's all around us and being soiled
17. what we are for treating the world carelessly
18. we still have _____ to fix things up
19. mail a protest here (abbreviation)
20. stand _____, it will soon be your turn

This puzzle was comparatively simple to compose. If you're interested in more complex puzzle composition the puzzle columns in *Games and Puzzles* magazine and *Games* magazine are probably for you. (See the Appendix for their addresses.)

How Do I Love You?*

This punning game consists of answering a question such as "How do I love you?" with a phrase that would be appropriate coming from people with different professions or special characteristics. For example, here are some answers to "How do I love you?":

cardiologist	– with all my heart
mortician	– to death
contortionist	– head over heels
optician	– at first sight
mathematician	– constantly
psychoanalyst	– in depth
person on a diet	– through thick and thin
astronaut	– from here to the moon

Here are some other questions that beg punning answers:

How do I loathe thee?
What do I wish for? (As a version of this, one could ask what particular types of people would wish for if they had three wishes.)
Where has my youth gone?
How cold was last winter?
Where would you like to go on vacation?

It is possible to answer these questions from the point of view of comic-book characters, movie stars, politicians, etc. For example, how would Jimmy Carter, Wonder Woman, Popeye, and John Wayne answer "How do I love thee?"

Catchy Combinations

A while ago I went to a store to buy some current 45-rpm records for my daughters. There were about 120 titles on display and I found myself reading them all with fascination. More than twenty were three-, four-, or five-word titles that contained the word "love" ranging from "To Sir with Love" to "Love Me Tender." Another twenty or so contained some form of the word "cry" (cried, crying, cries). Other words, like "dreaming" and "pretending" and "wishing," also occurred frequently. On the way home I started playing with making up titles of imaginary songs, restricting myself to a list of charged words like those above and limiting the length of the titles to five words. Recently I've been playing with these catchy combinations with friends, who in some cases have gone beyond making up titles and composed lyrics and melodies, turning titles into songs.

A good way to start, and one which focuses attention on the difference in meaning a preposition can give, and the creation of phrases, is to begin with lists of three-word titles, two words of which are identical. For example, starting with "Crying _____ you," with the middle word a preposition, the following titles, all with different meanings, result:

> Crying over You
> Crying at You
> Crying on You
> Crying with You
> Crying for You
> Crying about You
> Crying to You
> Crying above You
> Crying under You

It is possible to discuss the different meanings of each of these with particular attention to the difference between seemingly close titles like "Crying at You" (which seemed angry) and "Crying to You" (which was more imploring), and then to speculate on the kind of singer and group that would go along with each song.

It's possible to carry the crying motif further and explore other titles like:

> Crying out _____
> Crying on My _____

which yield among other variants:

Crying out . . .	*Crying on My . . .*
For Crying out Loud	Crying on My Pillow
I'm Not Crying out	Crying on My Knees
Crying out over You	Crying on My Time
Don't Cry out Loud	Cry on My Shoulders
I Can't Cry out Loud	Don't Cry on My Shoulders

Each of these titles suggests a melodrama or romance, a tale of love or jealousy or longing, and it's fun to make up stories that could go with the titles.

Here are some other words that easily lend themselves to song titles:

pretending	laughing	scheming
hate	dreaming	forgetting
help	waiting	care
longing	hoping	waiting

and in Spanish

corazon	amor	perdonare
camino	comprendeme	ultimo

Variations on "el ultimo _____" could include such examples as

el ultimo amor
el ultimo tren
el ultimo vez
el ultimo dia

While thinking about simple word combinations that lead to a variety of song titles, I came upon an ad for novels by Stephanie Blake that read:

After the sensational	*Flowers of Fire*
After the blockbusting	*Daughters of Destiny*
After the record-breaking	*Blaze of Passion*
The ultimate bestseller	*So Wicked My Desire*

That ad set out a formula that could be used for play with word combinations and constructions:

After the _____ _____ of _____
After the _____ _____ of _____
After the _____ _____ of _____
The ultimate_____ So _____ My _____

Here's a simple inversion of the ad:

After the mediocre	*Ladder of Rungs*
After the timid	*Heart of Cotton*
After the faltering	*Bladder of Gold*
The ultimate flop	*So Profound My Turnip*

Playing with this form is a wonderful way to think about the appropriateness of superlatives and the fit between nouns and adjectives (in _____ of _____) that leads to a serious, comic, or flat image.

This formula can be varied in any number of ways. Here are two. Try to make up others:

Two weeks ago you saw ＿＿＿＿＿＿＿

Last week you saw ＿＿＿＿＿＿＿

At last, this week you will see ＿＿＿＿＿

Now appearing for the ＿＿＿＿＿＿ time

on ＿＿＿＿＿＿＿＿＿＿＿＿

The (film) ＿＿＿＿＿＿ (title) ＿＿＿＿＿＿

    (novel)

    (play)

    (etc.)

Sentence Grids and Magic Sentence Grids*

In Chapter 1 I described letter grids and magic word squares. There is another form of grid that I have not seen anything written about but which is worth exploring. In this form of grid whole words are used instead of letters, and the object is to complete the grid with grammatical English sentences that make some sense (if you get too strict on exact meaning the constructions aren't so much fun). Here are some simple examples of sentence grids (complete these grids so that sentences are formed horizontally and vertically—punctuation can be used in any legitimate way and doesn't take up a square on the grid):

The			

	the		

		the	

			the

1

	the	

2

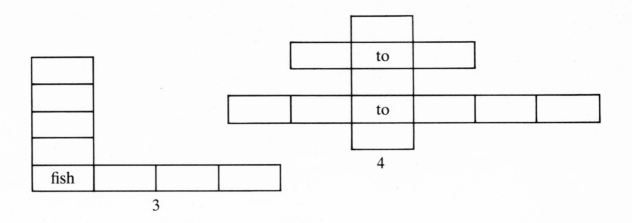

Possible solutions (there are others):

1. The colonel is dead.
   Did the general die?
   Hand me the ladder.
   Do not say "the."

2.   He
         likes
      playing
   kick "the" chair.

3. Did
   you
   catch
   a
   fish (?) make good eating.

4.   Try
      Go   to   Chicago.
           get
   I got   to   Chicago by sled.
   Chicago.

Of course there are dozens of variations that can be made up. There are also sentence square equivalents of word squares.

Simple Word Grids

The simplest word grid contains words which then can be recombined to make sentences. When making the grid it's sensible to include at least one noun, one verb, an article, and some conjunctions and prepositions. Here are a three-by-three and a four-by-four grid and some of the sentences they generate:

find	she	sky
swim	to	gray
and	went	the

1. She went to swim.
2. She went to find the gray sky.
3. She went to find and swim the gray sky. (This mythical statement contains all nine words.)

dog	go	fast	I
she	ran	am	angry
hit	a	and	went
at	fell	was	slowly

1. She was angry.
2. I hit a dog and fell slowly.
3. I was fast and she went slowly.

There are some interesting *challenges* that can be raised with regard to word squares.

How many possible three-word grammatical sentences can be generated by a three-by-three word square? The answer depends on the number of verbs, nouns, etc., in the square, as well as the fact that there are only nine words in the square. Because of that, the question cannot be answered in a purely mathematical way as could the question of possible words generated by a three-by-three letter square. The syntactic structure of English has to be taken into account for any configuration of nouns, verbs, etc., used to fill the square. This question then can be reduced to the question: Is there an optimal way to fill in a square so that the maximum number of grammatical sentences can be generated? (The same questions can be raised for four-by-four, five-by-five, etc., squares, and for sentences of four, five, six, etc., words in length.)

What are the best ways to distribute verbs, nouns, adjectives, adverbs, articles, prepositions, etc., throughout the square so as to generate long sentences? In a three-by-three word grid, how many nine-word sentences can be generated? How many sentences between nine and sixteen words long can you get out of a well-designed grid?

Additional Conditions

It's possible to make additional conditions on allowable sentences. For example, only sentences in which the words trace a connecting path could be allowed. In the four-by-four grid above, here are some allowed sentences:

I am angry fast.
She ran and fell.
She hit at a fell ("fell" meaning the hide of an animal).

Try to make a three-by-three grid with a connecting sentence nine words long. How many other connecting sentences can you get from the grid?

Try to make a grid with no connecting sentences (be sure the grid contains at least one verb and one noun).

Seeding the Grid

Larger grids with more interesting words naturally generate more interesting sentences. Below is a five-by-five grid constructed first by scattering a few nouns and *I, he, they, is, are, am, to, for, the,* and *have* about the grid. This is done to ensure enough flexibility in the grid so that sentences can be made. (There are other words that can be used to seed grids. A few are: *no, not, will, can, we, from, under, above, went, came.*)

After seeding the grid with words that guarantee that some sentences can be generated, the square was enriched by opening *The Shorter Oxford English Dictionary* at random and putting down the words my finger landed on. Whenever the word is unusual, the definition is written under the grid. How many sentences can you generate from this grid? I've found that this construction works best when sentences can be made using any order of words in the grid and when words like *the* and *and* can be repeated in a given sentence.

think	am	I	determination	renown
panther	manumit	is	handcuff	fancy
to	he	sour	have	for
hiss	snake	are	hang	the
and	itchless	game	they	fetch

(Definitions: *itchless*—free from itching; *manumit*—to set forth from one's hand, to release from slavery, to set free)

Here's one sentence using fourteen words and repeating "the" and "and":

I have to manumit the fancy itchless panther and fetch, handcuff, and hang the sour snake.

Magic Sentence Grids

Magic sentence grids are easier to make than magic word grids. Here's a four-by-four grid which contains four sentences that read the same across and down:

The	dog	is	weak
dog	the	fighting	men
is	fighting	good	will
weak	men	will	fall

In constructing the square, I began with the top sentence and put it on an empty grid:

The	dog	is	weak
dog			
is			
weak			

At that point, in order to use "dog" as the first word in a sentence, I had to consider it a verb (to dog someone) and therefore added "the" to the grid:

The	dog	is	weak
dog	the		
is			
weak			

Now it was necessary to add an adjective and a noun to complete the sentence, so I added "fighting" and "men" since they seemed promising for the last two sentences, which would then begin "is fighting _____ _____" and "Weak men _____ _____."

The	dog	is	weak
dog	the	fighting	men
is	fighting		
weak	men		

From here things were pretty simple. "Weak men will _____" made sense, and using the word "will" in the sense of good will completed the third sentence.

The	dog	is	weak
dog	the	fighting	men
is	fighting	good	will
weak	men	will	

Phrase and Sentence Variations

Completing the grid was simple. Whatever weak men will do can fit.

Good News/Bad News*

I'll end this chapter with a simple exercise in contrasts which can be used to generate strings of simple sentences. The idea is to make up two news items. The first should be positive, the kind of news people like to hear. The second item builds on the first and turns it into bad news. Here are a few examples:

Good News: I just bought a new plant.
Bad News: It turned out to be poison oak.

Good News: I just bought you a new digital watch.
Bad News: It got lost on the way home from the store.

Good News: We just sold the millionth copy of your new book.
Bad News: We can't sell the first 999,999.

Sense and Nonsense

Preliminary Distortion*

My daughter Tonia, who is twelve and reads quite well, showed me this quote from the *New York Times* (Nov. 30, 1978) which she thought was hilarious:

> President Carter announced today that he had placed a ceiling of $8.43 billion on the total value of American arms that could be sold in the 1979 fiscal year to nations not allied with the United States.

I didn't find anything funny about the quote, in fact what it contained seemed grim and depressing to me. I mentioned that to Tonia and she agreed but said that putting a ceiling on arms made her think of putting a floor on arms, of putting makeup on arms, of putting all kinds of things on arms. She added that she also thought of selling legs and eyes as well. Then she read a version of the sentence which she had concocted:

> President Carter announced today that he had placed an attic of $8.43 billion on the total value of American eyes that could be sold in the 1979 physical year to people blind toward the United States.

From there we proceeded to look through the paper, substituting phrases and words that distorted meanings and yet were connected in some way to the words they replaced, just as attic and ceiling, eyes and arms, physical and fiscal, people and nations are related through association or sound in the example above.

It might be fun to take reading texts, or sentences from newspapers or magazines, and systematically distort them through substitution. It's a good way to attend to nuances of meaning, to the use of images, and to the power a single word has to change the meaning of a complex sentence. Here's an example of what's possible. Consider the following ad:

GENTLEMAN'S COUNTRY ESTATE

39 plus acres, high elevation, privacy, country living, panoramic views yet 1½ hours from New York City.

MAIN RESIDENCE: superb, spacious, custom design, fieldstone ranch style home with a combination 50 × 24 feet living room & dining room, marble flooring in living room with raised fieldstone fireplace, master suite and family bedroom 26 × 13 feet with fireplace, bath, electric picture window, open beamed ceiling in living room & step-saver kitchen, game room carpeted and knotty-pine-paneled, library, laundry room, private rooftop sundeck.

Grounds are well maintained with an abundance of fruit trees and evergreens. Condition of property excellent. Rolling hills, large pond and some wooded area complements this estate. Offered at $500,000.

As an exercise in word substitution, I decided to replace as many words in the ad as I could by their opposites, using a thesaurus in order to enlarge upon the possibilities for substitution (for many people, an exercise like this is an excellent introduction to the thesaurus, an occasion to bring one out and explain its use). Here's part of my version of the ad:

HORRIDMAN'S SEWER HOVEL

$\frac{1}{39}$ minus inches, underground, thoroughfare, urban delights, subterranean views yet only $1\frac{1}{2}$ hours from a tree.

Deliberately breaking the rules of language or distorting the meaning of a word or sentence is a challenging exercise. There are many games with words where the imagination is set free from the constraints of grammar on the one hand and events in the real world on the other. Making up nonsense and being silly are ways of stepping away from the serious roles of everyday life and welcoming the unexpected and bizarre.

Perplexing Proverbs

Another form of rewriting consists of taking a simple statement and rewriting it in a complex, slightly pompous, overadjectivized form. When these are presented as a puzzle one can ask others to guess the originals.

Here are some outrageous complications of simple proverbs. They were sent me by Mike Sensena and Scott Garner, students at the Acacia School in Fullerton, California. Try to translate these statements into familiar proverbs. Be careful, they're tricky.

1. A rotating fragment of minerals collects no bryophytic plants.
2. Exercise your visual faculties prior to executing a jump.
3. Under no circumstances compute the number of your barnyard fowl previous to their incubation.
4. An excess of individuals skilled in the preparation of edibles impairs the quality of thin soup.
5. A feathered biped in the terminal part of the arm equals in value a pair of feathered bipeds in densely branched shrubbery.
6. A recently purchased implement for brushing away floor dirt invariably displaces the dirt most efficiently.
7. A timorous heart at no time succeeds in acquiring the beautiful damsel.
8. Everything is legitimate in matters pertaining to ardent affections and armed conflict between nations.

Answers:

Can you find a way to complicate these other proverbs?

A stitch in time saves nine.
Do unto others as you would have them do unto you.
Penny wise, pound foolish.
All's well that ends well.
The end justifies the means.

Here are two nursery rhymes to complicate:

Jack Sprat would eat no fat,
His wife would eat no lean,
And so between the both of them,
They licked the platter clean.

Jack be nimble, Jack be quick,
Jack jump over the candlestick.

The second one might begin: "Jack be dexterous, Jack be fleet. . . ."

The Oh Susannah Game

Remember the lines from "Oh Susannah"?

Oh it rained so hard the day I left
the weather it was dry
The sun so hot I froze to death
Susannah don't you cry.

The juxtaposition of opposites in the song can be used as the model for a group game using impossible juxtapositions. Let someone start with an assertion; for example:

I ate so much

Then the next person adds a line that contradicts the first:

> I starved to death

Then the third person continues the story:

> Then I went out

Then a fourth adds:

> When I stayed inside

And so on, continuing like this:

> That's why I loved you so
> My hate it knew no bounds

The first few times playing a game like this can seem dull and awkward. However, after a few times the story can get more interesting and the oppositions more striking.

There is a wonderful section in Iona and Peter Opie's classic *The Lore and Language of Schoolchildren* (London: Oxford Paperbacks, 1967), which has examples of word play in which words are substituted for their opposites or used in self-contradictory ways. The section is called "Tangletalk." Here are some of the Opies' analyses and examples:

> There is a difference between "nonsense" and "utter nonsense," and, curiously, "utter nonsense" often seems to be more laboured and self-conscious, although it is just as traditional.
>
> "As I walked down to the wayrail station, I met a bark and it dogged at me. I pulled a hedge out of a stake and necked its knock out."
>
> "You can say this when you are skipping if you like," says a 12-year-old Market Rasen girl. . . .
>
> The deliberate juxtaposition of incongruities, the "got the toothache in his toe" type of humour, is . . . characteristic of native English wit, and examples of both types of tangletalk have been found amongst children in different parts of Britain, only minor differences existing between the rhymes in one place and another:
>
> > One midsummer's night in winter
> > The snow was raining fast,
> > A bare-footed girl with clogs on
> > Stood sitting on the grass.
> > > Market Rasen
> >
> > It was a summer's day in winter,
> > The snow was raining down,
> > A bare-footed girl with clogs on
> > Stood sitting on the ground.
> > > Newcastle upon Tyne

A popular recitation of this type (versions from ten schools) may not be as modern as first appears, since it may have been a theatre not a cinema that the original hero visited:

I went to the pictures tomorrow
I took a front seat at the back
I fell from the pit to the gallery
And broke a front bone in my back.
A lady she gave me some chocolate,
I ate it and gave it her back.
I phoned for a taxi and walked it,
And that's why I never came back.

Kirkcaldy

I went to the pictures next Tuesday
And took a front seat at the back.
I said to the lady behind me,
I cannot see over your hat.
She gave me some well-broken biscuits,
I ate them and gave her them back;
I fell from the pit to the gallery
And broke my front bone at the back.

Enfield

It's fun to read these nonsense verses out loud and try to make up your own. Start simply with a few lines. Some beginning phrases that can get you right into the process are:

I went to _____
I took a _____
I fell from _____
We loved each other so we _____

Here are two of the best known tangle rhymes:

One fine day in the middle of the night,
Two dead men got up to fight,
Back to back they faced each other,
Drew their swords and shot each other.
A paralyzed donkey passing by
Kicked a blind man in the eye,
Knocked him through a nine-inch wall
Into a dry ditch and drowned them all.

'Tis midnight and the setting sun
Is slowly rising in the west.
The rapid rivers slowly run.
The frog is on his downy nest.
The pensive goat and sportive cow,
Hilarious, leap from bough to bough.

The Oh Susannah Game

99

Straight Questions and Crooked Answers

There are many funny ways of saying "Mind your own business." Iona and Peter Opie describe a number of them in *The Lore and Language of Schoolchildren*, which everyone concerned with language or children should read.

> Urchins seem to take a connoisseur's pleasure in evading questions which are inconvenient to them. If another child asks them their name and they do not want to give it, they say "Same as me Dad's." If the questioner persists, "What's your Dad's then?" they reply, "Same as mine." If asked "Where do you live?" they reply sharply "In a house." If asked "How old are you?" they reply "As old as my tongue and a little older than my teeth." Asked "What are you going to be when you grow up?" a girl replies "A woman I hope." It is part of the fun of such retorts that they adhere ostentatiously to the truth. And these prevarications baulk and irritate the questioner, without, perhaps, giving real offence. But should the children think a person is being unnecessarily nosey, or asking questions which are downright foolish, they are likely to give more impertinent answers. To one who asks inquisitively "What are you looking for?" they reply tartly "Looking for my shadow," or "Looking for last year's snow."
>
> "Where are you going?"
> "There and back again to see how far it is."
> "Where *are* you going?"
> "Daft, are you coming?"
> "Where have you been?"
> "To see my Aunt Fanny's ghost wrapped up in brown paper."
> "What did you do that for?"
> "To make fools spier (ask) and you're the first" (Kirkcaldy).
>
> And to people who ask an unanswerably stupid question, they recite:
>
> > "Twelve and twelve makes twenty-four
> > Shut your mouth and say no more,"
>
> or reply, "Does an elephant hate peanuts?" or "Can a wren take a crane for a lark?" or other inanity—it being well known that "Jolly silly questions deserve jolly silly answers."

It's fun to pose perfectly innocent questions and try to think up thoroughly crooked responses, or to act out dialogues with one person asking straight questions and the other inventing crooked answers.

One such question is "What's the time?" and there are crooked answers: Time you knew better. About now. Ten o'clock next Wednesday. Half past kissing time and time to kiss again. The same time as it was this time yesterday.

Some other questions you could start with are:

> What are you doing?
> Where are you going?
> How's the weather?
> What's your mother's name?
> How old are you?

Paradox

Paradoxes are statements or situations that seem to defy logic, and the word "paradox" itself means thought against itself or contrary beliefs. Some paradoxes appear to state two contrary things (like that Jesus is both man and god, mortal and immortal). Others appear true and are false or appear false and are true. There are paradoxical statements which are self-contradictory and others that seem to go against reason altogether. Paradoxes take one to the limits of language, to those areas where the usual rules don't seem to apply.

Paradox has a central role in religion, and especially in Christianity. How can a good god create evil? How can a person, Jesus Christ, be both man and god at the same time?

Paradox also plays a role in much poetry where the poet tries to deal with paradoxical ideas like: love can free and enslave at the same time; death can be a release from pain but not existing might be a greater hurt; or freedom leads to responsibility for action which then limits freedom.

Here are some paradoxical poetic statements:

> When my love swears that she is made of truth
> I do believe her though I know she lies.
> —Shakespeare, Sonnet 138

> Follow a shadow, it still flies you;
> Seem to fly it, it will pursue;
> So court a mistress she denies you;
> Let her alone she will court you.
> —Ben Jonson

There are also logical paradoxes which revolve about sentences or words that refer to themselves. Consider, for example, the statement:

The sentence in this box is false.

If that sentence is false, then it is true. If it is true, then it is false. So the statement is true and false at the same time and therefore self-contradictory. Yet it exists and provides an example of usage where the exclusivity of truth and falsity don't apply. There are many other versions of this paradox of self-reference. Here are a few:

1. Epimenides, who was from Crete, made the following statement: "All Cretans are liars." Was he telling the truth or was he lying?

2. There was a town which had only one barber. He shaved all and only those men in the town who didn't shave themselves. Did he shave himself?

3. Think of all the adjectives in English. Either they apply to themselves or they don't. Thus "short" is a short word but "long" is not a long word; "English" is an English word but "Spanish" is not a Spanish word. It's possible to divide all the adjectives in English into two classes: those that apply to themselves and those that don't apply to themselves. Adjectives of the first kind are called "autological" and those of the second kind are called "heterological." Now the question is whether the adjective "heterological" is itself heterological? If it is, then it applies to itself and is therefore autological. If it isn't, then it doesn't apply to itself and therefore is heterological, resulting in a paradox.

In addition to religious, poetic, and logical paradoxes, there are humorous paradoxes, like this one described in *Alice in Wonderland*. The Queen has just ordered the executioner to behead the Cheshire Cat, who at that point was just a grinning head:

> The moment Alice appeared, she was appealed to by all three to settle the question, and they repeated their arguments to her. . . .
> The executioner's argument was that you couldn't cut a head off unless there was a body to cut it off from: that he had never had to do such a thing before, and he wasn't going to begin at *his* time of life.
> The King's argument was that anything that had a head could be beheaded, and that you weren't to talk nonsense.
> The Queen's argument was that if something wasn't done about it in less than no time, she'd have everybody executed all around.

As an exercise, it is a challenge to list paradoxical situations where two contrary things are happening at once. For example, begin by making a list of opposites or contraries and see if you can imagine situations where they operate simultaneously. Here's a beginning:

1. hate and love
2. hot and cold
3. beginning and end
4. heaven and earth
5. asleep and awake

For these pairs:

1. Love/hate relationships are common.
2. You can have hot passion and cold feet at the same time.
3. The beginning of a new love and the end of an old one can occur simultaneously.
4. Heaven and earth can merge during states of earthly bliss.
5. There are many times (especially in school) when I am biologically awake and intellectually asleep.

Another exercise is to develop paradoxes of self-reference of your own. Better yet, read *What Is the Name of This Book: The Riddle of Dracula and Other Logical Puzzles* by Raymond Smullyan (Englewood Cliffs, N.J.: Prentice-Hall, 1978), the best book on paradox and logical puzzles I've seen, and then develop some of your own.

Here are two cartoons that show signs that are paradoxical:

It is possible to make up a whole series of signs with similar paradoxical content:

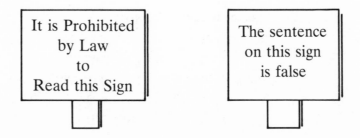

Here are a number of paradoxical problems taken from *Riddles in Mathematics: A Book of Paradoxes* by Eugene P. Northrop (New York: D. van Nostrand, 1944):

1. A bookworm starts at the outside front cover of volume I of a set of books and eats his way to the outside of the back cover of volume III. If each volume is one inch thick, how many inches will he travel?

2. A wealthy farmer left 17 beautiful horses to his three sons. He specified that the oldest was to get ½ of the horses, the middle to have ⅓ and the youngest ⅑. The sons didn't know what to do without calling in the butcher. Fortunately a friend arrived on horseback. He added his horse to the 17, making 18, and gave the oldest ½, which was 9, the middle son ⅓, which was 6, and the youngest son ⅑, which was 2. 9+6+2 made 17, so he took his own horse, the 18th, and rode away. How did that happen?

3. A clock strikes 6 in 5 seconds. How long does it take to strike 12?

4. A bottle and its cork cost $1.10 together. The bottle costs a dollar more than the cork. How much does the bottle cost?

5. A frog is at the bottom of a thirty-foot well. Each hour he climbs three feet and slips back two. How many hours does it take him to get out?

Answers:

1. One inch—look carefully to see where the front cover of volume I and the back cover of volume III are in the diagram.
2. The catch is that ½ + ⅓ + ⅑ do not add up to 1. They add up to ¹⁷/₁₈. The father was either a bad mathematician or somewhat evil.
3. 11 seconds—it is the intervals between strokes, and not the strokes, that take up time. There are 5 intervals in 6 strokes, and 11 intervals in 12 strokes.
4. The answer is not $1.00 for then the cork would be 10¢ and the

difference between the prices would be 90¢. The answer is $1.05 for
the bottle.

5. The answer is not thirty hours, as many people guess. It is
twenty-seven hours, for during the twenty-eighth hour he climbs
three feet and is out.

I'll conclude this section with a paradox invented by Lewis Carroll whose mastery of word puzzlements has possibly never been equalled. The paradox was described in a letter to his sister written in 1849:

> Which is the best, a clock that is right only once a year, or a clock that is right twice every day? "The latter," you reply, "unquestionably." Very good, reader, now attend.
>
> I have two clocks: one doesn't go *at all,* and the other loses a minute a day: which would you prefer? "The losing one," you answer, "without a doubt." Now observe: the one which loses a minute a day has to lose twelve hours, or seven hundred and twenty minutes before it is right again, consequently it is only right once in two years, whereas the other is evidently right as often as the time it points to comes round, which happens twice a day. So you've contradicted yourself *once*: "Ah, but," you say, "What's the use of it being right twice a day, if I can't tell when the time comes?" Why, suppose the clock points to eight o'clock, don't you see that the clock is right *at* eight o'clock? Consequently when eight o'clock comes your clock is right. "Yes, I see *that*," you reply. Very good, then you've contradicted yourself *twice*: now get out of the difficulty as you can, and don't contradict yourself if you can help it.

Carroll then adds this last comment:

> You *might* go on to ask, "How am I to know when eight o'clock *does* come? My clock will not tell me." Be patient, reader: you know that when eight o'clock comes your clock is right: very good; then your rule is this, keep your eye fixed on your clock, and *the very moment it is right* it will be eight o'clock. "But—" you say. There, that'll do, reader: the more you argue, the farther you get from the point, so it will be as well to stop.

Thank You for the Giant Sea Tortoise

New York magazine has nonsensical competitions. The magazine poses a silly question and judges the wildest and cleverest responses. Here are a number of the contest themes to work on, or try with your friends and students. They and many others are reprinted in a paperback called *Thank You for the Giant Sea Tortoise,* edited by Mary Ann Madden (New York: Lancer Books, 1971).

Thank You for the Giant Sea Tortoise

"Good Luck to the Drop-Out"
"So you've been elected President of the United States!"
"Congratulations to my son-in-law on joining the firm"

Above, unseemly greeting cards for unlikely occasions. Competitors were invited to supply greeting card messages for similarly odd occasions. Here are a few results of the competition:

"Thinking of You as You Picket"
"Hats Off to Your New Hairpiece!"
"Sorry to Hear about Your Allergy to Paper Products"

I Went on a Long Trip

I went on a long trip. Buzz and Mike went too. No girls or pets or parents allowed but there still wasn't all that much to do like swimming. You have to wear a uniform and a hat the whole time and the food was boring. I guess it was O.K. if you like sight-seeing. You can kick the moon dirt with your toe. We took some swell pictures. I lost my good camera. Everybody made a big deal when we got back. Next year I'm either going to Mars or getting a paper route.

Above, a composition by Neil Armstrong, age ten. Competitors were invited to submit an essay on this topic by a famous fifth-grader.

From Poland, With Love

Fiddler on the Porch
Eight Lives Cat Food
From Poland, with Love
The Socks of the Fisherman
Why Junior Can't Reed

Above, some near-miss nomers. Competitors were invited to submit suggested titles, product names, slogans, or what-have-you of a similar just-off-the-mark variety.

A Bird in Hand Is Worth Two in the Bus

"Look upon the rainbow and braise him who made it"
"A bird in hand is worth two in the bus"

Above, misprints due to the substitution or omission of a single letter.

Sense and Nonsense

Competitors were invited to submit similarly altered titles, quotes, aphorisms, and the like. Some responses:

"There's No Place Like Nome," "Wish You Were Her," "Up, Up, and Awry," *Love's Labours Cost,* "I've Got You Under My Ski," "A Rose is a Rose is a Ruse," "Wouldn't You Really Rather Have a Buck?" "I've Come to Bury Caesar, Not to Raise Him," *All's Well that Ends Wel,* and *A Comedy of Errers.*

The Pie Game Annual Expenses

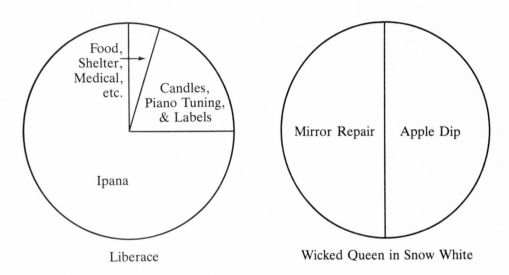

Liberace

Wicked Queen in Snow White

Above, the economists' favorite, the money pie. Competitors were invited to submit pies with characteristic annual expenses for a well-known person. Here are some responses:

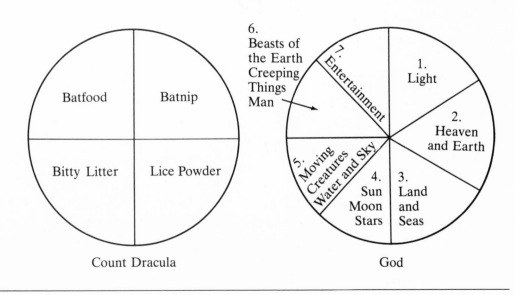

Count Dracula

God

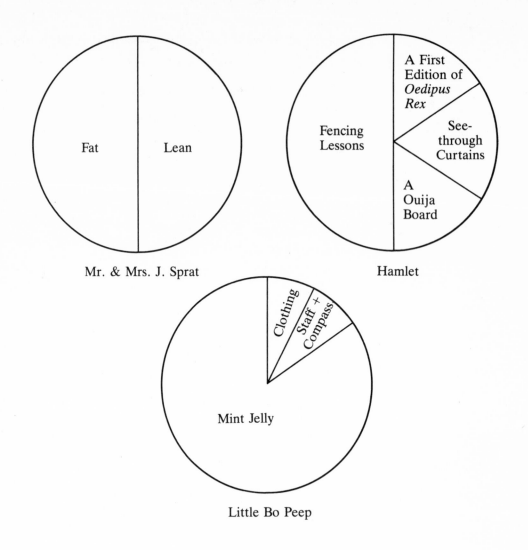

Fat | Lean

Mr. & Mrs. J. Sprat

A First Edition of *Oedipus Rex*

Fencing Lessons

See-through Curtains

A Ouija Board

Hamlet

Clothing

Staff + Compass

Mint Jelly

Little Bo Peep

A Selected Table of Contents to an Imaginative Journal

David LeCount teaches English at Menlo-Atherton High School in Atherton, California. Over the past six years he's produced some of the most creative material on the teaching of English that I've seen. Recently he sent me "A Selected Table of Contents to an Imaginative Journal," which is full of ideas and suggestions for play with the meanings of words and sentences. Each of his chapter headings can be the basis for writing exercises for people of just about any age.

A Selected Table of Contents to an Imaginative Journal

I. Questions I Can't Answer

   Examples:

   "Why can you see something better in the dark by looking immediately to the left of it?"

   or

   "Why do the spokes on a stagecoach wheel seem to be going backward when they hit a certain speed?"

   or

   "Why isn't the opposite of 'getting high' called 'getting low'?"

II. Words That I Have Made up, Their Derivation and Their Usage

   Examples:

   1. Twooter: (noun, street slang) a high-fidelity speaker that combines the bad qualities of woofers and tweeters with none of the good qualities. Sentence: "I would have gone out with him, but he had *twooters* in the back of his car."

   2. Cancer-Kire: (verb, Japanese hara-kiri) an ingenious method of committing slow suicide by sucking tobacco smoke into all of one's internal organs. Sentence: "In the third act of *Madame Butterfly,* Cio-Cio-San commits Cancer-Kire."

III. Phrases That I Enjoy Fooling Around With

   Examples:

   "Good fences make good . . . vantage points from which to spy on the neighbors."

   "A bird in the hand is worth . . . two gamehens in your shorts."

   "Silence is golden . . . but noise is diamond needles."

   "All I want for Christmas is my . . . sister in jail."

IV. Conversations or Portions of Conversations That Have Interested Me/Puzzled Me

   Examples:

   As I was riding home on the bus the other day, I overheard an old grandfather type whisper into the ear of a young, shapely blonde: "O.K. You can get the Iron Butterfly if you want."

   I sat next to a drunk and his wife on a park bench. I only overheard this: She: "After what you did, I wouldn't speak to you either." He: "How was I to know your mother planned to pay for it?"

Overheard in a railway station: "You may have gotten the children, but you'll never get my Maserati."

Overheard in church: "Pass the plate a little more slowly so they won't know if you put anything in."

V. Inventions That the World Still Badly Needs

Examples:

A device the length of a bacon strip that could, with little, razor-sharp blades, cut into the fatty edges of bacon strips so that they would never curl up while being cooked, and would, instead, lie flat.

A device to make the scratching of poison oak less pleasurable.

A tag license for identifying and registering werewolves.

A miniature knapsack that could be strapped to bats when they are used, during wartime, as homing pigeons in the dark.

A CB radio that works on solar power.

A biodegradable piton for mountain climbers who are aesthetically and ecologically conscious.

VI. Plots That I Think Would Make Surprising Stories (one paragraph each)

Examples:

A man discovers that his wife is having an affair with the plumber. In order to catch them in a compromising situation, he deliberately clogs the sink with beer cans and nostril hair. When he catches them together using this ingenious method, he draws a gun and forces the plumber to have his system cleared with his own snake. He charges the plumber $32 an hour, and sends him on his way. As for his wife, he puts Drano in her Bromo-Seltzer bottle.

A woman is elected president of the United States. Her first act as president is to require that all husbands stay at home all day long and care for the children on rainy days. She is impeached in a record one hour and six minutes.

An ant labors all spring and all summer to store food for the winter while his next-door neighbor, a cricket, sings and makes merry, urging his good friend the ant to do the same. The ant tells his good friend that he too should be laying up food, for all signs point to a very severe winter; nonetheless, the cricket ignores him, basking in the sun, playing his transistor radio, and drinking beer. Sure enough, the ant is right: the winter comes and is devastating. The smug ant opens his door to the poor cricket who is desperately begging for a handout, and hands him a cookie, saying, "It is always wise to prepare for our winters before they arrive." Hearing this, the cricket chokes the life out of the poor ant, takes over his domicile, wines and dines on his neighbor's food, smirks inwardly, and draws the fable to a close, thinking: "It is a far, far better thing that I do now, than I have ever done; it is a far, far better rest that he goes to than he has ever known."

VII. Observations About Human Beings or Nature

Examples:

My dog makes a ritual circle before he lies down in the grass, but he never does it in the house.

When my father is about to say yes to me, like that I can have the car Friday night, he always plays with the fat part of his ear. But when he is about to say no to my mom, he plays with his wallet in his back pocket.

Goats yawn sideways as well as up and down.

Hawks always seem to be hungriest between rain showers; that's when I see them the most. They also seem to hunt lower in the sky when it is windy.

VIII. Settings Where Stories Could Take Place or Places I Find To Be Most Beautiful

Examples:

I visited a beach this summer while I was in Hawaii that was made up of black volcanic sand. To one side of it, there was a cheap hotdog and souvenir stand; to the other side was a luxurious motel. In the middle of the beach there was a sign saying that it was against state law to take souvenir grains of sand from the beach. There were tiny shells, white, mixed in with black sand, like visible diatoms, like the teeth of some pygmy dinosaur who lost them years ago, volcanoes ago, when he was very young and teething on a lavastone.

There is a tree in the state park that is so contorted it looks like a witch played a game of "freeze" with her and left her that way forever. Rangers have had to put a fence around her trunk to keep people from carving their impermanence into her, and to keep them from touching her too roughly; now the beer cans rust around her at least at a spelled-out perimeter. Every now and then a tourist complains to the head ranger that he can't get close enough for "pictures."

A crowded bus depot somewhere in Nevada. A man who has not shaven for days glances at his watch. He walks to the cigarette machine, fumbles with the knobs, and looks around him. He puts no money in the machine, gets no cigarettes, and sits back down. The man sitting next to him, a balding man in his forties, shakes his head, and goes back to reading the *National Enquirer*.

IX. Exercises for Remaining Ignorant or Confused (Antiawareness Exercises)

Examples:

Walk into a local paperback bookstore and pick up a volume with your eyes closed. Keep the title hidden with a piece of paper, sit down and read every other page of it, and then plan your life by what you read.

Each morning as you wake up, remember what object in your room your eyes first focus on. During the day, look for those objects all day long, and count the number that you see while you are awake. Take this number and use it as your lucky number to find out how many letters your mantra should ideally have. Pick your mantra to correspond to the number of things you have seen that day, each thing corresponding to one letter. Each day you will pick a different object and a different mantra. In this way variety will give peace.

Run backward through a supermarket pretending you are a lobotomized beef.

Answer every question or statement you receive all day long with the statement: "You are blessed in believing so." Count the swearwords that you receive and this will tell you how many true friends you have.

X. Characters Who Should Be in Stories, Described

Examples:

A priest who is experiencing a crisis of faith decides to get away from it all and takes a trip to the Virgin Islands. He is tall, dark, and handsome, a fact which causes him to be mistaken for a secret agent by some freelance espionage agents who are trying to hide the fact that they are looking for atomic secrets to buy. The excitement and adventure of this world appeal to him a great deal, its pure mundane carnality, but he sincerely loves the spiritual truths of his religion.

A woman has four sons: one is killed in the Korean War, one is lost and presumed dead in a sailboat in the South Pacific, and one is retarded and commits suicide. The fourth son feels lost and is in search of his identity. What is the mother like who will help him the most?

A conservative businessman loses a son in a meaningless international incident, and decides to spend the rest of his life working in a hothouse experimenting with the heredity of flowers.

A high school student discovers that she has paranormal powers at a dance when she can cause different guys to ask her to dance in whatever order she wishes. She is mostly concerned with getting into college and does not feel right to use these powers on the college admissions officers; and yet she feels it foolish to have these powers that could get her in if it means that she is going to be rejected. What can she do experiencing this conflict?

XI. Four Solutions to Four Problems

Examples:

Problem #1: The insects of the world are becoming immune to DDT and are gradually taking over the world; and a time will come when no insecticide will be of any use.
Solution #1: Negotiate with them now while we still can. Give them the Amazon jungle, the Everglades, the Kalahari Desert, the Sudetenland, and Tonopah, Nevada, in exchange for leaving us alone. If they do not agree, blow up the earth to show them we are serious.

Problem #2: There is too much crime in America—in the cities, in the suburbs, in the country.
Solution #2: Pass a law which makes each person in the neighborhood legally and financially responsible for the criminal acts of anyone residing in the neighborhood. A victim residing anywhere else will be allowed to sue any and all of the crook's neighbors.

Problem #3: Fan violence in the sports arenas.
Solution #3: Block off all of the playing fields with double-thick glass, and allow no entryways for spectators to get onto the fields.

Problem #4: The potato chips I get are always crunched into small pieces because of their packaging.
Solution #4: Package potato chips in Styrofoam miniboxes that can be returned to the grocer's and reused.

XII. Puns I Have Known and Loved (?)

Examples:

Time flies like the wind, but fruit flies like banana.

This cemetery workers' strike is a grave business!

I know his poetry is bad but it could be verse.

And everybody knows about the optician who fell on his glass and made a spectacle of himself.

A Dictionary Game

This chapter concludes with a game that requires a dictionary. Dean Kahn introduced me to this group word game. A group (preferably six or more players) takes turns passing around a dictionary. The person with the dictionary chooses and announces a word nobody knows (if you know, or think you know, the word, speak up so another word may be chosen). While that person writes the real meaning on a piece of paper, all the others write a phony one on their pieces of paper. The definitions are passed to the announcer, who shuffles them and reads them aloud, trying to maintain a straight face.

The game is generally played one of two ways: seriously—real thought is given to creating convincing and plausible phony definitions; or (the way I prefer it) humorously—using the word's sound and structure to suggest hilarious meanings.

If you wish to keep score, each player receives two points for guessing the correct definition, and one point for each person who voted for the definition he authored.

Another way to score the game is to have everyone vote on the most convincing or humorous definition and score two points for that and one for a correct dictionary definition.

5

So to Speak–
Images and
Figures of Speech

Synecdoche
Personification
Simile
Metaphor
Understatement (Meiosis)
Overstatement (Hyperbole)

*Hands.** Since this book is about play and invention with language, I decided to introduce figures of speech through creating some fanciful and entirely speculative linguistic history. Let's start with the limbs we have coming out of our shoulders and project ourselves back to a time when there were no words for them. People had just realized that they had the power to name things and use words to describe actions, events, thoughts, and objects. They also discovered that they could use words to help them think about and plan their experience, and best of all to help them communicate with other people in more complex ways than they were accustomed to. Those limbs coming out of the shoulders were very important. They were used for pulling, dragging, splitting, hunting, throwing, and gathering. They were also used for eating, embracing, caressing, and healing. They were central to surviving, and beyond that to the creation and enrichment of culture. There had to be a word for them.

That word, roughly translated into English, was "arm." After some time passed, some people noted that there was a part of the arm that functioned as an independent unit. They noticed, for example, that you could rest most of the arm and still move those things at the end of the arm. You could hold and drop something without moving the arm, and even paint and sketch and carve small things using that thing at the end of the arm. It was as if it was an independent part of the whole with its own identity—and therefore needed a name. The name given it is roughly the equivalent of the English "hand."

As culture became more complex, as writing and crafts developed, as records began to be kept of economic transactions, and art was created to record and honor culture, the hand became more and more important. If people create with their hands, then the gods must also create with their hands. The hands of god became an important symbol, and whenever something unusual occurred, people began saying that the Lord's hand must be in it. (They had neighbors who disagreed and believed the gods created with their breath or with their words.)

If the gods had their hands in some events, so did people have their hands in things. The gods, having the power to create the world, also had the whole world in their hands, and when people felt exalted and godlike they said that they had the whole world in their hands.

At some point there was a famous boaster in this hypothetical society. He spent hours boasting about the game he could catch if only he could lower himself to go hunting. One day as he was boasting, a hunter passed by carrying a huge pheasant and one person, tired of hearing all the boasting, said, "A bird in hand is worth two in the bush." That putdown was so effective that it became a way to comment on all kinds of boasting having nothing to do with birds or hands.

The phrase "in hand" also became common usage. To have something "in hand" came to mean to have it under control, and politicians claimed that they had situations in hand or worried that other situations might get "out of hand."

The hand was used to wield a sword, and fighting at close quarters became "hand-to-hand combat." The hand was used to manipulate spoons and knives, and life on the margin of starvation came to be known as "hand-to-mouth existence." When people were given charity, they got a "handout," and if they acted ungrateful they were admonished, "Don't bite the hand that feeds you." When you controlled someone the way you controlled a pet dog or bird, people would say that you had them "eating out of your hand."

When people were prevented from using their hands, they became powerless. Tying someone's hands had a literal meaning and also came to mean making someone unable to act.

People played cards a lot during the cold winters, and the cards you held became your "hand." Your strategy for the game (and then for dealing with life situations) was known as how you "played your hand." Someone who made overaggressive moves and lost out was someone who "overplayed his hand." If you could outsmart someone, you could "force his hand."

In many cases "hand" came to stand for a whole person. For example, "I give up" could be expressed by "I throw my hands up"; to steal was "to have one's hands in the till," and to keep active in a group one "kept one's hand in." To be confused was "to have the left hand not know what the right one was doing." And given that it was noticed that the right hand was frequently more deft than the left hand, a person who was indispensable to your work was referred to as your "right hand."

The hand, being associated with creation and the gods, had special powers. Some people had healing hands. When you wanted to form a special group you "handpicked" them, and when you wanted to be recognized you raised your hand. When someone did something excellent and unexpected, people said "I've got to hand it to you, that's a good job."

A word was created from the root "hand" to mean something that was done by a skilled hand. That word, "handsome," was used to describe handcrafted objects that were particularly well made. Later it became applied to any well-made or fine-looking object. After some time it also came to be applied to the physical quality of people (especially men). To be handsome meant to be well made and physically appealing.

Another word, a verb, was created that meant to act with your hand. That verb, the equivalent of "to handle," also developed extended meanings so that people handle situations, other people, and ideas. A common way of expressing despair was "I can't handle it anymore." In some places hands were so identified with the self that one's name was one's "handle."

Not every simple descriptive word develops such a variety of uses and extensions of meaning as "hand" which lends itself to becoming an image of action because of its role in our life. As Montaigne said in one of his essays, "Behold the hands, how they promise, conjure, appeal, menace, pray, supplicate, refuse, beckon, interrogate, admire, confess, cringe, instruct, command, mock, and what not besides with a variation and multiplication of variation which makes the tongue envious."

However, "hand" is not unique in our language. The word "language" or "tongue" itself has many extensions (think of "tongue in cheek" and "a forked tongue"). The mouth, eyes, heart, and feet have their extended meanings and proverbial uses, as do animal names and other common words such as "house," "fire," "knife," and "air." Here are a few samples drawn from everyday language:

eye: evil eye
  the apple of one's eye
  open up one's eye
  bat an eye

  in the mind's eye
  to feast one's eyes on
  a private eye
  an eye-opener
  pull the wool over someone's eyes
  to have eyes in the back of
    your head

four-eyed
to make eyes at
out of the corner of
  one's eye
shut one's eyes to
the inner eye
keep in the public eye
starry-eyed
a sight for sore eyes
your eyes are bigger than
  your stomach

fire: ball of fire
  to fire someone
  hold one's fire
  to fire someone up
  keep the home fires burning
  to play with fire

to heap coals on the fire
set the world on fire
to build a fire under
  someone
out of the frying pan
  into the fire

air: to pass air
  to air one's opinions
  to give oneself airs
  into thin air
  to leave someone hanging in
    the air

to build castles in the air
to clear the air
to air dirty linen
  in public
to be up in the air about

The range and variety of these and other extended meanings of words and phrases have been studied for thousands of years, and they have been classified in many different ways from Aristotle's time to the present. The classifications have been made according to *figures of speech,* and for the sake of the exercises and games in this chapter, I'll use six figures which cover most extended nonliteral uses of words. These figures can be illustrated by some ways in which "hand" is used.

Synecdoche. In this figure a part is used to represent a whole. Most of the extended meanings of "hand" provide synecdochal uses of language. For example,

> They fought hand-to-hand.
> She's my right hand.
> I need a new hand to work with me.
> We have twenty good hands in our group.

In these forms the word "hand" and the phrase "right hand" represent whole people and not just hands. Here are some poetic examples of synecdoche:

> Farewell, thou child of my right hand, and joy;
> My sin was too much hope of thee, loved boy.
> > —Ben Jonson

> Two thousand souls and twenty thousand ducats
> Will not debate the question of this straw.
> > —Shakespeare, *Hamlet* 4.4.25

> Faces along the bar cling to their average day.
> > —W. H. Auden

Personification. In this figure an inanimate object, an abstract concept, or a nonhuman living creature is represented as if it is alive and endowed with human qualities or abilities:

> The car handled the curves well.
> The moon handed the sky over to the sun at dawn.

Here are other examples:

> Prudence is a rich ugly old maid courted by Incapacity.
> > —William Blake

> Mark how the bashful morn in vain
> Courts the amorous marigold
> With sighing blasts and weeping rain
> Yet she refuses to unfold
> > —Thomas Carew

Hey diddle diddle
The cat and the fiddle
The cow jumped over the moon
The little dog laughed to see such sport
And the dish ran away with the spoon.

Simile. A simile is an explicit comparison using the words "as" or "like":

They fought hand-to-hand like two wounded wolverines.
His hands moved like lead weights sinking to the bottom of the ocean.

Here's a classic extended simile from Homer (*Iliad* 4.275), perhaps the greatest master of this figure in written history:

As when a goatherd looks out from a watchtower of a hill over the sea and sees a cloud coming afar off over the sea, carrying with it much tempest, showing to him blacker than pitch, coming on driven by the west wind, and he shudders to see it and drives his flock into a cave, so appeared the march of the Greek warriors.

Here are a few more poetic similes:

> . . . turn away
> And like a laughing string
> Whereon mad fingers play
> Amid a place of stone,
> Be secret and exult.
> —W. B. Yeats

> That his hair is beautiful,
> Cold as the March wind his eyes
> —W. B. Yeats

> Poet, oracle and wit
> Like unsuccessful anglers by
> The ponds of apperception sit
> —W. H. Auden

Metaphor. Metaphor is a difficult figure to define. The simplest definitions of metaphor say that it consists of an implied comparison, and that the difference between metaphor and simile is the absence or presence of "as" and "like." Thus "Her hand is like a slender ivory sculpture" is a simile, and "her hand is a slender ivory sculpture" is a metaphor. However, there are many instances in which metaphor goes beyond being a comparison. For example, "He has bloody hands" doesn't imply a comparison between his hands and other hands that are bloody. The metaphor "bloody hands" has a meaning not implicit in "bloody" or "hands." Basically it means that he is guilty of some crime probably involving violence even though he did not necessarily administer the violence. Thus a dictator who orders someone executed has bloody hands even though he didn't pull the trigger.

Consider another word, "heavy-handed." To be heavy-handed is to deal roughly with a situation in a way that seems excessive. The sentence "You dealt with that child in a heavy-handed way" doesn't simply reduce to "You dealt with that child as if your hands were heavy." The merging of "heavy" and "hand" produces a new way of describing behavior. "Heavy-handed" is now a part of ordinary language, but it is likely that there was a time when it was considered a striking image. The same is true with "dirty hands," which means tainted and soiled in a moral rather than physical way.

The *Princeton Encyclopedia of Poetry and Poetics* (ed. Alex Preminger; Princeton, 1965) gives a broad definition of metaphor that encompasses cases where metaphor is not an implied comparison. According to this encyclopedia a metaphor is "a condensed verbal relation in which an idea, image, or symbol may, by the presence of one or more ideas, images, or symbols, be enhanced in vividness, complexity, breadth of implication." This broad definition accounts for the fusing of "heavy" and "hand," as well as of "dirty" and "hand." It also accounts for the possibility in our language of combining almost any two words and imagining a context in which they could enhance the meaning of the whole. For example, consider the following poem by William Butler Yeats:

> I made my song a coat
> Covered with embroideries
> Out of old mythologies
> From heel to throat;
> But the fools caught it,
> Wore it in the world's eyes
> As though they wrought it
> Song, let them take it,
> For there's more enterprise
> In walking naked. . . .

In the poem Yeats dresses and undresses his song, letting the fools take the superficial aspects of his song and keeping the naked substance. Here the metaphor of a coat to dress a song pervades the whole poem whose meaning emerges from the metaphor. The poem, interestingly enough, is close to a fable with the implicit moral "Don't mistake the package for the contents" and reminds me of some of the extended African riddles and proverbs that will be discussed in the next chapters.

Here are some other poetic metaphors which illustrate how the nonliteral juxtaposition of ideas, images, and symbols create metaphors which enhance the meaning of a work:

> Blasted with sighs and surrounded with tears,
> Hither I come to seek the spring.
> —John Donne

What sphinx of cement and aluminum
bashed open their skulls and
ate up their brains and imagination?
      —Allen Ginsberg, *Howl,* part II

Pour the unhappiness out
From your too bitter heart,
Which grieving will not sweeten.
      —Wallace Stevens

She sang beyond the genius of the sea.
      —Wallace Stevens

Finally, here are some metaphors picked out of the poems of Edith Sitwell:

Flames of the Laughing Sun
The dews of Death
The wooden chalets of the cloud
The sea in each fire
The universal blackness of Hell's day
The hammer of Chaos
The lunatic Wind

Hyperbole or Overstatement. This figure involves deliberate exaggeration, such as:

She was so strong she could handle Paul Bunyan as if he were a baby.
He was so handy he could make a Rolls-Royce out of Volkswagen parts.

Other examples:

She ate a ton of ice cream.
We had a million laughs together.
When she kissed me, I felt I could fly to the moon and back in a second.

Meiosis or Understatement. This figure is the opposite of hyperbole and involves deliberate understatement, such as:

Mohammed Ali is pretty fair with his hands.
I'll hand it to Einstein, he knew a bit about thinking.
Bob Hope occasionally liked to tell a joke or two.

Meiosis and hyperbole are forms of *irony,* as are sarcasm, mockery, joking, and false naïveté. The word "irony" comes from the Greek *eironeia.* In ancient Greek comedy there was a character who played the *eiron* role. An *eiron* was a weak but clever underdog who triumphed over the strong but stupid and boastful *alazon.* Socrates is a good example of an *eiron* as he pretended ignorance and raised questions that caused his opponents to make statements that were contradictory or absurd, thus refuting themselves.

Ironic statements usually say the opposite of what they mean. I've noticed that there is very little irony used in school texts and a great deal used informally by teachers and students when talking about each other. D students say they have great report cards, and teachers who have reputations for being mean and inconsiderate are referred to as Nice Mr. So-and-So or Gentle Mrs. X. Irony and indirection are powerful forms for commenting on reality and it makes sense to study them explicitly as well as use them correctly. In the next section on games and exercises with figures of speech, I'll suggest some ways of playing with irony.

Synecdoche

In a synecdoche a part of something stands for the whole, a head for a person or a wing for a bird. One way to begin playing with synecdoche is to pick out some wholes and make lists of their parts. Here are a few lists:

person		*car*		*bird*	*book*
intestines	head	wheels	names of	wings	pages
behind	eyes	steering	makers:	beak	binding
leg	ears	wheel	Ford,	eyes	cover
foot	mouth	accelerator	Cadillac,	tail	page
toes	nose	speedometer	VW,	claws/talons	numbers
fingers	neck	fenders	T-Bird,	feet	front
brains	chest	brakes	etc.	feathers	back
muscles	arms	bumpers	windows	crop	spine
hair	hands	radio	door	droppings	table of
navel	stomach	windshield	key		contents
heart		gas tank	ignition		index
		fuel	motor		title page
					publisher
					author
					editor

Then take some other wholes that might lend themselves to being described by the parts generated. As a start one can choose:

the country
a baseball team
the family

and begin playing with different ways of describing them. For example,

who is the   head of the country
eyes of the country
ears of the country
mouth of the country
stomach of the country
brains of the country
navel of the country
heart of the country
hands of the country

Once while discussing these particular synecdoches with friends we made distinctions between people who saw everything going on, who always listened and hardly spoke, who gossiped, and who organized things, etc. The discussion was both playful and serious. There were debates over the meaning of the navel of the country, and some awkward moments when we discussed where the stomach of the country might be located. Dealing with the figures was a way of thinking about the country and its structure as well as learning about nonliteral uses of language.

After thinking about the country in terms of a person, we shifted to considering the whole country in terms of a car. Who was the steering wheel, what was the fuel, where were the brakes located, what happened when the motor broke down? Starting from synecdoches it is possible to begin dealing with the extended metaphor of the country as a car. This symbolic thinking stretches the possibilities for analysis in a group context, and I've found that it can lead to more serious self-analysis and consideration of problems than literal fact-minded discussions. For example, I've found it easier to discuss discipline with students and with my children in the context of examining what the brakes of the class are and how the motor gets regulated than by talking more directly about what happens when things get out of hand. The figure seems to provide a nonthreatening vehicle for thought and discussion.

Some other wholes that can be analyzed to generate lists of parts are:

a flower   an ant hill
a beehive   a wolf pack
an airplane in flight   a government
a sailboat   an orchestra

These analyses can be applied to social groups, to businesses, to parties, political campaigns, races, etc.

Another interesting thing to do is collect synecdoches from everyday language and vary them. For example, here are a few common synecdoches:

> the head of the line
> the public eye
> to count noses
> to count heads

It would be interesting to speculate on the nose of the line, the ears of the line, the heart of the line. These ideas are not so absurd when you consider what happens on a line that has formed several days before a sports event or concert. It develops more than a simple head and tail.

Personification

Personification makes objects and abstract ideas come alive, and gives nonhuman things human qualities. Love and hate become people, rocks talk, and chairs and tables become alive. A good example of how elaborate a personification can be is Swinburne's portrait of Love:

> Love laid his sleepless head
> On a thorny rosed bed;
> And his eyes with tears were red,
> And pale his lips as dead.

It's fun to take such lofty abstractions and turn them into people: justice, vice, the spirits of the past, present, and future, life, death, irony, pleasure, or pain can all be personified. These personifications can lead to interesting improvisations. For example, all these abstract nouns can be written on scraps of paper and then people can pick a scrap, create a personification for that idea, and act it out. The others can guess what idea was portrayed at the end of the improvisation.

Once I was fortunate enough to teach a high school class in improvisation in the costume and prop room of a theater. We did our improvisations in full dress. We started with simple personifications (death in a black shroud, justice with scales and a blindfold) and then elaborated on the original improvisations. Instead of one death, six students characterized death in different ways. One student was a weaver who ended lines by breaking threads, another had a cage where she kept souls stolen from the living, etc.

After personifications of a single idea we developed skits with several ideas vying against each other. I got the concept for this from traditional poetic contests. In these contests there is a dialogue between two personifications, for example, between

summer and winter
body and soul
wine and water
country and city

where each personified idea tries in rhyme to prove its superiority. Our version of these contests was to have fights over a person's fate. Thus, life and death fought over a person, as did love and hate, justice and greed, pleasure and pain, etc. The person fought over entered the improvisation whenever he or she wanted to and led the skit to a conclusion by giving in to one side or getting them to fight so intensely that he or she could slip out of both their grasps.

In addition to improvisations with such abstract ideas it's possible to do improvisations (or mime) by animating inanimate objects. For example, you can start by posing a group of actors as dolls, tables, chairs, knives, spoons, plates, glasses, pots, pans, etc., and then at a given sign have them animate themselves and relate to each other. The objects can also be described in more detail and be made more interesting. Some objects that lend themselves to interesting improvisations are:

a discarded wedding dress
a broken drum
an old military jacket that's been through the wars
an old shoe with no laces
a cigar or cigarette butt
a radio
a shell found on a beach one summer
an empty ballpoint pen
a toothbrush

Each object has a story of its own to tell, and in groups they can develop stories. These histories and little dramas can be written out as well as acted.

There are other writing exercises that utilize personifications. Here are some themes that can be played with as an autobiographical sketch in the object's own voice, e.g.,

The Life History of a Coffee Table: "I was born in Brazil and California hundreds and thousands of years ago. Part of me is teak and part redwood, and they don't go well together. That's why I creak so much. . . ."

The Adventures of a Rolling Stone
From Factory to Junkyard—A 1952 Ford's Own Story
Interview with a Much Abused Statue—or Why Do the Pigeons Pick on Me?
Confessions of a Dishrag (or any other object)
The Life of a Liberated Shoe (or any other object)
Life in a Mixed Set of Silverware
"I Drank Too Much"—Confessions of a Cadillac

It is also possible to write out dialogues between personified objects and/or ideas. Some can be simple discussions about their lives or the way they observe people. Others can be arguments as to which is superior. Here are some possible ones:

dialogue between a new doll and a discarded doll
dialogue between time and space
dialogue between a car and a motorcycle
dialogue between a door and a window
dialogue between silence and noise

Simile

I usually introduce play with similes by starting with a list of similes to complete. People compare responses and then stretch out a bit, making the similes more elaborate and trying to have them express a range of attitudes from praise to ironic insult. The list usually consists of five or ten similes like these:

my love is like _____
she's as smart as _____
they're as funny as _____
he's as fierce as _____
he's as handsome as _____
she's as beautiful as _____
he's as tall as _____
she's as brave as _____
the army marched across the valley like _____

the boat moved through the water like _____

the car sped down the highway like _____

he's as fast as _____

they're as kind as _____

they're as cruel as _____

playing with him is as much fun as _____

getting cut is as painful as _____

The range of responses for any of these simile-forms is enormous. For example, consider these ways of responding to "he's as fierce as":

He's as fierce as a lion.

He's as fierce as a wolverine.

He's as fierce as a tiger.

He's as fierce as a Spartan warrior.

These four similes are all flatteringly positive. However, there are insulting possibilities:

He's as fierce as a mouse.

He's as fierce as a soggy tomato.

He's as fierce as a pillow.

He's as fierce as a marshmallow.

There are more complex responses that begin to qualify the nature and quality of fierceness to be attributed:

He's as fierce as a pit bulldog that smells blood (a pit bulldog is relentless, and when it gets its prey, it bites its ears or neck and holds on even if it is killed in the process; this simile describes tenacious ferocity).

He's as fierce as a wounded tiger (this is the wild ferocity of someone in flight).

He's as fierce as Herb's golden retriever (this is no fierceness at all; it's a bark with no bite).

Then there are really elaborate responses similar to the one I quoted before from Homer:

He's as fierce as water flowing from a quiet mountain stream becomes as it joins other streams and moves down to the sea, building up, cresting, and finally overflowing its banks and carrying everything away with it.

This simile is somewhat exaggerated but it does describe a person who does not look fierce on the surface, but someone who slowly builds to a fierceness that could sweep away everything in its path.

As some of these examples illustrate, even a very simple simile-form such as "he's as fierce as . . ." or "she's as smart as . . ." can generate an indefinite number of similes of different levels of sophistication. When playing with similes it is important to get a sense of the ways in which a simile has been elaborated. To facilitate this, I usually devote time to exploring the variations of one simile in some depth. I might start with this chart and fill it in:

she's as strong as

(+) positive	(−) negative
an ox	a whisper
an elephant	a pea
a cockroach	a cockroach
an ant	an ant

It is interesting that ants and cockroaches appear in both columns. In these cases it depends on what the creator of the simile intended. According to one person an ant may be strong because it can lift many times its own weight, while according to another it might be weak because it can't lift anything bigger than a twig. Neither simile is "wrong," but each is ambiguous and can be clarified through elaborations such as:

She's as strong as an ant who carries many times its weight without straining.

or

She's as strong as the puny ant who can't even move a pencil out of its way.

After filling in the chart and discussing the positive and negative similes, it makes sense to discuss ways of being strong and not being strong before going on to generate further similes. There are many different kinds of strengths and weaknesses—intellectual, emotional, spiritual, and physical—and it is probably possible to invent similes that embody them.

As a final exercise it is interesting to define a particular kind of strength (or love, or height, or whatever is being qualified by the comparison in the simile) and then try to make up similes that embody it. Here are a few examples:

Emotional strength: the ability to bear a great deal of stress without collapsing
Similes: She's as strong as a steel beam that bends under the weight it carries but never breaks.
She's as strong as a bridge that expands and contracts with heat and cold, and that sways with the wind, but is so well constructed that it never breaks.

Intellectual strength: the ability to analyze problems, to get right to the core of things

Similes: She's as strong as a diamond bit that bores through the hardest material and yet never loses its brilliance or shape. She's as strong as a shaft from a crossbow that flys straight to its target and passes on through.

Metaphor

I was once asked whether it was possible to give a metaphoric meaning to any adjective-noun combination imaginable. I'm not sure of the answer, but experimentation with words has led me to believe that there are no apparent limits to our ability to import metaphoric meanings to combinations that have no literal sense. For example, I experimented with the color of lies, beginning with a little white lie. A white lie is a small, insignificant lie made without intent to harm. What about these lies:

> a black lie
> a gray lie

and to run through the rainbow:

> a red lie
> an orange lie
> a yellow lie
> a green lie
> a blue lie
> an indigo lie
> a violet lie

There was no trouble assigning meaning to them:

a black lie	– an ominous, dangerous lie
a gray lie	– an old, sickly, familiar lie
a red lie	– one told with a flickering red tongue smacking of nastiness
an orange lie	– a luscious, tasty, citrus lie that is as interesting as it is vicious
a green lie	– a fertile, fecund one that gives rise to other lies
a blue lie	– a sexual lie

an indigo lie – a deep-blue lie, one that springs from unconscious motivation

a violet lie – a regal lie emerging from a person with authority

It wasn't difficult to invent these meanings since colors have so many psychological and physical associations that they bring the whole spectrum of these associations to the fusing of meanings that creates metaphor.

In playing around with the genesis of metaphor with some friends and students, a number of games have emerged. These games have no winners or losers. Basically they provide practice with the figurative use of language. They can provide an ease with metaphor that is useful for reading and studying poetry as well as analyzing the way metaphor is often misrepresented as literal truth in politics and advertising.

Game 1: Adjective-Noun Combinations

This game is for two people or two small groups (two, three, or four people). The first group makes a list of a dozen nouns. The second makes a list of a dozen adjectives. The group should be aware of the difference between literal and nonliteral uses of language. The lists are placed on a board or written on index cards. Then the people take turns choosing one adjective and one noun that do *not* make literal sense when combined (for example, "blue ball" and "warm soup" would not be allowed). Once players have chosen, they make up a meaning for their combinations and write sentences using their metaphors. A round ends as the players read the meaning and sentence for their words.

This description of the game seems dry. However, the game can be quite lively if the players are willing to stretch out and think of possible meanings for their words rather than trying to get the "right" meaning and "right" metaphor. Here is part of a round of the game that I played with my son Josh and my daughter Erica:

adjectives	*nouns*
slimy	frog
weary	city hall
purple	box
thoughtful	book
fast	letter
dreadful	piano
cool	earth
tasty	person

Erica's first choice was a tasty person. According to her definition, a tasty person is "one who has good taste or a precise taste, a very picky taste on what he or she likes." Her sentence was "In order to come to this restaurant you must be a tasty person." Her response surprised me as I immediately associated "tasty person" with a cannibal's dinner, with someone who would taste good in a stew. Erica's use of taste in the sense of sensitivity in choosing things was logical but not usual. The meaning of taste she used probably was initially a metaphoric extension of "taste" meaning the way things feel to the tongue.

One of Josh's responses also was somewhat unexpected. He chose "dreadful frog" and defined it as a frog who is very sad and scared. Dreadful for him meant being full of dread (a metaphor) rather than inducing dread or being terrible, which is the common meaning of the word. Some of the other combinations we chose were:

slimy city hall—a city government that oozes with corruption
purple letter—one that someone writes to brag about something
thoughtful piano—a piano that practices your lessons for you, a player piano
weary earth—earth tired of wars and storms and earthquakes

This game can be complicated by letting players choose two or more adjectives and nouns. For example, the rules can be modified so that on each turn players choose any combination of four words on the list. Here are some possibilities:

a dreadful, slimy, purple city hall—a government that is terrible, lying, and outrageous in its pompous self-righteousness

a fast, cool, thoughtful box—a good talker who responds quickly and well to any verbal challenge (e.g., "Don't insult him. He's got a fast, cool, thoughtful box")

Game 2: Metaphoric Phrases

There are a number of metaphoric phrases like "the trail of tears," "the valley of death," and "a pot of gold" that are commonly used in our language. Adopting their forms

a _____ of _____
the _____ of _____

it's possible to play with these phrases in the same way Game 1 used adjective-noun combinations.

Start with any list of nouns and make up phrases, define them, and use them:

silver	pot	street	anger	seat
money	knife	city	play	walk
cry	smile	fear	cushion	work

Here are some phrases:

a city of fear	the smile of fear	the anger of play
a city of play	a cushion of work	the walk of smiles

Game 3: Metaphoric Actions

One can cut through an argument, cut red tape, swim through a sea of words, have thoughts race through the mind, sell someone on something, and pay one's dues. These actions are metaphoric, describing ways of doing things in nonliteral ways. Verbs can be used so that they describe such metaphoric actions. For example, here are some common verbs and a few of their metaphoric usages:

to walk – to walk the plank
    to walk all over someone
    to walk the chalkline
    to walk the floor

to beat – to beat the band
    to beat into someone's head
    to beat one's brains out
    to beat the game

to play – to play politics
    to play possum
    to play the game
    to play second fiddle

to look – to look daggers at
    to look down one's nose at
    to look for a needle in a haystack
    to look someone in the eye

It is possible to take any list of verbs and examine ways they can be used to describe metaphoric actions. Try these:

to swim	to cry
to talk	to believe

In order to focus the process of developing metaphors, the following forms are convenient as starting points:

to _(verb)_ to the
to _(verb)_ for
(verb)ing in the _____

For example,

to swim to the moon
to swim for the devil

swimming in the air

Here are some metaphors made with the above verbs. Can you find meanings for them:

> to swim to the bathtub
> to talk to the clouds
> to cry to a stone
> to believe for the papers
> crying in the closet
> talking in a pot

It is also possible to approach the creation of action metaphors by beginning with a verb and trying to create metaphoric equivalents of it. For example, the following could be metaphoric equivalents of "to exaggerate":

> to walk to the moon
> to talk to the mountains
> to lift the Empire State Building
> to weave a tree
> to kiss the heavens

Try to create metaphors for the following:

to lie	to love	to doubt
to congratulate	to risk	to defend
to attack	to hesitate	to support

Strictly speaking, the invention of metaphors is not a game. It is play with language within a gamelike context, i.e., it is not done for any goal other than the pleasure and learning it provides. Sometimes it is difficult to begin to play with words when there is no apparent outcome—no test results or rewards. Yet for adults and schoolchildren such play is the equivalent of the baby's babbling and sorting out sounds. It leads to an extension of one's command of language. The ability to create metaphor makes it possible to extend one's language, to say more about the complexity of experience than literal language allows. It helps articulate one's own way of perceiving and living in the world.

Game 4: Extended Metaphors

An extended metaphor is an elaborate nonliteral description of an idea, feeling, person, event, or place. Emily Dickinson's poem "Hope" is an extended metaphor:

> Hope is the thing with feathers
> That perches in the soul,

And sings the tune without the words,
And never stops at all.

And sweetest in the gale is heard;
And sore must be the storm
That could abash the little bird
That kept so many warm.

I've heard it in the chillest land,
And on the strangest sea;
Yet, never, in extremity,
It asked a crumb of me.

There are a number of ways in which extended metaphors can be developed. Starting with a feeling, idea, person, event, or place, a group can take turns describing it, each person adding to the previous person's phrase (this is also a good individual exercise). For example:

a feeling: Doubt is the thing
  that floats backward and forward at the same time
  that sinks and swims but is never in water
  that is ashamed to sing and ashamed to be silent

an idea: Justice is
  a saint dressed as a beggar
  something hidden under the bed or in a drawer
  a liquid that moves to its level
  a stream that is stronger than the rocks and soil in its path

a person: W. C. Fields is
  a red light bulb
  a sneer
  a lover of what others hate
  and a hater of what others love

a natural event: The hurricane was
  ten babies crying
  a hundred children screaming
  a thousand parents sighing
  a million grandparents mourning

a historical event: The Civil War was
  a family quarrel
  a family suicide
  a family show
  a family disease
  a family famine
  a personal death

a place: New York is
    an anthill
    a beehive
    the hometown of the lemming
    a vacation spot for roaches
    a haven for hell

A second way to develop extended metaphors is to take two structurally related concepts or things and compare them in detail using the following form:

X is a *Y* in these ways: (1), (2), (3), etc.

Here are some possible exercises using the form:

An ant community is a city in these ways: (1), (2), etc.
A baseball game is a love affair because: (1), (2), etc.
A game of chess is war because: (1), (2), etc.
A game of checkers is war because: (1), (2), etc.

As a variant of this it's possible to analyze differences and complete statements like:

A game of chess is not war because: (1), (2), etc.
A game of chess is not a game of checkers because: (1), (2), etc.
A game of chess is not a love affair because: (1), (2), etc.

There is another way to develop extended metaphors that occurred to me after rereading Langston Hughes's "A Dream Deferred":

What happens to a dream deferred?
Does it dry up
like a raisin in the sun?

Or fester like a sore—
And then run?

Does it stink like rotten meat?
Or crust and sugar over—
like a syrupy sweet?

Maybe it just sags
like a heavy load.

Or does it explode?

It is possible to use this structure for other questions:

What happens to an old love?
What happens to an old enemy?
What happens to lost hope?

What happens to childhood?
What happens to a wasted effort?
What happens to a battle lost?
What happens to a battle won?

I like to try my hand at answering these questions metaphorically. It is not important to create a poem. Developing a metaphor can be a way of thinking through a problem, of finding out what you think and feel. For example, recently sixty miners lost a strike and their jobs at the Blue Diamond Mines in Kentucky after three years of being on the picket lines. I had supported the strike. Creating an extended metaphor helped me work through my feelings about what to do to help them

What happens to a battle lost?
  Does it vanish like smoke?
or get swallowed in quicksand?
Does it lose all shape like melted clay
Or return to its original conviction
  like scattered iron filings when
    new energy from a magnet comes into its field?

Understatement (Meiosis)

Understatement (meiosis) is basically a form of irony that is used to give the impression that something is less in size or importance than it really is. Sometimes it can be very simple. For example, if you ask someone how she feels after having a child or being married or winning a prize and she smiles and says "Miserable," she is employing meiosis. Sometimes meiosis can pervade a whole poem, as it does in this four-line poem by Sarah Cleghorn, where the meaning is deliberately understated in a naïve way:

The golf links lie so near the mill
That almost every day
The laboring children can look out
And see the men at play.

A more complex example of understatement is W. H. Auden's "The Unknown Citizen":

The Unknown Citizen
(*To JS/07/M/378*
This Marble Monument
Is Erected by the State)

He was found by the Bureau of Statistics to be
One against whom there was no official complaint,
And all the reports on his conduct agree
That, in the modern sense of an old-fashioned word, he was a saint,
For in everything he did he served the Greater Community.
Except for the War till the day he retired
He worked in a factory and never got fired,
But satisfied his employers, Fudge Motors Inc.
Yet he wasn't a scab or odd in his views,
For his Union reports that he paid his dues,
(Our report on his Union shows it was sound)
And our Social Psychology workers found
That he was popular with his mates and liked a drink.
The Press are convinced that he bought a paper every day
And that his reactions to advertisements were normal in every way.
Policies taken out in his name prove that he was fully insured,
And his Health-card shows he was once in hospital but left it cured.
Both Producers Research and High-Grade Living declare
He was fully sensible to the advantages of the Instalment Plan
And had everything necessary to the Modern Man,
A phonograph, a radio, a car and a frigidaire.
Our researchers into Public Opinion are content
That he held the proper opinions for the time of year;
When there was peace, he was for peace; when there was war, he went.
He was married and added five children to the population,
Which our Eugenist says was the right number for a parent of his generation,
And our teachers report that he never interfered with their education.
Was he free? Was he happy? The question is absurd:
Had anything been wrong, we should certainly have heard.

Rather than make up games employing meiosis it's probably sensible to use poems like Auden's to point out the way one can say something and mean another thing. As an exercise it is also possible to make up questions like Auden's "Was he free?" and "Was he happy?" and try to give a number of understated answers to them. Some questions and answers might be:

Was seeing the *Mona Lisa* interesting? About as interesting as

> eating a banana
> getting a haircut
> watching television

How did you feel meeting the president? It was just the same as

> taking a walk
> meeting my brother
> taking a nap

What was it like hearing that you won the Nobel Prize? Nothing to it. Just like

> eating toast for breakfast
> getting my phone bill
> getting a call from my uncle

Overstatement (Hyperbole)

Hyperbole consists of bold exaggeration, often expressing strong emotion. Hyperboles like "He's raging like a tornado," "She's strong as an ox," "They're fighting against the waves and the very ocean itself"—which are metaphors—are not meant to be taken literally.

It's interesting that, according to the *Princeton Encyclopedia of Poetry and Poetics,* hyperbole is common to all the literatures of the world. It seems that exaggerating is not the special province of any particular people.

It is possible to play at exaggerating. I vaguely remember a radio show called "Can You Top This?" where comedians competed telling more and more absurd jokes. A hyperbole version of "Can You Top This?" would consist of making more and bolder (and perhaps more absurd) exaggerations. Starting from simple sentences like "She's strong" or "They are angry," a series of hyperboles can be built up:

> They are angry.
> They are angry as a tornado.
> They are angry as a dozen tornadoes.
> They are angry as a dozen tornadoes ripping across a small, defenseless prairie town.

> She's strong.
> She's strong as a mountain.
> She's strong as an unmovable mountain.
> She's strong as an unmovable mountain that stands in majestic isolation dominating all the hills and valleys around.

Another way to play with hyperbole is to use the form:

> not all the _____ can _____ from _____

The form is used by Shakespeare in *Richard II:*

> Not all the water in the rough rude sea
> Can wash the balm from an anointed king.

Here are some versions:

Not all the hounds of hell can chase me from my true home.

Not all the ghosts and demons that inhabit the Congress can scare me from my convictions.

Not all the money on earth can dissuade me from following my conscience.

A simpler exercise with hyperbole can use the form:

not all the _____ can _____

Not all the water in the sea can drown his grief.

Not all the tea in China can satisfy her thirst.

Not all the Rolls-Royces on earth can persuade him to junk that '62 Ford.

6

Riddles, Proverbs, and Fables

Riddles
Proverbs
Fables

Riddles*

The earliest known riddles were found written in cuneiform on clay tablets. They came from Babylonia and are over 5000 years old. Nobody knows how far back into history the habit of riddling dates, although some scholars think it may be one of the earliest forms of thinking. Riddles are challenges, questions that have unexpected and often amusing answers. They pop up throughout the world's literature, appearing in the Bible, in medieval texts, in Moslem and Hindu writing, as well as in nursery rhymes such as:

> Humpty Dumpty sat on the wall,
> Humpty Dumpty had a great fall,
> All the King's horses / all the King's men,
> Couldn't put Humpty Dumpty together again.
> What was Humpty Dumpty?   (an egg)

This riddle is believed to be thousands of years old and is told throughout Europe. Humpty is known as "Boule-boule" in France, as "Hillerin-Lillerin" in Finland, and as "Etje-Papetje" in part of Germany. The egg has many other names throughout Europe and the riddle is only one of dozens of riddles that depend on the nature of the egg. For example, there's the following Scottish children's riddle:

> A wee, wee hoose
> Fou, fou o' meat
> Neither door nor window
> To let you in to eat.
> What is it?   (an egg)

This riddle is strikingly similar to a Bantu riddle told in East Africa:

What is the white hut which has no door?   (an egg)

and to the following one told to me recently in California:

What is a house with no doors and windows but with gold inside? (an egg)

Not only are riddles spread around the world. They have a habit of persisting, of being handed down over the generations and possibly even being reinvented every hundred years or so. Iona and Peter Opie in *The Lore and Language of Schoolchildren* tell of two riddles they heard from twelve-year-olds in England in the 1950s:

How deep is the ocean?   —A stone's throw.

How many balls of string would it take to reach the moon?   —One, if it was long enough.

They found the same riddles (although with somewhat different spelling and phrasing) in a riddle book *Demaundes Joyous* which was "Enprynted at London in Flete strete at the sygne of the sonne" by Wynkyn di Worde in 1511:

What space is from ye hyest space of the se to the depest   —But a stones caste.

How many calves tayles behoveth to reche frome the erthe to the skye   —No more but one and it be longe ynough.

The riddles illustrated so far portray a basic feature of most riddles: they are metaphors, unusual and unexpected comparisons and contrasts. The egg is a person or a house, the ocean is as deep as a stone can sink, a string can be stretched to the moon. All of these are mini-poems, condensed images.

Many African riddles are explicit about the metaphoric nature of riddles. There are riddle contests where the riddle presents an image and the audience takes turns guessing the answer. For example, here are a few East African riddle/images and their answers:

Birds which gaze on a place not near	(the eyes)
Two children disputing leadership	(the heels)
Ten boys with their hats on the back of their heads	(the fingers)
The old lady who cries when knocked by a child	(a drum)
A little child's sweet gruel	(sleep)
Mother is small but she knows how to cook nice food for me	(a bee)

Zulu riddles are extended metaphors and are sometimes amazingly complex. Here's one as an example, with its explanation (taken from Harold Courlander's *A Treasury of African Folklore,* pp. 474–5):

Riddle
Guess you: a man who lives in the midst of enemies every day, where raids are made without ceasing; and he is alarmed when the army sets out, knowing that he is then in the midst of death; he has no forest to which he can escape. He escapes only by the enemy retiring. He then eats food, saying: "Ah! escaped this time! I did not think that I could escape from the midst of the army." He has no children, because he lives in the midst of enemies, saying, "No; it is well that I should live by myself, and then when an alarm is given, I may be ready to escape."

Explanation

The tongue is a man which is in affliction because it is in the midst of enemies; the teeth are the enemy; for when the teeth are eating, the tongue is often injured whilst they are fighting with the food, that they may grind it. The tongue, then, is not happy, for when the teeth are chewing food, the tongue continually moves from side to side between the teeth, and is on its guard when the food is killed; for the food is constantly killed by the teeth; but the tongue is not killed by them for it is known, it is a man of that place; but it continually meets with an accident, for there is fighting in the place where it dwells; it is happy before the food is eaten; but when the food is being eaten, it knows that it is in the midst of danger, and is about to be injured, without having had any charge made against it; it dies because the battle is fought in its presence. There, then, is the man who is in the midst of enemies, the tongue.

Riddles play many different roles. Sometimes riddling is purely for fun. At other times it is a teaching device. Melville J. and Frances S. Herskovits describe some of the complex functions of riddling in Dahomean society in their *Dahomean Narrative* (published by Northwestern University Press):

The Dahomean riddle is expressed with economy. Its appeal lies not only in the hidden meaning of the solution, but more especially in its double entendre, the play on words that is so important an element of Dahomean everyday communication. . . .

A period of riddling prefaces all storytelling sessions. For the adults it is a warming-up time, a keying to attention, that keeps them occupied until latecomers arrive. For the children it has the special function of memory training, and is so recognized by the adults. To be present at one of these children's storytelling sessions, presided over by one of their age mates, and listen to the answers to the riddles coming with lightning rapidity is like hearing a drill in the multiplication table. Of the double entendre the children get nothing, though at certain points they will laugh in imitation of their elders. It is this double entendre that gives the riddle its importance in the rites for the dead. For the dead, who are being sent away from the world of the living, must savor all that gave them pleasure when alive; so at wakes the old men show their mastery in introducing riddles with the broadest innuendo, the greatest subtlety, and the sharpest suggestiveness. Some of these elements, unfortunately, are blurred or lost in translation.

Some of the riddles asked at these sessions are:

Hole within hole, hair all round, pleasure comes from inside. (Answer: A flute being played by a bearded man)

A thing leaves the house bent over and returns home straight. (Answer: A water jar)

A thing is naked going out, but returning, the body is covered with clothes. (Answer: Corn)

My father eats with his anus and he defecates through his mouth. (Answer: A gun)

A large hat in the midst of weeds. (Answer: A latrine)

One thing falls in the water with a loud voice, another falls in the water with a soft voice. (Answer: A bottle of oil, a carrying basket)

Charles Frances Potter, who wrote the article on riddles in the *Funk and Wagnalls Standard Dictionary of Folklore, Mythology, and Legend* (New York: Funk and Wagnalls, 1972), described how he learned through riddles:

I have sat by the stove of a winter night and given the answers to the riddles my father and mother alternately asked me as they went through the catechism their parents had taught them. It was part of my education, and much more interesting than the lessons in grammar school. It was much more mind-stretching, for the answer to each new riddle was not given me until I had tried long and hard and turned the given situation every which-way seeking the solution. . . .

Perhaps it was the neatness of the packages in which the lore was given which appealed to me. L. W. Chappell, on page 227 of B. A. Botkin's *Folksay* 1930, recognizes this very point: "Riddles, perhaps even more than most types of traditional lore, have a way of 'staying put'. Their vigorous compactness of form seems to give them a peculiar hold on the popular imagination and in many cases to insure their preservation for centuries." . . .

Then again, like all children, I was intrigued by the peculiar combination of beauty and mystery on the one hand and absolutely logical factual reasoning on the other. The riddle was a puzzle and a challenge and a nut to crack. We called it cracking riddles, too, and we cracked nuts at the same time, and one seemed to help the other.

Adults use riddles too. Oedipus had to answer the riddle of the Sphinx in order to save Thebes (What walks on four legs in the morning, two in the afternoon, and three in the evening? Answer: people—as babies they crawl, they walk on two legs in their prime, and toward the end of life use a cane as a third leg), there was a riddle contest at Samson's wedding feast, as well as at Roman and Greek feasts. In fact, the riddle Hesiod asked Homer is supposed to have worried Homer to his death. The riddle, which still exists in communities throughout the world, refers to a fisherman's reply to the question "What did you catch?" The answer is:

> What I caught I left behind,
> What I brought, I didn't find.
> What was the catch?

(Answer: ǝɔᴉl)

There are many folktales where a marriage or the salvation of a kingdom or the acquisition of treasure depends on answering riddles correctly. As an example, there are versions throughout Europe of the tale of the clever peasant girl. Stith Thompson, in his book *The Folktale* (New York: Holt, Rinehart and Winston, 1946), describes the most common version of the tale:

> A peasant finds in his field a golden mortar and tells his daughter that he plans to take it to the king. She advises very strongly against this, because she says the king will demand the pestle also. It turns out as she has predicted, and the peasant in his distress bemoans the fact that he did not obey his daughter. The king inquires about what he means, and hears the whole story, whereupon he insists upon having the daughter come to court. Another opening of the story begins at the court itself, where two peasants must give answers to questions propounded by the judge. One of them answers correctly as his daughter had advised him. This comes to the attention of the king, who wants to see her. When the clever girl arrives at the court, he assigns her various tasks and propounds various questions. She must come to him neither naked nor clad, neither by day nor by night, neither washed nor unwashed, or the like. She comes wrapped in a cloth, or at twilight, or with only part of her body washed, or otherwise carries out the paradoxical order. . . . She weaves a cloth with two threads, hatches out boiled eggs, or carves a fowl so as to give the appropriate pieces to all members of her family. After she has successfully passed all the tests, she marries the king. One day as she sees him make a manifestly unjust decision about the possession of a colt, she advises the owner how to act so as to show the king the absurdity of his decision. The king is incensed at her meddling with his affairs and casts her out with the permission to take with her only that one thing which she holds dearest. She takes with her the sleeping husband, who is so moved by this touch of affection that he forgives her.

Even the simplest, most common riddles like "Why did the moron throw the clock out the window?" (answer: to see time fly) or "What goes up when the rain comes down?" (answer: an umbrella) involve tricks of language or unusual juxtapositions. Children delight in them and often use them to get the better of adults. I remember one day my children were sitting around the table telling riddles. As I came into the room Josh asked me "What is black and white and red all over?" I knew that one, I thought, and answered confidently "a newspaper." He said no, the answer was "a skunk with diaper rash," to which my daughters added "a penguin with pimples" and "a zebra with measles." (Another reply I heard during the 1960s was a civil rights march.) They threw me off and I was resolved to be cleverer the next time. Erica threw one at me: "A zebra with wide stripes married a zebra with narrow stripes. They had a son with no stripes. What did they call him?" I toyed around with several answers—a stripeless zebra, a blank something, a clear something—but nothing seemed right so I gave up. Erica's answer was "Milton." She had caught me again, this time for trying to be too clever.

I've often wondered how many riddles are known by people at any party or meeting. A good way to find out is to ask. In fact, the easiest way to introduce riddles is to suggest that people try to stump you (or each other) with riddles. From there it's possible to write up riddles and even publish a neighborhood riddle book. It's also possible to make up riddles, especially if you have examples of different types of riddles available. Here's a partial list of different types of riddles with some suggestions about how to create new ones:

True Riddles

A true riddle according to Iona and Peter Opie (in *The Lore and Language of Schoolchildren*) describes an object or creature in a deliberately obscure way. The solution to a true riddle fits the description exactly and usually resolves some paradox stated by the description. Some examples the Opies heard from English children are:

What goes up when the rain comes down?   —An umbrella.

What can go up a chimney down but can't come down a chimney up?   —An umbrella.

What goes up but never comes down?   —Smoke (according to boys in Dublin); Your age (according to boys in Knighton).

What holds water yet is full of holes?   —A sponge.

What gets wet when drying?   —A towel.

What goes to sleep with its shoes on?   —The milkman's horse.

Some examples I've heard from American schoolchildren are:

What goes up and down but doesn't move?   —A staircase, a ladder, the temperature, a road that goes over a hill.

A boy and a girl had birthday cakes. The girl had eight candles and the boy seven. Which candles would burn longer?   —None, candles burn shorter.

What has eyes but doesn't see?   —A potato.

What grows in winter and dies during summer and has its roots upward?   —An icicle.

What runs around the lawn but never moves?   —A fence.

There are also African examples of true riddles. Here are a few from Peter Farb's *Word Play* (New York: Alfred Knopf, 1974):

Statement: Invisible
Response: The wind, or your thoughts, or my dead grandfather
Statement: Little things that defeat us
Response: Mosquitoes, or fleas, or lice

These African riddles can be used as the basis of a riddling game. One person gives a one-word description or a sentence and then others take turns creating answers that fit the descriptions. For example, here is a list of some words and some responses:

Statement	Response
silent	my love, a sculpture of a person
fast	your mouth, a good time
wicked	his smile, a storm in summer
angry	the wind, waves
gentle	a soft bed
lonely	the last bird, the moon when no stars are out, me when my parents got separated
powerful	water, a baby crying (because grownups do what it wants them to do)

Another way to invent true riddles is to begin with objects, list their characteristics, and then try to make up some puzzling combination of these characteristics. For example, starting with water the following qualities could be listed: strong, can break rocks, can wash away trees, flows around things, even soft things can move through it. Combining some of these, the following riddle emerges:

What is so strong it breaks rocks and uproots trees and yet is so gentle that your hand can move through it without being hurt?   —Water.

Here are some other possibilities:

Word	Characteristics
food	gets cut and stabbed by knife and fork, gets ground up by teeth, gets digested

Possible riddle: What gets stabbed and cut and ground up and doesn't get hurt?   —Food.

Word	Characteristics
the moon	waxes and wanes, shines and lights up earth but doesn't have light of its own

Possible riddle: What lights up others but has no light of its own?
—The moon.

Homonym Riddles

There is a series of riddles that depend on the fact that there are pairs of words in English that sound the same, are spelled differently, and have different meanings. One I came upon recently is:

What's the difference between two policemen and two butchers?
—The policemen meet on the beat, and the butchers beat on the meat.

Homonym riddles are a good way to get children to learn homonyms and exercise some ingenuity in playing with shifts of meanings. Here's a list of homonyms to play with:

allowed – aloud	flee – flea	mail – male	seller – cellar
all – awl	fore – four	need – knead	stake – steak
bail – bale	foul – fowl	pail – pale	steal – steel
bear – bare	great – grate	peek – peak	teem – team
beer – bier	hail – hale	plain – plane	tier – tear
boar – bore	heel – heal	reel – real	vial – viol – vile
can't – cant	here – hear	sail – sale	wear – ware
deer – dear	holy – wholly	seem – seam	weak – week
dough – doe	leek – leak	seer – sear	waist – waste
fare – fair	made – maid	seize – seas	right – rite – write

Using the format "What's the difference between *X* and *Y*?" and beginning with homonym pairs, here are some riddles:

Homonym pair	*Riddle*
dough/doe	Why are a gambler and a hunter the same? —Because they both shoot the dough/doe.
flee/flea	What's the difference between a robber and a dog? —One tries to flee the cops and the other tries to cop the fleas.
waist/waste	Why are a fat person and a garbage collector the same? —They both work to eliminate the waist/waste.

Punning riddles are extensions of homonym riddles. Puns use words that suggest two or more meanings or use words of the same sound with different meanings. A simple old punning riddle goes:

What is put on a table and cut but never eaten? —A deck of cards.

Here's a collection of pun riddles to share. They were drawn from various sources as well as from conversations with children. In my experience people pick up the knack of punning quickly and on hearing these riddles create their own variations.

What stays where it is when it goes off?   —A gun.

What would happen if a girl ate bullets?   —She'd grow bangs.

What did one candle say to the other candle?   —We're going out tonight.

Why does the rain fall in sheets?   —To cover the riverbed.

What goes out without putting its coat on?   —Fire.

What has a neck but can't swallow?   —A bottle, a turtleneck sweater.

What has teeth but can't bite?   —A comb.

What has legs and arms but can't walk or hold things?   —A chair.

What has fingers but can't use them?   —A glove.

When is a door not a door?   —When it's ajar.

Finally, here are some riddles collected by the Opies which involve homonyms, double puns, and in some cases rhymes:

What is the difference between a jailer and a jeweler?   —One watches cells and the other sells watches.

What is the difference between a ball and a prince?   —One is thrown in the air and the other is heir to the throne.

What is the difference between a letter ready for posting and a lady going along a road?   —One is addressed in an envelope and the other is enveloped in a dress.

What is the difference between a big black cloud and a lion with toothache?   —One pours with rain and the other roars with pain.

What is the difference between a lazy schoolboy and a fisherman? —One hates his books and the other baits his hooks.

What is the difference between an angry circus owner and a Roman hairdresser?   —One is a raving showman and the other is a shaving Roman.

What is the difference between a cat and a comma?   —A cat has its claws at the end of its paws and a comma has its pause at the end of a clause.

Catch Riddles

A good riddler likes to vary things. A catch riddle is one that catches you off guard because it has a simple, straightforward answer. They work best when mixed in with other riddles that require thought and ingenuity. For example, consider this sequence of three riddles:

What did the chicken say when it got out of the egg?   —Marmalade (ma me laid).

What did the beaver say to the tree?   —It's been nice gnawing you.

Why did the clown wear red, white, and blue suspenders?

The first two riddles depended on word play so it's natural to look for a similar clever variation of meaning or sound. The catch, however, is that the answer is "to hold up his pants."

Here are some more catch riddles:

What is the first thing that happens when a dozen elephants fall into a river?   —They get wet.

If you went over a cliff what would you do?   —Fall.

Which boy in the school wears the largest hat?   —The boy with the largest head.

What makes more noise than a pig under a gate?   —Two pigs under a gate.

What smells most in a perfume factory?   —The nose.

Why did the chicken cross the road?   —To get to the other side.

This last riddle is so much of a cliché that people make up clever answers that catch out the catch riddle. Some are:

to hitchhike to town
because the light changed
to buy a six-pack
to watch time fly

It's easy to make up catch riddles but it takes some skill to know when to use them. It's fun to set up riddling matches where two teams of three persons each take turns asking riddles. Each person asks five riddles and the team that stumps the other the most gets a riddler's badge or patch or some equally appropriate antic reward. There's one rule that turns out to be necessary—a unanimous vote of the players on one team can disqualify a riddle for being too obscure or too much like a factual question. As an example: "Where's the largest pizza in the world?" could be excluded if the answer is meant to come from the *Guinness Book of World Records*.

On the other hand if the intended answer is "in some people's stomachs," the riddle would be acceptable.

Surreal Marriages

Some riddles depend on creating the most unlikely combinations, yielding almost surreal metaphors. For example:

What's purple and plugs in?   —An electric prune.

What's green, faster than a bullet, and can stop a train? —Superpickle.

What would you get if you crossed a porcupine and a skunk?   —A smelly pincushion.

If a cat ate a lemon, what would it become?   —A sourpuss.

What do you get when you cross an owl with a goat?   —A hootenanny.

What do you call a werewolf in a Dacron suit?   —A wash and werewolf.

It's easy to create variations on these riddles. Superpickle can become Batpickle, Wonderpickle, or The Lone Pickle, with the following variations:

What's green, wears a cape, and solves crimes with the boy wonder?

What's green, carries a magic lasso, and wears gold bracelets?

What's green, wears a mask, and rides a white horse?

There are also variations on the electric prune: the electric pickle, banana, or squash. My children's favorite is: What is green with white freckles and plugs in?   —An electric zucchini.

An interesting exercise is to make a list of animals, fruits, characters, vegetables, or things and see if combinations of the words lead to riddles. Here is one set I tried with some friends:

yellow	red
turtle	car
black	white

What's red and black and has a hole in it?   —An anarchist bagel.

What do you get when you cross a turtle and a car?   —A mobile home.

What's black and red and yellow?   —Burnt toast with ketchup and mustard, a Chinese anarchist, a cowardly anarchist.

What's black and white and black and white and black and white?
—A zebra, penguin, skunk (or to be a bit religiously mischievous, a nun) falling down a flight of stairs.

Extended Metaphor Riddles

Zulu riddles are basically extended metaphors. The one cited earlier in this chapter listed over eight characteristics of the teeth in metaphoric form. Here are some more Zulu riddles (from Harold Courlander's *A Treasury of African Folklore*) which are equally elaborate:

1. Guess you: a pumpkin plant; it is single and has many branches; it may be hundreds; it bears many thousand pumpkins on its branches; if you follow the branches, you will find a pumpkin everywhere. You will find pumpkins everywhere. You cannot count the pumpkins of one branch; you can never die of famine; you can go plucking and eating; and you will not carry food for your journey through being afraid that you will find no food where you are going. No; you can eat and leave, knowing that by following the branches you will continually find another pumpkin in front; and so it comes to pass. Its branches spread out over the whole country, but the plant is one, from which springs many branches. And each man pursues his own branch, and all pluck pumpkins from the branches.

A village and the paths which pass from it are the branches, which bear fruit; for there is no path without a village; all paths quit homesteads, and go to homesteads. There is no path which does not lead to a homestead. The pumpkins are villages from which the paths go out.

2. Guess you: a man whom men do not like to laugh, for it is known that his laughter is a very great evil, and is followed by lamentation, and an end of rejoicing. Men weep, and trees and grass; and everything is heard weeping in the tribe where he laughs; and they say the man has laughed who does not usually laugh.

Fire. It is called a man that what is said may not be at once evident, it being concealed by the word "man." A riddle is good when it is not discernible at once. We say "a man," because it is not liked that the fire, even indoors where it is kindled, should cause its sparks to start out and fall on the clothes. The owner of the clothes cries because it burns; and when he sees a hole in it, he cries again. Or if food is being cooked, if the fire is large the pot may be put on, and be burned by the fire, and the pot burn the food. So the man laughs, that is the fire. And the people cry. Again, if a spark is cast into the thatch of the hut, it is seen by the fire; all the men will come together when the flame of the fire appears, and burns the house with the things which are in it; and there is a great crying; and the goats are burnt, and the calves; and the children are burnt. The cows cry, crying for their calves which are dead; men cry, crying for their goats; the wife and husband cry, crying for their children which are burnt; and the children cry for their father who has been burnt, having died whilst fetching his precious things from the burning house, and the house fell in on him; and the husband cries, crying for his wife who has been burnt; she died when she was fetching her child which was in the house, and was burnt together with it; and the trees cry, crying for their beauty which is lost, being now destroyed by the fire, and the trees are shrivelled and withered, and their beauty gone; and the cattle cry, crying for the grass, because they no longer have anything to eat, but are dying of famine. This, then, is the laughing of fire.

3. Guess you: a man who makes himself a chief; who does not work, but just sits still; his people work along, but he does nothing; he shows them what they wish, but he does nothing; his people do not see, he sees for them, they are blind, the whole of his nation; he alone can see. They know that though they cannot see, they see by him; for they do not go without anything they want; he takes them by the hand, and leads them to where there is food, and they return with it to their homes; but he touches nothing, for he makes himself a chief; he remains a chief forever, for his people are supported by him.

At first there was a dispute, and his people said: "You cannot be our king and do nothing; we cannot see the power of your majesty." He answered them, saying: "Since you say I am not a chief, I just sit still, and look on the ground. Then you will see that I am truly a chief, for if I look on the ground the land will be desolate; you will fall over precipices and into pits; you will be eaten by wild beasts through not seeing them; and die through famine, being unable to find food; because you dispute with me, you are blind."

So they see that he is a chief, and say: "Let us acknowledge openly that he is our king that we may live. If we die of famine, that majesty which we claim for ourselves will come to an end. We are kings by living." So he was acknowledged a chief, and reigned; and the country was peaceful.

And he is a man that never washes; he just sits still. And when he is ill even with a slight illness all his nation is troubled, and dies of famine; and the people are afraid to go out of their houses, because they would fall over precipices and be dashed to pieces. They long for him to get well at once; and the people rejoice when he is well.

[Answer] The eye.

These riddles are metaphoric ways of exploring the nature of things. Cities, social organizations, human organs, plants, animals, and natural phenomena are paired in complex ways, illuminating both. I can think of many other parallels that can be spelled out through extended metaphor:

a spider's web and a piece of cloth
a bus full of people and a mushroom cap full of spores
a human society and a bee hive
a writer's life and the life cycle of a plant

an echo and a conversation where nobody listens to anybody else

I've played around with elaborating an extended metaphor riddle using the parallel between a novel and the life cycle of a plant, working in Zulu style:

> Guess you: a plant that grows and then is completed, one of many ·seeds, some which never grew, others which froze or washed away, a slow-growing plant that took long to flower, which emerged in beauty for a while, then goes to seed only to open up the chance of further plants and flowers coming into being.

> Answer: ǝɟᴉꞁ (s,ʇsᴉʇɹɐ) s,ɹǝʇᴉɹʍ ∀

The Zulu are not the only ones who ask extended metaphor riddles. Here's one in a more antic mood that was transcribed in Tennessee in the late 1800s:

> On this hill there was a green house. And inside the green house there was a white house. And inside the white house there was a red house. And inside the red house there were a lot of little blacks and whites sittin' there. What place is this?   —A watermelon (Bedford County, Tennessee).

And finally here are two contributions of Lewis Carroll's. The first is uncanny in its similarity to the Zulu riddles. Carroll called it "An Explication of the Enigma (Proposed by Bishop Samuel Wilberforce)":

> I have a large Box, with two lids, two caps, three established Measures, and a great number of articles a Carpenter cannot do without. —Then I have always by me a couple of good Fish, and a number of a smaller tribe, —besides two lofty Trees, fine Flowers, and the fruit of an indigenous Plant; a handsome Stag; two playful Animals; and a number of a smaller and less tame Herd: —Also two Halls, or Places of Worship; some Weapons of Warfare; and many Weathercocks: —The Steps of an Hotel; The House of Commons on the eve of a Dissolution; Two Students or Scholars, and some Spanish Grandees, to wait upon me.
>
> All pronounce me a wonderful piece of Mechanism, but few have numbered up the strange medley of things which composed my whole.

Here's Carroll's explication:

The WHOLE, —is MAN.

The PARTS are as follows:

A large box – The Chest.
Two lids – The Eye lids.
Two Caps – The Knee Caps.
Three established Measures – The nails, hands, and feet.
A great number of articles a Carpenter cannot do without – Nails.

A couple of good Fish – The Soles of the Feet.
A number of smaller tribe – The Muscles (mussels).
Two lofty Trees – The Palms (of the hands).
Fine Flowers – Two lips (tulips), and Irises.
The fruit of an indigenous Plant – Hips.
A handsome Stag – The Heart (hart).
Two playful Animals – The Calves.
A number of a smaller and less tame Herd – The Hairs (hares).
Two Halls, or Places of Worship – The Temples.
Some Weapons of Warfare – The Arms, and Shoulder blades.
Many Weathercocks – The Veins (vanes).
The Steps of an Hotel – The Insteps (inn-steps).
The House of Commons on the eve of a Dissolution – Eyes and Nose (ayes and noes).
Two Students or Scholars – The Pupils of the Eye.
Some Spanish Grandees – The Tendons (ten dons).

Finally there's Carroll's fish riddle from *Through the Looking Glass* with its solution, which so far as I can tell includes just about all the techniques and tricks used in the riddles described in this section. The riddle:

"First, the fish must be caught."
That is easy: a baby, I think, could have caught it.
"Next, the fish must be bought."
That is easy: a penny, I think, would have bought it.

"Now cook me the fish!"
That is easy, and will not take more than a minute.
"Let it lie in a dish!"
That is easy, because it already is in it.

"Bring it here! Let me sup!"
It is easy to set such a dish on the table.
"Take the dish-cover up!"
Ah, *that* is so hard that I fear I'm unable!

For it holds it like glue—
Holds the lid to the dish, while it lies in the middle:
What is easiest to do,
Un-dish-cover the fish, or dishcover the riddle?

The solution:

First pull up the fish.
It can't swim away: for a fish this is funny!
Next 'tis bought; and I wish
That a penny was always its adequate money.

Make it ready to eat—
Fetching pepper and vinegar won't take a minute.

Dish with cover complete,
Of lovely shell china, already 'tis in it.

Now 'tis time we should sup.
What's one only, you dolt? Set a score on the table!
Take the dish-cover up—
With mere finger and thumb you will never be able.

Get an oyster-knife strong,
Insert it 'twixt cover and dish, in the middle;
Then you shall before long
Un-dish-cover the OYSTERS—dishcover the riddle!

As an exercise to explore, try to create riddles similar to Lewis Carroll's "Enigma" using this form:

the whole to be guessed	*the parts to be guessed*	*the metaphor*
e.g., a car	steering wheel	a person
	wheels	brain
	brakes	legs
	headlights	thinking
		eyes

The description:

A wonderful way to be carried,
it has a brain and
    four legs
    it can think
    and use its eyes to pierce the darkness.

Proverbs

I grew up in the same house with my grandparents who were born in Poland and who spoke Yiddish most of the time. Whenever I caused trouble or fought with friends or felt unhappy or rejected, my grandmother had a saying that addressed the issue in a way that enabled me to save face and gave me insight into the situation. For example, when one of my friends ridiculed me my grandmother's response was "Stay away from a billy goat's front, a horse's behind, and a fool's everyside." At other times she would respond to situations with proverbs like:

A person that can't dance says the band can't play.
Don't rejoice when you knock someone down—but don't pick him up either.

Your health comes first—you can always hang yourself later.
Poverty isn't a disgrace—but it isn't an honor either.
If I try to be like someone else, who will be like me?

These proverbs were natural coming from my grandmother. They didn't seem like clichés or formulas for behavior so much as provocations to think and laugh and not take oneself too seriously. I find it harder to use English proverbs with a straight face since they seem like clichés to me. However, statements that are trite and preachy to me often seem like marvelous metaphors to young children. I remember telling Josh, who was five at the time, that there was a park just a stone's throw away from our vacation house. He paused, looked thoughtful for a minute, and then asked whose throw, his or mine. Measuring distances by a stone's throw was a new and interesting idea, only he wanted to know how the measure was standardized.

There is a whole series of phrases like "a stone's throw" that can be explored and varied. Some are:

in a nutshell	in one ear and out the other
on one's coattails	in one's blood
in glass houses	in one's hair
in a lather	in one's shoes
in a dither	in shape
in full swing	in the money
in Dutch	in the dark
in one's element	in the groove
in one's mind's eye	on the wagon
ins and outs	on the band wagon
in step with	on the heels of
in the air	on the nose
in the nick of time	on the fly
on the brain	on the wrong foot
on the chin	on top of the world
on the make	on one hand
on the level	off balance
on one's high horse	off one's rocker
on the warpath	off-color
on one's chest	to take one's breath away
in hand	to take in stride
in hot water	to take one's life in one's
in left field	hands
in nothing flat	by the seat of one's pants

These phrases embody images even though some of them are so worn out and clichéd that most adults avoid them or think of their metaphoric meaning as almost literal. This isn't so for children. These phrases are often striking to children since they can picture the literal meaning and often haven't encountered the metaphoric use of the phrase. For children, people sit on high horses, live in grooves, get hit on the nose. Try yourself to get back to the literal meaning of these sentences:

He tried to ride on my coattails.
She put the whole situation in a nutshell.
They get in my hair.
We sure are in the groove.
You hit it on the nose.

It would be interesting to ask children to draw pictures of what those sentences said literally and then to consider what the metaphoric meaning of the phrase might be. Sometimes it is useful to introduce metaphor using ordinary language rather than trying to come up with startling verbal juxtapositions or famous poetic metaphors. Metaphoric thought is not confined to poetry and the making of images is not confined to poets or other special people.

It is possible to experiment with image and metaphor by taking one of the common phrases above and varying it, and then finding meanings for the created images. For example: "in a nutshell" can be varied to produce "in a coconut," "in a molehole," and "in a volcano," so that "He put his ideas in a volcano" could mean that he expanded on his ideas in a broad context and even then they were likely to overflow the vehicle he chose. An image like this one can illustrate how compact complex ideas can be made through the use of image and metaphor. Thus, "in my hair" can be varied to "in my ear," "in my navel," "in my mouth," etc.

Another way to explore this basic use of image and metaphor in everyday language is to pick a part of the body or natural object like the sun or moon or stars, or animals, and examine the various ways in which it is qualified to expand our possibilities of communicating thoughts and feelings. For example, consider these occurrences of the word "heart":

a heavy heart	after one's own heart
hearts and flowers	at heart
lose one's heart	know by heart
to be heartsick	eat one's heart out
to be heartless	do one's heart good
search one's heart	at the bottom of one's heart
get to the heart of a thing	break one's heart
cross one's heart	find it in one's heart

with all one's heart
set one's heart on
heart of gold
heart in the right place
wear one's heart on
   one's sleeve

have heart
take heart
to one's heart's content
heart in one's mouth
heart goes out to you
heart and soul

(Note: A good source for proverbs, phrases, and clichés is *A Dictionary of American Idioms* by Maxine Tull Boatner, John Edward Gales, and Adam Makkai, published by Barron's Educational Series.)

As exercises, one can try to list occurrences of images using words like: hand, foot, eye, ear, nose, hair, etc. Animals also provide a rich source of ordinary images. Here are a few. Try to find more, to make up your own, and to explicate the ones you've listed:

dog	son-of-a-bitch dirty dog works like a dog dog's life	*ass*	silly ass assinine mulish stubborn as a mule mulatto
wolf	wolf your food wolf ticket	*horse*	works like a horse
fox	foxy sly as a fox	*sheep*	sheepish fleeced
pig	eats like a pig hog, hoggish	*goat*	scapegoat
bat	old bat bats in the belfry batty (bats) blind as a bat	*cat*	catty cat house pussy tomcat cool cat kitty (of money)
fowl	cock rule the roost chick waddles like a duck fat as a hen old hen to be chicken (cowardly) silly goose to goose fat as a goose	*fish and shellfish*	big as a whale a whale of a time drinks like a fish sharkskin (fabric) slippery as an eel card shark a shrimp clam up clammy hands

birds		monkey	
	bird (girl)		monkey business
	rare bird		monkeyshines
	stool pigeon		monkey around
	ball hawk		
	it's for the birds	cow	
	hawk-eyed		chewing one's cud
	gullible		contented as a cow
	ravenous		bullshit
	to gull		
	eat like a sparrow	insects	
	(or bird)		ants in your pants
	eagle eye		a hornets' nest
	an old crow		busy as a bee
	cuckoo (crazy)		a fly in the ointment
	bird-brained		don't bug me
			bees in your bonnet

Many proverbs are basically images that serve to provoke thought and comment upon life. This is especially true of African proverbs. In many parts of Africa "talking in proverbs" represents the wisdom and thought of a people. According to Professor Ida Ward (quoted in *Hausa Ba Dabo Ba Ne* by A. H. M. Kirk-Greene, published by Oxford University Press, Ibadan, Nigeria):

In law the proverb seems to classify a court case, to provide a precedent, to generalize a particular action; in family life it regulates the attitude of one member of the family to another; it helps in the education of children; and in social intercourse it smooths out difficulties and adds pith to the well known accomplishment of the African conversation.

The following are some proverbs from different parts of Africa with explications of some of them. First, here are a few Hausa proverbs (from Hausa-speaking peoples of Nigeria):

The blind man has no eyes so he says the eye smells [this is like our "sour grapes"].

A blind man does not worry about breaking a mirror.

I ran away from a show, I entered a downpour [like our "out of the frying pan and into the fire"].

"I entered but I did not take" will not save a thief.

The meat that has fat will be known when it is put close to the fire.

Fulfilling your needs is better than gaining a profit.

Give a stranger a drink and you will hear the news.

Sin is a dog which follows its owner.

It is the tortoise's fate not to be able to climb into the sky.

The elephant's footprint obliterates that of the camel.

Here are some Yoruba proverbs taken from *Owe L'Esin Oro—Yoruba Proverbs* by Isaac O. Delano (published by Oxford University Press, Ibadan, Nigeria):

If the ear does not hear malicious mischief the heart is not grieved.

The eagle flying high in the sky does not know that those on the ground are looking at him.

It is through sheer stupidity and inexperience that a rat challenges a cat to a fight.

Instead of the lion becoming the servant of the leopard, each one will go out on visits separately.

A hare's mouth is too small for a bridle [a way of saying that a problem is too difficult for you].

The rain forms dark clouds in the sky for the sake of those who are deaf; it rumbles for the sake of the blind [warnings are given to people in different ways].

It is a thief who can trace the footsteps of another thief over a rock.

Finally here are a few more Yiddish proverbs taken from *Yiddish Proverbs* edited by Hanan J. Ayalti (published by Schocken Books):

He that is fated to drown will drown—in a spoonful of water.

If God were living on earth, people would break his windows.

He that can't endure the bad, will not live to see the good.

Look for fancy bread and you lose the plain.

Better a good enemy than a bad friend.

Hell shared with a sage is better than paradise with a fool.

Truth never dies, but lives a wretched life.

Reason is a slowpoke.

One fool can ask more questions than ten sages can answer.

It is interesting to think of situations where these proverbs might be explicable, discuss them, and then write them down. Some of the situations can be actual, others fictional involving animals or imaginary creatures. These latter tales are versions of another traditional form of commenting on life, fables.

It is also fun to make a list of proverbs that are the opposites of each other. Here are some pairs of opposites:

> Too many cooks spoil the broth.
> The more the merrier.
>
> A stitch in time saves nine.
> Better late than never.
>
> Distance makes the heart grow fonder.
> Out of sight, out of mind.

Fables*

> "The next time you write a fable about me," said the ass to Aesop, "make me say something wise and sensible."
>
> "Something sensible from you!" exclaimed Aesop; "What would the world think? People would call you the moralist, and me the ass!"

The fable is a short tale with a specific point; it is not a tale told merely for the sake of telling. The form seems to be as old as writing itself, although it is by no means confined to cultures with a written tradition. The earliest known fables come from Sumerian literature and date as far back as 2200 B.C., about the time of the earliest recorded riddles. Most of the Sumerian examples are condensed and are as close to proverbs as they are to fables. Two examples involve the fox, a traditional figure in more recent fables.

> He did not yet catch the fox yet he is making a neckstock for it.

> The fox, having urinated in the sea, said, "The whole of the sea is my urine."

There are common myths about what fables are and about the attitudes toward life they represent. Fables are commonly considered to be moral tales with lessons of goodness to teach children. This idea has been encouraged by many versions of Aesop's and La Fontaine's fables rewritten specifically for children which twist the complex intentions of their authors into simple moralistic conclusions. Nothing could be further from the nature of fables, which are commentaries on human actions and interactions that range from the cynical through the indifferent to the silly. The moral fable is but one of a diverse and motley species. Consider, for example, this cynical fable written by one of my students:

> Once a boy was standing on a huge metal flattening machine. The flattener was coming down slowly. Now this boy was a boy who loved insects and bugs. The boy could have stopped the machine from coming down, but there were two ladybugs on the button and in order to push the button he would kill the two ladybugs. The flattener was about a half inch over his head. Now he made a decision—he would have to kill the ladybugs. He quickly pressed the button. The machine stopped, he was saved, and the ladybugs were dead.
> *Moral: smash or be smashed.*

As one reads a lot of fables, a sense of theme and variation arises. For example, starting with a basic moralistic fable, one finds the following versions of the same fable: (1) ironic (the theme is inverted so that, for example, punishment causes more pain to the punisher than to the punished); (2) cynical (misery triumphs and that is all there is to it); (3) wise (distance, restraint, and intelligence are the prime virtues); (4) humorous (the humor of the situation is all, there is no point—sorry about that); (5) moralizing (there is a right and wrong and the right wins); and (6) straight (something happens and there is no explanation beyond that).

Fables employ animals and objects as well as humans to represent types of people or character traits. For example, the fox is often the crafty man and the peacock the foolish boaster. An innkeeper may be used to represent greed and a peasant to represent naïveté. The symbols may not be consistent, for the peasant can also represent native shrewdness and the innkeeper fatal oversophistication. The animals and objects in fables talk and act in ways that embody the human types they are chosen to portray. There is no fantasy involved, nor any belief that they do talk or can do the things they are described as doing. They are merely used to enable the author of the fable (who usually keeps himself hidden) to make his comment on the life of the animal man.

There is as much play in the creation of fables as there is in riddling. For example, if there is a fable with the moral "A friend in need is a friend indeed," there's likely to be one with the opposite moral, "A friend in need is a pain in the neck"; if one fable teaches that "Time heals all wounds," another will teach that "Time wounds all heels." Here's a list of proverbs from traditional fables as well as ones written recently by young people that give a sense of the range and variety of experiences and feelings commented on in fables:

Antimoralizing and Cynical Proverbs

Don't believe what the teacher says.
If you live as humans do, it will be the end of you.
A deaf audience is better than none at all.
Don't get it right, just get it written.
The flash that flashed always turns to ashes.
My Pop is bigger than your Pop!!!
Don't break your arm patting yourself on the back.
If someone has been bad to you, give him a taste of his own medicine.
A friend in need is a pain in the neck.
Never believe a relative.
Do unto others before others do unto you.
Women are like the sea, which smiles and lures men onto its sparkling
   surface, then snuffs them out.
If only he had had no friends, he might have reached old age.
Happiness is a First National City Bank!
It is not so easy to fool little girls nowadays as it used to be.
Don't believe your children because they might get you in trouble.

Be Careful, Deliberate

Don't play with fire.
It is better to ask some of the questions than to know all the answers.
He who hesitates is sometimes saved.
Don't eat animals you don't know.
Never trust a dog—friendly or not.
Don't nibble at anyone's cracker but your own.
Don't smile if you don't have teeth.
Never pick on anyone who's bigger than you.
Never flirt with a lady whose husband is a fighter.
Never have too much furniture.
Don't play around with anything of importance.
Don't play games with smart little girls who have guns.
A bird in the hand is worth two in the bush.
Don't put all your eggs in one basket.
Never try to take someone out of a cage or you might get locked in.
Each man, to save his life, would never take more than one loving
   wife.
Don't shine your head too much.

The Truth in Generalities

As a priest is, so is the parish.
Consort with bad men and you will be hated just as they are, even

though you yourself do no injury to those around you.

As the twig is bent the tree is inclined.

Show me a man's friend and I'll tell you who he is.

All's Hopeless Anyway

There is no safety in numbers, or in anything else.

You may as well fall flat on your face as lean over too far backward.

The world is like a candy jar. If you try to take a piece, you might get a stomach ache.

Don't bother, or you'll be hurt.

If you are ugly, stay ugly.

Ashes to ashes, and clay to clay: if the enemy doesn't get you your own folks may.

Open most heads and you will find nothing shining, not even a mind.

Boasts, and the Consequences of Boasting

And oft it happens, that we hear him boast of what he ought to blush for most.

A barking dog is never a good hunter.

Although your rap is strong,/ Your words may be wrong,/ So have some slack, brother,/ Before it's all gone!

Never brag or you will surely lose.

The noblest study of mankind is Man, says Man.

Never count your chickens before they hatch.

Justice Wins Out, or Does It

You can fool too many of the people too much of the time.

It's better to be a dirty cat than a dirty dog.

Crime does not pay.

Give the people what they think they want.

Get a good mask and the part plays itself.

Don't trick anyone into doing something you can do yourself.

One who dishes it out better know how to take it.

Nothing in life is to be feared, it is only to be understood.

Those who laugh last laugh best.

Don't Try to be Something You're Not or Take the Consequences

Don't wish to be a monkey because you like bananas a lot.

You can't very well be king of beasts if there aren't any.

He who lives another's life another's death must die.

One man's meat is another man's poison.

It is better to have bad breath than no breath at all.

Be Clever about Determining Others' True Natures

Beware of people who ask for criticism when it's praise they want.
Never trust a lion even if he's your friend.

Be Good and Kind; These Are Their Own Reward

A dog does not forget for three years the kindness of three days.
One true friend is worth more than a million false friends.
Two wrongs don't make a right.
One good turn deserves another.
Every dog has his day.

Be Safe

Better to be old than bold!
Safety in numbers.

Importance of Doing Things at the Right Time

For everything there is a season.
Let not him who injures me when living shed tears for me when dead.
A stitch in time saves nine.

There are certain character types that frequently appear in fables. There are tricksters, hustlers, fools, boasters, bullies, weaklings, and innocents, as well as less extreme personalities. In a study of hundreds of fables I did for the Teachers and Writers Collaborative with Karen Kennerly (her *Hesitant Wolf and Scrupulous Fox,* published by Random House, is the most thorough and serious collection of fables I know, and is an excellent resource) we found that almost all fables dealt with one or another of these eleven themes:

1. Trickery and tricksters
2. On not being content with oneself
3. The weak versus the strong with a digression on the nature of war
4. On generations
5. Sour grapes
6. Punishment and revenge
7. Curiosity
8. Man and the animals or the meaning of humanity
9. Honesty and deceit
10. Boasts
11. Tests and contests

It would take a whole book to discuss and present all the fables that deal with any of these themes. However, as an example of how fables can deal with an important human subject in depth and with humor, irony, cynicism, and wisdom, consider these treatments of the nature of war. The first is by James Thurber, from his *Fables for Our Time* (New York: Harper and Row, 1952):

The Rabbits Who Caused All the Trouble

Within the memory of the youngest child there was a family of rabbits who lived near a pack of wolves. The wolves announced that they did not like the way the rabbits were living. (The wolves were crazy about the way they themselves were living, because it was the only way to live.) One night several wolves were killed in an earthquake and this was blamed on the rabbits, for it is well known that rabbits pound on the ground with their hind legs and cause earthquakes. On another night one of the wolves was killed by a bolt of lightning and this was also blamed on the rabbits, for it is well known that lettuce-eaters cause lightning. The wolves threatened to civilize the rabbits if they didn't behave, and the rabbits decided to run away to a desert island. But the other animals, who lived at a great distance, shamed them, saying, "You must stay where you are and be brave. This is no world for escapists. If the wolves attack you, we will come to your aid, in all probability." So the rabbits continued to live near the wolves and one day there was a terrible flood which drowned a great many wolves. This was blamed on the rabbits, for it is well known that carrot-nibblers with long ears cause floods. The wolves descended on the rabbits, for their own good, and imprisoned them in a dark cave, for their own protection.

When nothing was heard about the rabbits for some weeks, the other animals demanded to know what had happened to them. The wolves replied that the rabbits had been eaten and since they had been eaten the affair was a purely internal matter. But the other animals warned that they might possibly unite against the wolves unless some reason was given for the destruction of the rabbits. So the wolves gave them one. "They were trying to escape," said the wolves, "and, as you know, this is no world for escapists."

Moral: Run, don't walk, to the nearest desert island.

There are other outcomes of war represented in fables, yet on the whole war is considered inevitable and a bad bet. It symbolizes the weakness and fundamental irrationality of man. A poignant fable on the inevitability of war was written by Franklin Foster, a sixth-grade student in New York City, who didn't think he had written a "proper" fable.

Once upon a time there was two men who were always fighting so one day a wise man came along and said fighting will never get you anywhere they didn't pay him no attention and they got in quarrels over and over again. So one day they went to church and the preacher said you should not fight and they got mad and knock the preacher out
    Can't find no ending.

There are fables that deal with avoiding warfare. The plight of the neutral is often depicted as well as that of the individual who does not believe in a given war and attempts to avoid participation. The next examples deal with this theme. The first is Lenny Jenkin's rewriting from a fable by James Reeves, from *Aesop* (New York: Henry Z. Walck, Inc., 1962); the second is by Grace Paley and appeared in *Ikon* 1, no. 3 (July 1967).

Birds, Beasts and Bat

Not too long ago one of the higher-ups among the hawks spotted a succulent fish in a stream far below him, and began his dive for it. He had been flying high, for by the time he got there, a bear had the fish hooked on one paw and was about to take a bite out of it. "Get your dumb paws off that fish," screeched the hawk, "it's mine." "You must be kidding," said the bear, and with one swipe of his free paw he broke the hawk's right wing. The hawk limped off through the brush, cursing and screaming. "I'm not gonna forget this—I'll be back with a few of my friends and we'll see how tough you are then, fat stuff!" The hawk gathered his friends, and the bear gathered his friends, and before anybody realized what was happening, a full-scale war between the birds and the beasts had begun. Every creature in the world took sides, except for one.

"I figure it this way," said Bat to himself: "I'll see which side looks like it'll come out on top, and join that one." He knew that with his leathery wings he could easily pass for a bird, and with his ears and claws he could pass for a beast.

Bat made himself a tricky reversible soldier's uniform, with bird insignia on one side and beast insignia on the other. When the beasts looked as if they would wipe out the bird forces, Bat turned his uniform beast-side out and joined them, screaming "God is on our side" and "Liberate the air!" He killed all the tiny birds he could find. When the birds had the upper hand, Bat went home, reversed his uniform, and flew back into the fray crying "God is on our side" and "Liberate the land!" He killed all the mice and other little animals he could find.

The war was fierce and bloody, and went on for many months. At last the beasts and birds, tired of fighting and sick of bloodshed, decided to make peace. Both sides wrote and signed many complicated treaties and documents, and set up all kinds of commissions and organizations to make sure there would never be another war. I am sorry to tell you that despite all the promises, there were other wars anyway, as silly as this one and even more horrible. But whether they were at peace or war, from that time on neither side would have Bat.

"You fought for the beasts," screamed the Eagle, King of Birds, "so you must be one. Go live with your friends. And never let us catch you flying in our air again!"

"You were on the side of the birds," roared the Lion, King of All Animals, "so, of course, you are a bird. Go live with them, and never let us catch you on land again!"

After all this Bat became so confused and unhappy that he himself no longer knew if he was bird, beast, or anything at all. From that time until today, rejected by all sides, he has sneaked around at night, and lived in dank caves and old barns. He can fly like a bird, but he never sits in trees, singing in the sunlight. Nobody knows exactly what kind of creature he is, and nobody cares.

If you try to sit on two chairs at once, you'll end up on the floor between them.

The Sad Story about the Six Boys
About To Be Drafted in Brooklyn

I

There were six boys in Brooklyn and none of them wanted to be drafted.

Only one of them went to college. What could the others do?

One shot off his index finger. He had read about this in a World War I novel.

One wore silk underpants to his physical. His father had done that for World War II.

One went to a psychiatrist for three years starting three years earlier (his mother, to save him, had thought of it).

One married and had three children.

One enlisted and hoped for immediate preferential treatment.

This is what happened next:

II

The boy who enlisted was bravely killed. There was a funeral for him at home. People sat on boxes and wore new sackcloth as it was one of the first of that family's bad griefs. They ate and wept.

Then, accidentally, due to a mistake in the filing system, the married father of three children was drafted. He lived a long time, maybe three months, and killed several guerrillas, two by strangulation, two by being a crack shot, and one in self-defense. Then he was killed as he slept in the underbrush, for other people think they ought to act in self-defense too.

A couple of years later, the boy who had gone to the psychiatrist for three years and the boy in the silk underpants were reclassified. Because of their instabilities, they had always been against killing. Luckily, they never got further than the middle airlane over the very middle of the Pacific Ocean. There, the mighty jet exploded, perhaps due to sabotage, distributing 133 servicemen in a blistery blaze to their watery graves.

As the war went on and on, the college boy became twenty-six years old. He was now in his eighth year in college. He could not remember the name of his high school when he applied for his first job. He could not remember his mother's maiden name which is essential to applications. Nervousness ran in that family and finally reached him. He was taken to rest in a comfortable place in pleasant surroundings where he remained for twelve years. When he was thirty-eight, he felt better and returned to society.

Now, the man with the shot-off index finger:

III

Even after four years, he didn't miss that finger. He had used it to point accusingly at guilty persons, for target shooting, for filing alphabetically. None of these actions concerned him anymore. To help him make general love, he still had his whole hand and for delicate love, his middle finger.

Therefore he joyfully married and fathered several children. All of them had shot-off index fingers, as did their children.

That family became a peaceful race apart. Sickness and famine didn't devastate them. Out of human curiosity they traveled and they were stubborn and tough like the feathery seeds of trees that float over mountain barriers and railroad valleys. In far places the children of the children of the man with the shot-off index finger gathered into settlements and cities and of course, they grew and multiplied.

And that's how at last, if you can believe it, after the dead loss of a million dead generations, on the round, river-streaked face of the earth, war ended.

Here are a number of fables written by elementary and high school students showing that the art of creating fables is by no means lost:

The Head Man

This guy was born, but he was just a head. So he went to a witchdoctor and he said, "I don't want to be just a head." The witchdoctor put up his hands and went puff and turned him into a hand.

Then the guy ran around hollering, "I don't want to be a hand!"

There is a moral to this story:

"You should have quit while you were a head."

—Mark Vecchoise

The Swan and the Elephant

In the deepest part of the African jungle, there was a swan who swam in the lake. A few feet away, the swan saw a couple of elephants who were horsing around. Every day Tarzan would come around and feed the swans and the elephants. Tarzan swung over to the elephants, and gave the elephants large chunks of meat. Don, the swan, was a bit curious about why he and his pals were always getting the little pieces of meat while the elephants always got the large chunks of meat. And Don was the bragger of the group. He was always saying, "Hey guys, look at how slender my neck is. Did you ever see such white fluffy feathers? Nobody can swim faster than me. I'm the perfect swan." But there was one thing he couldn't brag about. This was his food. "I'm the handsomest animal in the animal kingdom, and look, it wouldn't be enough to last a crow two bites. And guess who gets the large chunks of meat? That stupid trumpeting elephant Horton and his dumb kid, Dumbo. I could fly just as easily as he, if I wanted to. I'm going to do something about this." Don swam over to Horton and said, "Horton, come here a minute. You know what I'm going to do for you, old pal, old friend, old buddy. I heard some of the other animals calling you fatty. Now you don't want your son to be ashamed of you? Tell you what I'm going to do. I'll put you on a diet.

Riddles, Proverbs, and Fables

174

Then you'll go back to your slim three tons instead of that overweight ten tons. I'll take half of your meat and you eat the other half and you'll be slim in no time. O.K., Horton?" "All right, Don," said Horton. Don had a little trouble taking the meat back to his part of the lake, but he made it. Now Don had something new to brag about. "Well! Well! Well! Tarzan sure gave you little pieces of meat. Look what I have. I tricked that dumb elephant Horton. He is the most foolish animal here." But Horton wasn't stupid. He knew what would happen to Don, and it did. Don had a big piece of meat. He took one bite and tried to swallow the meat but his slender neck wouldn't let it go down and his throat burst and he never bragged again.

    Moral: One man's meat is another man's poison
or
Don't bite off more than you can chew.

—Theresa Brown

The Fox and the Grapes

One day a ferocious bunch of grapes were hanging idly on a grape vine. There weren't any ordinary grapes because each grape had a different personality. All of their personalities resulted in a demolition squad of grapes.

    A very unconcerned fox came walking by without a care in the world. Suddenly he was frightened by the grapes which were making an attempt to eat the fox. The grapes tugged at the vine so as to stretch far enough to reach the fox. But each time the fox would move an inch away. The grapes were grunting and large beads of sweat rolled off them in a river-like fashion. The grapes were at the end of their vine; they could stretch no further. Then at that moment the fox appeared even more delicious than before. Unable to control their desire for fresh meat, the grapes stretched with all their might until the vine broke. The grapes lay on the ground and were later eaten by the fox.

    Moral: It doesn't pay to stretch your neck out
or
Don't stretch until you come to the end of your vine.

—Donald Gea

The Man and the Lion

Once upon a time there was a man who defied his king so that the king sentenced him to die. But before they could do this he escaped and ran into the woods where he met this lion who had a nail in his paw. The man felt sorry for the lion and took the nail out; the lion said he was grateful for what the man had done, and he would always be a friend of his. So the man bid the lion good-bye and left, but when leaving the wood he was captured by the king's soldiers. They brought him back and he was sentenced to death in the arena.

    When they brought him to the arena he saw the lion whom he had made friends with. He was telling the lion not to eat him because they were friends, but the lion said he was very hungry. He jumped upon the man and ate him.

Moral: Beware of friends who make false statements.

—Edward Montes

Try to write some fables yourself. One way to begin is to take a traditional fable, change the moral, and then modify the fable to suit the new moral. Another way is to begin with a moral and create a tale to illustrate it. A third way is to start writing a tale about a few animals and see where it'll take you.

7

Play Songs
and Play Poems

Bouncing-ball Rhymes and Games
Jump-rope Rhymes
Color Rhymes
Counting Rhymes and Rhythms
Song, Dance, and Play
Response Games
Memory-response Games
The Hand Game

Playing, singing, and rhyming often go together. As a child I learned dozens of games from my friends, and my own children learn variations of these games from their friends. So far as I can tell, a whole series of games is passed from generation to generation without adult interference or conscious teaching. Just the other day my daughters were playing what I call a "jumping around" game. It consisted of one person chanting:

> Mailman, mailman do your duty
> Here comes Miss American Beauty
> She can do the pom pom, she can do
>   the splits,
> She can stop you from doing this . . .

The chanter waves her arms back and forth when she says "pom pom" and then begins a split, slowly going into a full split, while the other players try to imitate. Anyone who fails is out. After the splits, the chanter tries other bodily contortions to try and get everyone out.

This game is structurally the same as one I learned watching my pupils in Harlem seventeen years ago. There the play poem was:

> Policeman, policeman do your duty,
> Here comes Diane the American beauty,
> She can wiggle, she can wobble,
>   she can do the twist,
> Bet anything she can't do this . . .

The wiggle, the wobble, and the twist are dances and the chanter does each in turn when she calls them out. Then comes the challenge "Bet anything she can't do this . . ." and the chanter does a complex combination of dance steps. The other players try to imitate her. If they all succeed she's out. If not, she goes again, getting more elaborate as she tries to drive the others out of the game.

Both these versions of the game are played with great noise and excitement. One is a gymnastics contest and the other a dance contest. They require no equipment and can be played in the schoolyard, on the streets, in a room. Most play songs and play poems require very little by way of equipment or preparation so long as the players know the rhymes and rhythms. Here's a sampling of different types of games involving songs and poems:

Bouncing-ball Rhymes and Games*

A favorite city game consists of bouncing a rubber ball and turning your leg over the ball without touching it as it comes up. As an eight- to twelve-year-old I wouldn't go anywhere without my ten-cent pink Spalding, and I knew dozens of rhymes and game variations. Sometimes one used the right leg exclusively, sometimes one switched from the right to the left leg or hand (to bounce the ball). The experts could almost vary their hands and legs at will and reminded me of the way Marquis Haynes of the Harlem Globetrotters handled a basketball.

Here are some rhymes which end up in counting how many times you can turn over the ball without hitting it or dropping it:

Down by the river,
   down by the sea
I kissed someone
   and they kissed me
1, 2, 3, . . .

Dennis the Menace
   had a gun
He shot a man in
   the boodie
How many shots did
   he shootie?
1, 2, 3, . . .

Here's a rhyme inspired by an old fairy tale:

Cinderella dressed in yella
Went upstairs to kiss a fella
By mistake she kissed a snake
How many doctors did it take?
1, 2, 3 . . .

And here's a kitchen rhyme:

I was born in a frying
   pan
Just to see how old I
   am,
1, 2, 3, . . .

Charlie Chaplin sat on
   a pin.
How many inches did it
   go in?
1, 2, 3, . . .

There are other versions of this game using a ball and a rhyme. One consists of saying the rhyme and then throwing the ball up in the air and clapping your hands first once, then on the next turn twice, etc. The person who claps the most times before missing the ball wins. Another

Play Songs and Play Poems

180

version consists of throwing the ball against a wall and clapping or counting before catching it on the rebound.

Jump-rope Rhymes*

Jump-rope rhymes exist almost everywhere in the world and are recited while children jump rope. Often the rhymes give instructions on how the jumper is to jump. For example, in

> I'm a little sailor girl dressed in blue,
> Here are the orders that I must do,
> Salute to the captain, bow to the queen
> And turn my back on the submarine

the turners are the captain and the queen, and the children waiting turns are the submarine. The jumper must do a half turn on each jump.

Here's another one with instructions:

> Old lady, old lady, turn around, around
> Old lady, old lady, touch the ground
> Old lady, old lady, shine your shoe.

This rhyme indicates when one jumper is to leave and another one to take up a turn:

> On the mountain lives a lady
> Who she is I do not know
> All she likes is gold and silver
> All she wants is ice cream cones
> Jump in, my darling, jump out, my baby.

It's interesting to note that all the bouncing-ball rhymes are also simple jump-rope rhymes. Often with such simple rhymes, which end up by counting how long a person will jump, before counting the jumper will say "salt" or "pepper," or perhaps "cold" or "hot." These terms indicate whether the rope is to be turned slowly (salt and cold) or quickly (pepper and hot).

Some rhymes use the word "pepper" to signal to the turners to go as fast as possible and challenge the jumper to keep up. Here are two:

> Able, Able set the table,
> Don't forget the salt, ketchup, mustard
> "Pepper."

Buster Brown went uptown
With his pants upside-down.
He had a nickel,
He bought a pickle,
The pickle was sweet.
He bought some meat,
The meat was hard.
He bought a card
And on the card it said
"Hot pepper."

Color Rhymes

Sometimes rhyming itself can be a game. Here are some color rhymes that many children play with and vary endlessly:

Black, black,
You got a Cadillac.

Brown, brown,
you a clown
Turn yourself
upside-down.

Brown, brown,
go to town
Turn your bridges
upside-down.

Red, red,
go to bed
Eat up all your
gingerbread.

White, white,
Sleep all night

Blue, blue,
you got the flu
Nobody wanta
play with you.

Green, green,
you got a submarine
Wipe your head in
gasoline.

White, white,
Get married tonight.

Yellow, yellow,
Kiss a fellow.

Add new colors and see what you come up with. Begin new lists using animals or directions like:

Up, up
you live in a cup.
Down, down
get out of town

East, east
let's have a feast.
West, west
now it's time to rest.

Play Songs and
Play Poems

Counting Rhymes and Rhythms

In *Africa Counts* (Boston: Prindle, Weber, and Schmidt, 1973), Claudia Zaslavsky describes a number of African children's counting rhymes and rhythms:

Children in Africa, as in other parts of the world, learn finger counting rhymes even before they are aware of the number sequence. Some rhymes go only to five, while others continue as far as twenty. Most stop at ten, corresponding to the number of fingers. In some areas the rhymes are based on a twelve system or give special emphases to multiples of three or four.

Here is a popular five-finger Swahili verse, with an element of daring, translated freely: "Let's go!—Where?—To steal!—What about the police?—I'm out of this!" The counting begins with the little finger and ends at the thumb; with each phrase a finger is ticked off.

Many rhymes have nonsense words, or words that are obsolete or of foreign origin. The children of the Taita Hills, in southeastern Kenya, sing counting rhymes with words having no obvious meaning. According to John Williamson, an African adult made the discovery that some of these words had once been in the local language, but had been obsolete for a century. Amazingly, they were preserved in the children's songs. The children sing these words to a simple tune when they play games and even use verses in their arithmetic work. In some districts they accompany the song by bending down the fingers of the right hand with those of the left, beginning with the little finger, and then continuing with the little finger of the left hand. These gestures are absolutely unrelated to the formal system of finger counting of the Taita people.

Counting songs are among the first items of the Venda children's musical repertory. They, too, accompany the words by counting on the fingers. Using their right index finger, they first tap the little finger of the left hand, then each consecutive finger until the thumb is reached. Counting on the right hand starts with the thumb and proceeds to the little finger, each in turn being grasped by the thumb and first finger of the left hand. Sometimes the child claps his hand when he reaches ten. The actual number words embrace several languages besides Venda: Thonga, Sotho, Afrikaans, English.

Venda children use a counting song to choose a child to perform an unpleasant task—the last one is the loser. The children good-humoredly shout "Witch" at the odd child.

A special Venda song for counting legs is a jumble of several languages and nonsense syllables. The children sit in a row with their legs outstretched in front of them. The singer points at each leg in turn as he goes down the row reciting the verses and comes back in the opposite direction when he reaches the end of the row. The leg which is tapped on the last word, *mutshelwa*, "guilty one," is withdrawn, and the singer begins again with the first leg in the row. Clever children can calculate where to sit in order to be counted out satisfactorily so that they are not last, or if they are counting, how to work it so that a particular person is selected. Here is a free translation of the verses:

> This one is a child who is just beginning to
>   stagger about,
> This one is the sound of small reed-pipes,
> The reed-pipe of Mangayengaye,
> Masulu kungwa-kungwa, the calabash.
> Carried the chief's pitch-pipe,
> And it became bewitched, it is the guilty one.

In a Shona game, played as they sit around the fire at night, the children must listen carefully and count accurately. While an older man recites certain verses in a rhythmic pattern, the children count the number of principal beats. The teacher may vary his speed, speaking rapidly, then slowly. Or he may enunciate the words very distinctly, so that the audience loses the rhythm. All this is accompanied by a great deal of laughter and clapping. The losers are subjected to some good-natured mocking at the hands of the star students.

It's possible to play these games with your children as well as ask them to show how they choose leaders for games or decide who's first or last in a game. There are many American street games that are similar to these African ones. For example, William Wells Newell in his book *Games and Songs of American Children* (first published in 1883) describes American counting rhymes:

There are various ways in which children decide who shall begin in a game, or, as the phrase is, be "it." When this position is an advantage, it is often determined by the simple process of "speaking first." So far as can be determined when all are shouting at once, the first speaker is then entitled to the best place. Otherwise it is the practice to draw straws, the shortest gaining; to "toss up" a coin, "heads or tails"; or to choose between the two hands, one of which holds a pebble.

The most interesting way of decision, however, is by employing the rhymes for "counting out." A child tells off with his finger one word of the rhyme for each of the group, and he on whom the last word falls is "out." This process of exclusion is continued until one only is left, who has the usually unpleasant duty of leading in the sport. All European nations possess such rhymes, and apply them in a like manner. These have the common peculiarity of having very little sense, being often mere jargons of unmeaning sounds. This does not prevent them from being very ancient. People of advanced years often wonder to find their grandchildren using the same formulas, without the change of a word. The identity between American and English usage establishes the currency of some such for three centuries, since they must have been in common use at the time of the settlement of this country. We may be tolerably sure that Shakespeare and Sidney directed their childish sports by the very same rhymes which are still employed for the purpose. Furthermore, German and other languages, while they rarely exhibit the identical phrases, present us with types which resemble our own, and obviously have a common origin. Such a relation implies a very great antiquity; and it becomes a matter of no little curiosity to determine the origin of a practice which must have been consecrated by the childish usage of all the great names of modern history.

Here are some of these early American counting rhymes:

Onery, uery, hickory, Ann,
Fillison, follason, Nicholas John,
Queevy, quavy, Virgin Mary,
Singalum, sangalum, buck.

—Philadelphia

Onery, uery, ickory, a,
Hallibone, crackabone, ninery-lay,
Whisko, bango, poker my stick,
Mejoliky one leg!

—Scituate, Mass. (about 1800)

Eny, meny, mony, my,
Tusca, leina, bona, stry,
Kay bell, broken well,
We, wo, wack.

—Massachusetts

Stick, stock, stone dead,
Set him up,
Set him down,
Set him in the old man's crown.

—Philadelphia

Apples and oranges, two for a penny,
Takes a good scholar to count as many;
O-u-t, out goes she.

—Philadelphia

Song, Dance, and Play

Sometimes song, dance, and play go together. Here is an account of a game involving song and dance which is popular in Appalachia. It is taken from Jesse Stuart's moving book about his experiences teaching in mountain schools in rural Kentucky, *The Thread That Runs So True* (New York: Scribner's, 1970). The scene described here takes place in a one-room schoolhouse on Stuart's first day teaching.

While enrolling my pupils, I made some temporary changes in seating arrangements. I often put a pupil without books beside a pupil with books, if they were in the same grade. As I enrolled the pupils, I tried to remember and familiarize myself with each name. I tried to get acquainted with my pupils. I found them very shy. I was a stranger among them, though I had grown up under similar circumstances with equivalent opportunities. There were approximately thirty miles separating their Lonesome Valley from my W-Hollow. But I was a stranger here. . . .

When I dismissed my pupils for the first recess, a fifteen-minute period between the beginning of the school day and the noon hour, I was amazed to see them all jump up from their seats at the same time and try to be the first out of the house. Big pupils pushed past the little ones and there was so much confusion and disorder, I knew they would never leave the room like this again. Why were they running? I wondered. I had a few minutes' work to do before I could join them on the playground. Before I had finished this work, I heard the tenor of their uneven voices singing these familiar words:

> The needle's eye that does supply,
> The thread that runs so true,
> Many a beau, have I let go,
> Because I wanted you.
>
> Many a dark and stormy night,
> When I went home with you,
> I stumped my toe and down I go,
> Because I wanted you.

I walked to the door and watched them. They had formed a circle, hand in hand, and around and around they walked and sang these words while two pupils held their locked hands high for the circle to pass under. Suddenly the two standing—one inside the circle and one outside—let their arms drop down to take a pupil from the line. Then the circle continued to march and sing while the two took the pupil aside and asked him whether he would rather be a train or an automobile. If the pupil said he'd rather be an automobile, he stood on one side; if a train, he stood on the other of the two that held hands. And when they had finished taking everybody from the circle, the two groups faced each other, lined up behind their captains. Each put his arms around the pupil in front of him and locked his hands. The first line to break apart or to be pulled forward lost the game.

Fifteen minutes were all too short for them to play "the needle's eye." I let recess extend five minutes so they could finish their second game. It had been a long time since I had played this game at Plum Grove. These words brought back pleasant memories. They fascinated me. And my Lonesome Valley pupils played this game with all the enthusiasm and spirit they had! They put themselves into it—every pupil in school. Not one stood by to watch. Because they were having the time of their lives, I hated to ring the bell for "books." I lined them up, smaller pupils in front and larger ones behind, and had them march back into the schoolroom.

Moving from the Appalachian American tradition to West Africa (Ghana specifically), here's a dance/chant game drawn from Esther Nelson's valuable resource *Dancing Games* (New York: Sterling, 1973).

Che Che Koole

Each line of this very versatile chant from Ghana is sung first by the leader, and then answered by the group. Sing it loud and clear and forcefully. When the group answers, it is in exact imitation of what you sing and what you do.

In this version, start by singing the chant through once. The second time, clap as you sing, but clap 4 even beats to each measure, even though all the music is not even. The third time you sing it, clap in the rhythm of the music. After going through the chant three times, the children should know the words well enough to start moving as they sing.

Begin the dance in a circle, with you—the leader—in the center. Clap and sing the first line. The children answer, also clapping the rhythm. Repeat this pattern through the entire chant. Then silently count to yourself 4 beats, with no sound and no movement.

The second time through, stamp the rhythm with your feet as you sing. When the children answer, they stamp the rhythm, too, but this time they move toward the circle center. Use the same pattern for the next line. On the third line, turn in place as you stamp, and when the children answer, have them finish their turns facing the outside of the circle.

When the fourth answer comes, they start moving back to their places, out from the circle center. At the end of the fifth line answer, they turn and face the inside of the circle. Complete the chant again with 4 counts of silence.

The third time, move your head on each of the 4 counts of the first line. The children imitate this, in place. On the second line, move your shoulders; on the third, your arms; on the fourth, your hips, and last, your feet, stamping out the rhythm in place. Follow with the 4 counts of silence.

The fourth time through, combine the last two patterns. Have the children (on their answer) stamp their feet in rhythm as they move toward the circle center, but on the first line add the head movement, then shoulders, add arms with the turn, hips moving back, and finally just the feet as they return to place on the last line. Finish the chant with 4 counts of silence.

Finally, do the chant in place, but let the children take over the movement completely. While they stamp the rhythm with their feet, they add any sharp body movements they want. This involves singing, counting out the rhythm, possibly turning, and moving the body all at the same time, and it is quite complex, so only attempt it with older children, starting at age eight.

Variation: For younger children, just sing the chant and the answer, and then clap it out. Try it walking toward the center and out again. Keep it simple and just enjoy using your voice fully and defining the rhythm with hands and feet.

Don't feel that you must restrict yourself to these patterns. Experiment with other movement possibilities and even rhythm possibilities. You might try a chorus of drummers, who beat out the rhythms as the group dances and then explore other individual rhythmic improvisations.

Here are the words and music for this dance/chant game:

	pronounced:
Che Che Koole	Chay Chay *Kool*-ay
Che Ko Fi Sa	*Chay* Koe *Fee* Sah
Ko Fi Sa Langa	Koe *Fee* Sah Lahnga
Manga Tu Langa	Mahnga *Too* Lahnga
Aye, A Ye De	Ay, Eye *Yay* Day

Finally, here are two games from Richard Chase's delightful collection *Singing Games and Playparty Games* (New York: Dover, 1967). The first dance game is also a kissing game, a version of which I remember playing in junior high school when there were no adults around. The second, which is more a dance than a game, I've done with kindergarteners and high school students and adults. I learned it from Country Joe McDonald who played it for us in class. He called it "Do-the-Hootchie-Cootchie" and had the students, my student teachers, the parents present, and even me, dancing, singing, and playing.

King William

1. King Will-iam was King James's son, from the roy-al race he sprung.

He wore a star up-on his breast, Star of the East and Star of the West.

2. Go choose you East, go choose you West,
   choose the one that you love best.
   If she's not here to take her part,
   choose you another with all your heart.

3. Down on this carpet you must kneel,
   sure as the grass grows in the field,
   and now you rise upon your feet—
   hug her quick and kiss her sweet.

Formation: A single ring with all hands joined. Partners not necessary. One boy stands in the center.

Step: A brisk march with a good lifting lilt.

Figures: 1. The ring circles left, clockwise.
  2. The ring circles right. The boy in the center chooses a girl and takes her into the center.
  3. Action: The boy and girl kneel down facing each other and holding both hands. They stand up when the song says so, and then the boy does exactly as the fourth line directs, if the girl will let him! That's all there is to this game.

Here's another version of the last two lines of verse one:

Upon his breast he wore a star
like the points of the compass are.

The girl chooses another boy to stand in the center. She and the first boy take places in the ring. Repeat as many times as there are boys present, or as many times as the company wishes.

Sometimes the boy gets his kiss. Sometimes he doesn't.

King William is, to be sure, a game for home parties when all the crowd know each other well.

I first learned this game in North Carolina. The first time I played it was at Folly Cove on Cape Ann, Massachusetts.

Hullabaloo

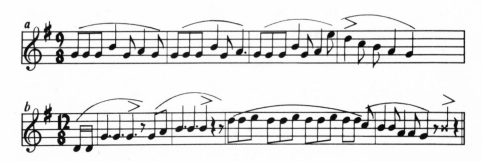

Formation: A single ring for any number. All hands joined. Or all the boys in one ring, and all the girls in a ring outside the boys' ring. Or the other way around if there are more boys than girls. And if there is a great crowd wanting to play, several concentric rings may be formed: a ring of about six girls in the center, a ring of about twelve boys outside these six girls, another ring of girls around the twelve boys, and a big ring of boys in the last outside ring. This rings-within-rings formation is ideal for a whole school to dance together in a single folk game at some Spring Festival or May Day.

Step: A quiet walk, brisk enough to be lively, for verses 1 through 4. For verses 5 and 6 galop sideways, or skip. Part *a* is in a three-beat rhythm, and the accent changes from right to left. Stop on "summer" and bring feet together (ft) on "night."

Hull- a- ba- loo- by   loo- by,
 (R)   (L)   (R)

     hull- a- ba- loo- by   light
      (L)   (R)   (L) . . . etc.

   . . . on   a   sum- mer   night.
       (L)   (R) (stop)   (ft)

Hullabalooby looby,
hullaballooby light.
Hullabalooby looby
on a summer night.

1a

All circle left. Hands joined. Hesitate on "summer," so you can stop, *all together,* on the word "night."

Put your right hand in,
put your right hand out.
Shake it a little, a
  little, a little,
and turn yourself about.
  WHOO!

1b

Thrust right hand toward center on the "in." Raise it overhead on the word "out." Shake it overhead.

The turn on the last line of Part *b* is done each time thus:

       . . . and . . . turn your-self a - bout. WHOO!

(Take weight on *left* foot
and *spring* onto)   (R)   (L)   (R)   (L)

    Do this R L R L with four bouncy steps, not just a whirl on one foot. Swing the right foot up with a little kick on "WHOO!"

Hullabalooby looby,
hullabalooby light.
Hullabalooby looby
on a summer night.

Boys circle left, while
girls circle right.

Put your left hand in,
put your left hand out.
Shake it a little, a
    little, a little,
and turn yourself about.
    WHOO!

Same as for 1b but with
left hand.

Hullabalooby looby,
hullabalooby light.
Hullabalooby looby
on a summer night.

All tiptoe toward cen-
ter, hands joined.
Jump, landing with both
feet on the word
"light." Move out again.

Hull- a- ba- loo- by loo- by,
(To center—R)   (L)   (R)

hull- a- ba- loo- by   light.
        (L)   (R) (spring) (*land*)

Hull-a-ba-loo-by loo- by
(Out again—R)   (L)   (R)

on   a   sum - mer   night.
     (L)   (R) (no jump, just ft)

Put your right foot in,
put your right foot out.
Shake it a little, a
    little, a little,
and turn yourself about.
    WHOO!

Right foot thrust
toward center, heel
on the ground. Then
thrust out behind, toe
on the ground. Keep
hands joined.

Hullabalooby looby,
hullabalooby light.
Hullabalooby looby
on a summer night.

All move in toward
center, jump, and move
back out again,
as for 3a.

Put your left foot in,
put your left foot out.
Shake it a little, a
    little, a little,
and turn yourself about.
    WHOO!

Same as for 3b, but
with left foot. Don't
let go hands.

Hullabalooby looby,
hullabalooby light.
Hullabalooby looby
on a summer night.

Everybody galop side-
ways to the left.
Don't get going so hard
you can't stop *all*
together on "summer *night*."

Put your ugly mug in,
put your ugly mug out.
Shake it a little, a
    little, a little,
and turn yourself about.
    WHOO!

5 b

Put your face in,
leaning forward. Then
lean way back. Shake it,
nodding up and down.

Hullabalooby looby,
hullabalooby light.
Hullabalooby looby
on a summer night.

6 a

All boys galop left,
while all girls galop
right. Stop *all together*
on the last note.

Put your whole self in!
Put your whole self out!
Shake it a little, a
    little, a little,
and turn yourself about.
    WHOO!

6 b

IN OUT

Let go hands and jump
in, landing on "in!"
Jump back and land in
place on "out!" "Shake
it" with four springs on
both feet. And turn
with R L R L as before.
This ends the game.

A₁ & A₂   Note: play B after A each time   Piano setting by Hilton Rufty

steps: R   L   R   L   R   L   etc.

B a bit faster

A₃ & A₄

tiptoe   R   L   R   L   R!ft   R   L   R   L   R   ft
         FORWARD   BACK

A₅ & A₆

Play thus: A₁ B, A₂ B, A₃ B, A₄ B, A₅ B, A₆ B.

Lady Gomme tells us that this game has been known since the time of King Henry VIII. And she says it may be even older than that. In King Harry's day it was a "grotesque country dance" for grownups.

William Wells Newell, one of the first scholars to collect these old handed-down games, says that in America this folk-game was done "politely and decorously" as a regular ballroom dance, but when it was done by children (making fun of grownups, maybe?) it was always "an antic and loony romp."

So, you can act like a "loony looby" when you play this game, if you wish. Walk wobbly and loose-jointed, but of course keep time with the tune! Another name for the game is "Ugly Mug."

Response Games

Response games involve fast questions and answers. The idea behind these games is to trick or confuse people into giving the wrong answer. Probably the most popular response game is "1, 2, 3, and a zing, zing, zing." In this game each player is given a number except the one who is the leader. Then the group chants "1, 2, 3, and a zing, zing, zing" and the leader begins the questioning:

Leader:	Number 1.
#1:	Who me?
Leader:	Yes you.
#1:	Couldn't be.
Leader:	Then who?
#1:	Number 5.
#5:	Who me?
Leader:	Yes you.
#5:	Couldn't be.
Leader:	Then who?
#5:	Number 9.
#9:	Who me?
Leader:	Yes you.
	(etc.)

The game keeps increasing speed. When players don't respond to their number or give a wrong answer, they drop out until the leader and only one other person are left.

Another response game begins by matching two simple phrases. For example:

1 gotta run
2 ain't true
3 not me
4 no more
5 that's jive
6 couldn't be

A leader is chosen and each person is given a number. Then the leader calls out numbers and the other players have to give their phrases. A good leader, by playing with pace and repetition, can trick almost all the players. When someone gives the wrong response he or she drops out of the game until only one person is left.

It's easy to make up your own responses for the game. For example, start with letters instead of numbers and use animal sounds instead of phrases:

A woof
B meow
C moo
D oink-oink
E quack-quack
(etc.)

Or use numbers and attach physical actions to them instead of words:

1 jump
2 spin around
3 do deep knee bends
4 raise right arm
5 raise left arm

Peggy Kreuter introduced me to a more active response game called "Chemasit" that is played by groups of children of the Kipsigis people who live in Kenya. Chemasit is the name of a hairy monster that is supposed to live in the forest and eat children. When children cry, they are told that unless they are quiet, Chemasit will come and eat them.

In this game all the children walk along in a silent line behind the leader, who is Chemasit. They chant together "Sait Chemasit?" which means "What time is it, Chemasit?" Chemasit answers by telling the things that people do every day, such as "It's time to milk the cows," or "It's time to sweep the house." Unexpectedly one time Chemasit says "It's time to eat," and turns and chases all the children. The one who is caught and "eaten" becomes the next Chemasit.

Memory-response Games*

In contrast to Chemasit, here's a game that just involves verbal responses. I learned it from Ira Altschuler. The idea is that you start with a simple description and proceed to develop increasingly elaborate images. The game is for two players. The first person begins with a simple description that starts with the word "one." For example, "one motorcycle." The second person repeats that image, then the first person repeats it and adds a second image beginning with the word "two." The idea is for one person to create a list, and for both of them to memorize and repeat the list. For example:

	Person 1	*Person 2*
Turn 1:	one wormy apple	one wormy apple
2:	one wormy apple	one wormy apple
	two smoking hams	two smoking hams
3:	one wormy apple	one wormy apple
	two smoking hams	two smoking hams
	three icy isolated islands	three icy—I forget

Here's an example of a list that got to ten images before one of the players went out:

one bird
two TVs
three ladies watching "Mod Squad"
four kids doing math quietly in Alabama Louisiana
five men climbing in the Sierra Nevadas
six porpoises walking in the streets of Palm Springs eating peaches
seven girls in bikinis in Hawaii
eight people holding oil

nine moms walking in the street on the Rockies on a Sunday morning
    eating bananas
ten hairy people taking naps on the Amtrak line

It seems best if the first images are simple and you increase in complexity as you go along. Here's the beginning of another list:

one hen
two ducks
three squawking geese
four Limerick oysters
five corpulent porpoises
six brass monkeys from the ancient sacred crypts of Egypt
seven . . . well, I forgot

The Hand Game

As a child I remember a guessing game one of the older men on the block would play with anyone who came along. He had two buttons, one black and the other white. He put one in each hand and then passed his hands back and forth, swaying and talking, switching the buttons from one hand to the other. Occasionally he'd sing in Yiddish or tell a joke. The game was to guess which hand held the black button when he stopped moving. Younger children who guessed correctly won an ice cream. He bet money with the teenagers. As I remember he lost very few ice cream cones or bets. What with the chanting and jokes, and his swaying back and forth, skillfully shifting and concealing the buttons, it was impossible to follow their paths.

I was amazed to discover recently that this game I witnessed (and tried out once or twice) in the Bronx in the 1940s is a simple version of the Native American hand games that were played by at least eighty-one tribes belonging to twenty-eight different linguistic stocks on the American continent before Columbus was born. According to Stewart Culin in his 800-page book *Games of the North American Indians* (New York: Dover, 1975), the game's wide distribution "may be partially accounted for by the fact that, as it was played entirely by gesture, the game could be carried on between individuals who had only the sign language in common" (p. 267).

The hand games were not as simple as the ones I witnessed. Usually two groups of men or women played against each other. The players would sit or stand in two lines facing each other. Buttons were sometimes used, but more often it was animal bones, one of which was marked in some way to distinguish it from the other one. Each team would take a turn passing the bones. One of the players in the middle would hold out the bones for the other team to see. Then he and his team would start swaying from side to side, bringing closed fists together, passing or pretending to pass the bones from one person to another. The object of the game was for the other team to guess where the bones were. After a few minutes any player on the other team could call out and play would be frozen. If the guess was correct, the guessing team would get points; if not, the hiding team would get them. The game trained manual dexterity and perception. The players on one side had to know how to pass or fake passing the bones; the others had to watch as keenly as they watched for the animals they were hunting or the tracks they were trying to follow. Often the game was primarily psychological. The presence of a bone was revealed by someone's face rather than his or her hand.

The game was not played in silence. Central to the game were the spectators, who were also participants. Behind each team were their supporters whose role was to sing and chant and recite poems and tales as the players swayed and passed the bones. Often a game was won by the chorus whose chants and verse reduced the opponents to listening and looking away for a second. The chorus and the players were inextricable parts of the game. The songs and poems were as much a part of the game as the dexterity of the players out front. Everyone present was part of the game.

I've never seen the hand game played by Amerindians but the idea of a group game involving song, movement, deception, dexterity, and psychological perception is intriguing. I've begun experimenting with groups of students and with some friends, trying to recreate a version of the hand game. Basically we've begun with two teams of five or six people standing facing each other. One team hides the bones and the other tries to guess their position. A player in the middle of the line begins with one bone in each hand. The bones are chosen so that they are rectangular and are almost as big as the fist of the smallest player in the game. The team passing the bones hums and begins swaying back and forth, and the players begin passing the bones. After a minute the other team can stop the action at any time and guess the location of the bones. Each one guessed correctly gives the guessers one point. Each one guessed incorrectly gives the hiding team a point. The first team to get ten, twelve, or some designated number of points, wins.

There are several things I notice during attempts to play the game:

1. At first the humming was done very awkwardly, without much conviction. After a while the intensity increases, and in some cases players chant such things as: "Bones, who's got the bones?" "Here they are, there they go," etc. These simple chants become elaborated into rhymes like:

> Here they are, there they go
> Where they are, you don't know
>
> Watch my hand, watch my eye
> You'll never guess till the day you die.

2. The first time the game is played it is often very frustrating. The chanting, swaying, and bone passing are hard to coordinate. Players have to get to know their teams, and learn how to pass the bones without looking at each other. They have to chant and move and at the same time pretend they are holding the bones. It takes a number of times working at the game to generate the excitement that can result from a well-played hand game.

3. Passing the bones is not easy and practice is needed for a team to work well together.

4. People have to learn how to control their fists so that every fist on the passing team looks like it could be holding a bone.

5. The game gets quite heated after a while, and as skilled teams develop, roles become diversified. Some people lead the chant, others stay in the middle and orchestrate the passing of the bones. Some become defensive specialists and have their skills of perception. Some teams are better at guessing than passing, and vice versa. And finally, song, chant, and movement are combined in the hand game in a way that no other game I've encountered approaches.

6. If it is hard to get a game going, a few drums, whistles, triangles, and rattles will help.

A game somewhat similar to the bone game could be called the Whole Body Game. One person, "it," leaves the room and the rest of the group chooses a leader whose movements the rest of the group has to mimic, making it look as if everyone in the group is making each movement simultaneously. "It" has to guess who the leader is by observing the group.

8

Codes and Ciphers

Some Basic Vocabulary
Cipher Systems
A Few Transposition Ciphers
Codes

Some Basic Vocabulary

Secret codes have been in existence for at least 3000 years, and it's possible that they developed right along with writing. As soon as people learned to write messages it seemed that they also learned how to conceal them. In *The Codebreakers* (New York: Macmillan, 1967), David Kahn gives a comprehensive thousand-page history of secret communication, and describes dozens of codes and ciphers. Kahn introduces some of the basic vocabulary of cryptanalysis (the deciphering or breaking of codes and ciphers) which is, not surprisingly, similar to the one I used to describe word transformations in Chapter 1 since codes and ciphers are transformations of the whole alphabet.

The message that is to be put into secret form is called the *plaintext*. There are two basic transformations of the plaintext: *transposition* and *substitution*. In transpositions the letters in the plaintext are jumbled. Thus the plaintext message GUESS MY SECRET can be transposed in a number of different ways: RESEYMUSSTEGC, for example, or CGETS-SUMYESER. In transpositions the letters retain their identity—the Es are still Es, the Ts still Ts.

In substitutions the letters of the plaintext are replaced by other letters or symbols. Thus GUESS MY SECRET might become 1345579548640 or ABCDDEFDCGHCL. In substitutions the letters retain the same positions they had in the original message.

It's possible to combine transpositions and substitution to double-jumble a message. Thus the word

MESSAGE

can be changed by substitution to

1233452

and then by transposition to

3254321

Substitution systems rest on the concept of a *cipher alphabet* which gives the equivalents used to transform the plaintext into the secret form. Here's a simple cipher alphabet using the usual alphabet in reverse:

Plaintext letters: A B C D E F G H I J K L M N O P Q R S T U V W X Y Z
Cipher letters: Z Y X W V U T S R Q P O N M L K J I H G F E D C B A

The plaintext message CAB would then read XZY.

Most ciphers have a *key*—a word, phrase, or number which specifies such things as how symbols are arranged in a cipher alphabet or how a transposition is to be made. For example, in the above cipher the *key number* could be "26," indicating that the twenty-sixth letter is substituted for the first, etc. The *key letter* "Z" could also do.

In cryptanalysis a distinction is made between a cipher and a code. In a *cipher* the basic unit is the letter. Each letter is replaced by a unit in the cipher alphabet. A *code,* on the other hand, consists of thousands of words, phrases, letters, or syllables which replace these different elements. Thus in a code the following replacements can exist:

COME	0101
GO	0201
-ING	0202
OUT	3012

Thus OUTGOING would be represented by:

3012 - 0201 - 0202

and COMING OUT by:

0101 - 0202 - 3012

Computer languages are codes that are designed to make certain parts of English compatible with the structure and functions of computers. There's also a commercial code used in business to save money on telegraph cables.

Finally, the process of putting a plaintext into secret form is called *enciphering* or *encoding* the message. The reverse process—going from the secret message to the plaintext—is *deciphering* or *decoding.*

Cipher Systems*

Simple Substitution Codes*

Simple substitution codes replace one letter with another one. No complex shifts or deceptive symbols are used. Two simple substitution codes are (1) the backward substitution code, which was described above, and (2) the single-shift code. The single-shift code consists of shifting all the letters of the alphabet one place to the left and then putting the *A* at the end of the cipher alphabet:

Plaintext: A B C D E F G H I J K L M N O P Q R S T U V W X Y Z
Cipher: B C D E F G H I J K L M N O P Q R S T U V W X Y Z A

In the single-shift alphabet CAT would be encoded DBU. Obviously there can be double- and triple-shift alphabets, in fact twenty-five shift alphabets. It's possible to use a key letter to indicate which shift alphabet is being used. The key letter of a shift alphabet would then be the letter that is to replace A. Thus key letter K would indicate that the following cipher alphabet is being used:

Plaintext: A B C D E F G H I J K L M N O P Q R S T U V W X Y Z
Cipher: K L M N O P Q R S T U V W X Y Z A B C D E F G H I J

It's possible to include the key letter in the message. Thus if it is agreed that the key letter is to be the last one in the message, MKDK would indicate that shift alphabet K is being used, and deciphering that, the message is CAT. If two people agree on a particular placement for the key letter, they can keep changing ciphers without others' being aware of it. Thus if the key letter is to be the third in the message, MKKD would mean cipher message K, CAT. Similarly, DBBU would mean B, CAT.

Once you understand how to use key letters or key numbers it is possible to find ways to keep messages secret from anyone who doesn't know how the key is being used.

The shift alphabet beginning with D is one of the first documented uses of secret messages. Julius Caesar used this cipher when writing to Cicero and other friends. Because of this, all the shift substitution ciphers are called *Caesar's alphabets.*

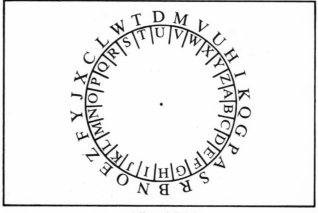

Alberti Disk

Shift substitutions can be encoded and decoded easily by making a code wheel (called an Alberti disk) like the one shown here. The disks can be made out of cardboard and held together by a tack or clip. To set a code, just move the A on the inner disk to the letter which will be its equivalent in the code. In the diagram, K stands for A. Then use the inner disk to spell out your message, putting down the code equivalents. NO in code A=K would be YJ.

Key-Word Substitution Codes

Pick any word that does not have any letter repeated. For example, these words would do:

PLANE

CAB

Then write a plaintext alphabet and under the first letters write the key word you've chosen. Then after the key word write the alphabet, dropping only those letters that appear in the key word:

Plaintext:	A B C D E F G H I J K L M N O P Q R S T U V W X Y Z
Cipher:	P L A N E B C D F G H I J K M O Q R S T U V W X Y Z
Cipher:	C A B D E F G H I J K L M N O P Q R S T U V W X Y Z

The key-word ciphers here have one obvious problem. Too many of the letters in the plaintext alphabet are their own equivalents. Thus with CAB as a key word, twenty-three of the letters are unchanged, which doesn't make for much secrecy. One way to fix that is to make a second substitution after the key-word substitution, consisting of reversing the order of all those letters that are the equivalents of themselves. Thus the CAB cipher alphabet would read:

C A B Z Y X W V U T S R Q P O N M L K J I H G F E D

Polybius' Checkerboard

An ancient Greek writer Polybius devised a system of substitution that has become widely used for a number of ciphers. First he arranged the letters in a five-by-five grid (which can be accomplished by putting two letters in the same cell (in this case I and J):

	1	2	3	4	5
1	A	B	C	D	E
2	F	G	H	IJ	K
3	L	M	N	O	P
4	Q	R	S	T	U
5	V	W	X	Y	Z

and numbering the columns and rows. Thus each letter can be represented by two numbers (3,1) where 3 is the column number and 1 is the row number. Thus CAT would be 31-11-44.

Polybius suggested that this way of enciphering letters could be used as a signaling system using torches. The left hand could represent columns;

the right, rows. Thus two torches in the left hand and one in the right would mean B.

There are many different variants of Polybius' checkerboard and it is easy to make up one's own codes using a five-by-five grid. Here are some variants:

	1	2	3	4	5
1	Z	Y	X	W	V
2	U	T	S	R	Q
3	P	O	N	M	L
4	K	IJ	H	G	F
5	E	D	C	B	A

1

2

	A	B	C	D	E
A	A	F	K	P	U
B	B	G	L	Q	V
C	C	H	M	R	W
D	D	I	N	S	X
E	E	J	O	T	YZ

3

Here's CAT in the three ciphers:

(1)   35–55–22   (2)

(3)   AC–AA–DE

The Shadow Cipher

In the 1940s and 1950s there was a radio program that began with a sinister voice saying "Who knows what evil lurks in the hearts of men? The Shadow knows!"

The Shadow was created by Maxwell Grant, who wrote twelve Shadow novels (available from Pyramid Books, 919 Third Avenue, New York, NY 10022) and who edited *The Shadow* magazine during the 1930s.

The Shadow is Lamont Cranston, an ordinary mortal and not a superhero in the usual sense. On a trip to the Orient he learned the secret of clouding people's minds and appearing invisible.

Shadow stories are more mystical than most mystery stories and

Cranston has a secret identity like Bruce Wayne. The Shadow knows people's hearts and has a highly developed intuition. He is also a master of ciphers. Many Shadow stories depend on secret messages, and often simple ciphers are used to mislead people and conceal more complex ones. One interesting cipher used as bait in the book *Chain of Death* consists of the following pictorial equivalents for the alphabet:

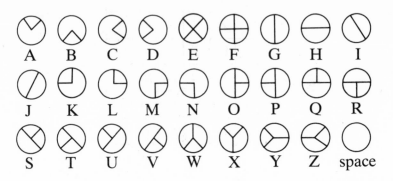

This cipher is not difficult to decipher if a long message is given. However, the Shadow is an expert at giving a simple twist to a cipher that makes it complex. In the case of this cipher four new symbols are introduced:

Turn Page

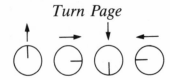

The function of these symbols is to indicate the way the other symbols have to be turned before you can decipher them. Thus ⊖ is H. ⦶ ⊖ and ⊖ ⦶ are also H. (Note that the page should be returned to its original position before using each new position symbol.) Here is a message written in the cipher without the special symbols:

Here is the same message using them:

The Triangle Cipher

Martin Gardner describes a neat coding device in his book *Codes, Ciphers and Secret Writing* (New York: Archway Paperbacks, 1974), which is the best volume to use if you want a clear exposition of many codes, some much more complex than the few described here.

The Rotating Triangle in Three Positions

To make this handy little coding device, first draw an equilateral triangle in the center of a sheet of paper. The alphabet, plus a circled period, is lettered in proper sequence around the outside of the triangle. The letters must be equally spaced as shown on the diagram here.

Draw an identical triangle on a sheet of thin cardboard. The alphabet, plus a circled period, is written on the inside edge of its three sides, but in a random order. Draw an arrow pointing to one of its corners. Cut out the cardboard triangle and place it on the paper triangle. Now it is possible to have three different cipher alphabets using the device.

Binary Ciphers* The binary number system has two symbols, 0 and 1. Using these symbols, all of the numbers can be represented as powers of two using the following place values:

2^n	. . .	$2^4 = 16$	$2^3 = 8$	$2^2 = 4$	$2^1 = 2$	$2^0 = 1$

By putting a zero or one in each column you can generate all the numbers by adding up the values of the rows that have 1s in them. Thus all the numbers from 1 to 10 are represented in the chart below:

$2^3 = 8$	$2^2 = 4$	$2^1 = 2$	$2^0 = 1$	sum
			0	0
			1	1
		1	0	2
		1	1	3
	1	0	0	4
	1	0	1	5
	1	1	0	6
	1	1	1	7
1	0	0	0	8
1	0	0	1	9
1	0	1	0	10

The number 26 is represented as follows:

11010 $[1(2^4) + 1(2^3) + 0(2^2) + 1(2^1) + 0(2^0) = 16 + 8 + 0 + 2 + 0]$

The alphabet can then be represented by binary numbers:

A =	0	F =	101	K =	1010
B =	1	G =	110	L =	1011
C =	10	H =	111	M =	1100
D =	11	I =	1000	N =	1101
E =	100	J =	1001	O =	1111

P = 10000	T = 10100	X = 11000
Q = 10001	U = 10101	Y = 11001
R = 10010	V = 10110	Z = 11010
S = 10011	W = 10111	

This is a simple cipher. It's possible to use other substitution ciphers, to shift letters, and in many other ways make this binary cipher more complex. I've found that introducing the binary number system to people is easy in the context of talking about it as a cipher.

Lewis Carroll's Alphabet Cipher

```
  A B C D E F G H I J K L M N O P Q R S T U V W X Y Z
A a b c d e f g h i j k l m n o p q r s t u v w x y z A
B b c d e f g h i j k l m n o p q r s t u v w x y z a B
C c d e f g h i j k l m n o p q r s t u v w x y z a b C
D d e f g h i j k l m n o p q r s t u v w x y z a b c D
E e f g h i j k l m n o p q r s t u v w x y z a b c d E
F f g h i j k l m n o p q r s t u v w x y z a b c d e F
G g h i j k l m n o p q r s t u v w x y z a b c d e f G
H h i j k l m n o p q r s t u v w x y z a b c d e f g H
I i j k l m n o p q r s t u v w x y z a b c d e f g h I
J j k l m n o p q r s t u v w x y z a b c d e f g h i J
K k l m n o p q r s t u v w x y z a b c d e f g h i j K
L l m n o p q r s t u v w x y z a b c d e f g h i j k L
M m n o p q r s t u v w x y z a b c d e f g h i j k l M
N n o p q r s t u v w x y z a b c d e f g h i j k l m N
O o p q r s t u v w x y z a b c d e f g h i j k l m n O
P p q r s t u v w x y z a b c d e f g h i j k l m n o P
Q q r s t u v w x y z a b c d e f g h i j k l m n o p Q
R r s t u v w x y z a b c d e f g h i j k l m n o p q R
S s t u v w x y z a b c d e f g h i j k l m n o p q r S
T t u v w x y z a b c d e f g h i j k l m n o p q r s T
U u v w x y z a b c d e f g h i j k l m n o p q r s t U
V v w x y z a b c d e f g h i j k l m n o p q r s t u V
W w x y z a b c d e f g h i j k l m n o p q r s t u v W
X x y z a b c d e f g h i j k l m n o p q r s t u v w X
Y y z a b c d e f g h i j k l m n o p q r s t u v w x Y
Z z a b c d e f g h i j k l m n o p q r s t u v w x y Z
  A B C D E F G H I J K L M N O P Q R S T U V W X Y Z
```

As a last substitution cipher, here's a difficult one that Lewis Carroll invented in 1868. Carroll described the cipher as follows:

Each column of this table forms a dictionary of symbols representing the alphabet: thus, in the A column, the symbol is the same as the letter represented; in the B column, A is represented by B, B by C, and so on.

To use the table, some word or sentence should be agreed on by two correspondents. This may be called the "key-word," or "key-sentence," and should be carried in the memory only.

In sending a message, write the key word over it, letter for letter, repeating it as often as may be necessary: the letters of the key-word will indicate which column is to be used in translating each letter of the message, the symbols for which should be written underneath: then copy out the symbols only, and destroy the first paper. It will now be impossible for any one, ignorant of the key-word, to decipher the message, even with the help of the table.

For example let the key-word be *vigilance,* and the message "meet me on Tuesday evening at seven," the first paper will read as follows—

v i g i l a n c e v i g i l a n c e v i g i l a n c e v i
m e e t m e o n t u e s d a y e v e n i n g a t s e v e n
h m k b x e b p x p m y l l y r x i i q t o l t f g z z v

The second will contain only "hmkbxebpxpmyllyrxiiqtoltfgzzv."

The receiver of the message can, by the same process, retranslate it into English.

N.B.—If this table be lost, it can easily be written out from memory, by observing that the first symbol in each column is the same as the letter naming the column, and that they are continued downwards in alphabetical order. Of course it would only be necessary to write out the particular columns required by the key-word: such a paper, however, should not be preserved, as it would afford means for discovering the key-word.

Here's the encipherment of CAT using the key word DOG:

Write key word over message:

DOG
CAT

Look in column D for encipherment of letter C = F
Look in column O for encipherment of letter A = O
Look in column G for encipherment of letter T = Z

Thus CAT is enciphered as FOZ.

A Few Transposition Ciphers

Combinations of Simple Transpositions

Here are a few simple transpositions:

1. reverse the letters in a message so that HELP ME becomes EMPLEH;
2. switch every other letter so that HELP ME becomes EHPLEM;
3. reverse the order of words in the message so that HELP ME becomes ME HELP; or
4. switch the first and last letters of each word in a message so that HELP ME becomes PELHEM.

There are other simple transpositions. However, these transpositions don't conceal a message as well as substitution ciphers unless they are combined and the message is scrambled several times. For example, it's possible to (1) reverse the words in a message; (2) switch the first and last letters in the reversed message; and (3) write the result of step 2 backward. Under these three transformations HELP ME becomes (1) ME HELP, (2) EM PELH, (3) HLEPME.

Experiment with combinations of simple transpositions and try to find which ones effectively scramble the original messages, are difficult to decipher, or hide less than the effort merits. In the example of triple transposing HELP ME to HLEPME one wonders whether it was worth the effort. However, with a longer message it might work. For example,

IT DOES NOT WORK

becomes:

(1) WORK NOT DOES IT
(2) KORW TON SOED TI
(3) IT DEOS NOT WROK

This doesn't seem too secret. The second stage of the transpositional process hides the message best for both examples. It might be best to stop there or at least try something else for the third stage. This is illustrative of how interesting codes are developed—inductively, through trial and error, and then generalization. It's useful to experiment that way and experience how innovations often develop through trial and error rather than logical deduction.

Horizontal Transposition Ciphers

To make up this cipher, first write down your message. Then break up the message into blocks of seven letters each (the choice of seven is arbitrary) and arrange them in rows. The two As at the end of the message below are just to fill up the last row. For example if we start with the plaintext "The treasure is in the doghouse," here's how it breaks down into blocks of seven:

THETREA
SUREISI
NTHEDOG
HOUSEAA

Now, to get the coded message, take the letters backward, in blocks of five, off the list above:

AERTE HTISI ERUSG
ODEHT NAAES UOH.

To decipher, all you need to know is that the original message was broken up in blocks of seven. Take the first seven letters of the coded message and write them backward. Then take the next seven letters, etc.

It's interesting to note that this transpositional cipher is basically a way to create anagrams of sentences.

Codes*

Codes consist of lists of words, letters, phrases, or syllables along with codewords or code numbers that replace them. They are quite different from ciphers although in ordinary conversation codes and ciphers are both often referred to as codes. A good example of a code was used by Benedict Arnold during the American Revolutionary War. Arnold, who at that time was head of West Point, passed military secrets to the British using a code that depended on Blackstone's *Commentaries,* an English legal classic. Each word in a message was first to be found in the *Commentaries.* Then the code number of the word consisted of three parts—the page the word was on, the line it was on, and the number of words separating it from the margin on that line. Words that couldn't be found in the book were spelled out, with the letters noted by the page, line, and number of letters the given letter was away from the left margin. This last series of numbers had a stroke through the final number of each group to indicate it was a letter and not a word.

After a while this system became tedious and Arnold switched to the *Universal Etymological English Dictionary* as words were arranged alphabetically and therefore much easier to locate.

The *Dictionary* and the *Commentaries* were Arnold's *codebooks.* Codebooks provide the list of words that are used in the code. If you do not know which codebook someone is using, it is just about impossible to decode the message. With sophisticated mathematics and computers to help, ciphers are easier to break than codes with secret codebooks. That's why so many mystery and spy stories revolve around the theft of codebooks.

Any dictionary can be used as a codebook, and any group of people can make up their codeword or code number equivalents to develop their own secret codes. For example, a word can be represented by three numbers:

page it is on   column it is in   line it begins

To complicate things more, it is possible to add the following twist:

page on	column in	line it begins
-2	$+3$	$+6$

There are clearly an unlimited number of ways a dictionary can be used to generate codes. There are also other codebooks that are more convenient for any particular use. For example, in 1845, the year after Samuel F. B. Morse sent the first telegraph message, Morse's lawyer Francis O. J. Smith published a commercial code entitled *The Secret Corresponding Vocabulary; Adapted for Use to Morse's Electro-Magnetic Telegraph.* This code was then assigned varying ciphers so that telegraph operators and casual readers couldn't understand secret business messages. Another book published in 1804 was entitled *A Dictionary; to Enable Any Two Persons to Maintain a Correspondence, with a Secrecy Which Is Impossible for Any Other Person to Discover.* The dictionary was a small book listing words and syllables in alphabetical order. These entries were to be numbered in some serial order by correspondents, omitting every tenth number to further decrease the possibility that two sets of correspondents might use the same code.

Most codes have specific functions and don't need to draw upon a whole dictionary. The list of words or numbers used for a given code is called its *nomenclator.* For example, the following short nomenclator is for a code some youngsters made up for their secret club:

John   Thursday
Robert   Friday

Allan	Saturday
meet	Sunday
not meet	hour
Monday	clubhouse
Tuesday	home
Wednesday	school
	AM, PM, 1, 2, 3, 4, 5, 6, 7, 8, 9, 0

After developing their nomenclator the boys and girls had to construct codewords for them as well as choose codenames for themselves.

The choice of a codename can be fun. It can also be a delicate and sensitive matter. During World War II Winston Churchill wrote the following about the choice of codenames for battles in which many people would be killed (found in David Kahn's *The Codebreakers,* p. 502):

> I have crossed out on the attached paper many unsuitable names. Operations in which large numbers of men may lose their lives ought not to be described by code-words which imply a boastful and overconfident sentiment, such as "Triumphant," or, conversely, which are calculated to invest the plan with an air of despondency, such as "Woebetide," "Massacre," "Jumble," "Trouble," "Fidget," "Flimsy," "Pathetic," and "Jaundice." They ought not to be names of a frivolous character, such as "Bunnyhug," "Billingsgate," "Aperitif," and "Ballyhoo." They should not be ordinary words often used in other connections, such as "Flood," "Smooth," "Sudden," "Supreme," "Fullforce," and "Fullspeed." Names of living people—Ministers or Commanders—should be avoided, e.g., "Bracken." . . .
>
> 2. After all, the world is wide, and intelligent thought will readily supply an unlimited number of well-sounding names which do not suggest the character of the operation or disparage it in any way and do not enable some widow or mother to say that her son was killed in an operation called "Bunnyhug" or "Ballyhoo."
>
> 3. Proper names are good in this field. The heroes of antiquity, figures from Greek and Roman mythology, the constellations and stars, famous racehorses, names of British and American war heroes, could be used, provided they fall within the rules above. There are no doubt many other themes that could be suggested.
>
> 4. Care should be taken in all this process. An efficient and a successful administration manifests itself equally in small as in great matters.

In the case of codenames for members of the children's club the case was naturally simpler. They wanted names that would reveal some aspect of themselves, although not be too obvious. They chose names that were similar to CB radio codenames: John became Big Red; Robert, Orange Raider; and Allan, Swift. Then they constructed codewords for the rest of the list:

meet	– abbl	hour	– ppsl
not meet	– quei	1	– abcl
Monday	– rrlt	2	– dclf
Tuesday	– pllt	3	– rtst
Wednesday	– rroo	4	– wwtl
Thursday	– mnno	5	– pglz
Friday	– rrot	6	– zlgp
Saturday	– floz	7	– zyzp
Sunday	– rftu	8	– xtxz
clubhouse	– rwrw	9	– xtuv
home	– wlrt	0	– tlmn
school	– psts	AM	– zfff
		PM	– pzzz

With the exceptions of the codenames the codewords were all four letters long. Thus the message

Robert meet John clubhouse Friday 3 PM

would be encoded

ORANGERAIDER ABBL BIGRED RWRW RROT RTST PZZZ

No amount of substituting letters in the codewords could lead to a deciphering of the message. If no one else has the codebook, you have a solid secret language.

It's possible to make up codes for different functions. For example, it's possible to make up nomenclators and codes for the following situations:

to give directions to a hidden treasure
to pass a love note so that parents won't understand it if they intercept it
to arrange a secret meeting
to describe the time, place, and strategies to take place in a battle
to list the contents in a safe
to send a secret formula or recipe to another person
to warn a person that someone is about to attack him.

There are a number of ways to develop codewords. One way is simple: decide on the length of codewords and combine letters arbitrarily as in the example above. It's important in that case not to repeat codeword combinations.

It is also possible to be more systematic too. For example, you could list combinations of letters and choose from the list in some systematic way. Here's the beginning of a potential list of four-letter codewords:

aaaa	bbbb	cccc
aaab	bbba	ccca
aaac	bbbc	cccb
aaad	bbbd	cccd
•	•	•
•	•	•
•	•	•

You could then choose every fourth word as a codeword, or pick in any other way from the list.

9

Pictographic Systems of Writing

Kiowa Pictograms
Hieroglyphics
Some Other Pictographic Systems
Symbols and Proverbs
Chinese Character Writing
Picture Sequences and Diagram Stories
Comic Books

Kiowa Pictograms

After playing with codes and ciphers it is possible to go a step further and investigate the nature of writing systems in general. It's also possible to invent writing systems. I was particularly struck by this possibility recently when I visited a classroom where at least four languages (English, Spanish, Vietnamese, and Chinese) were used. The seven- and eight-year-old students were all monolingual and were having a hard time communicating with each other. In the class I noticed one group of four or five children who were sitting around and drawing. They seemed to be having a delightful time and so I went over to their table. They were in the process of inventing their own writing system. One of the children had drawn a man, another added a car. A third child drew an arrow leading from the man's arm to a store that had been drawn on the corner of the paper. Under the store there were pictures of soda cans and candy bars. Finally each of the children had drawn a figure intended, I think, to represent himself and under the figure had drawn a number of lines indicating how much money he had. These children who couldn't speak to each other had found a way to communicate through pictures and were planning a trip to the neighborhood store.

It occurred to me that picture writing might be an interesting way to introduce people to the use of symbols to express ideas, as well as a way to help them understand that language is created all the time and is not static. I had seen a list of Native American pictorial symbols and found a book, *Indian Picture Writing* by Robert Hofsinde (New York: Wm. Morrow, Morrow Junior Books, 1959), that contained over 200 pictograms, so I decided to explore this writing. It is interesting that Amerindian writing developed precisely because different groups spoke different languages.

Here's a list of some Kiowa pictograms:

walk   fear   cloud   house   brothers

dead   eat   come   strong   day

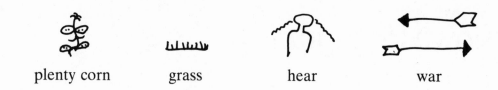

plenty corn   grass   hear   war

These symbols can be combined in many ways. For example, "day" ⌒⊃ can be multiplied ⊃⊃ to make "days." The same symbol backward ⊂⌒ can mean "the past." "War" ▷——▷, through the addition of "strong" ⋈, can indicate a major war among nations ⋈. A house with a cloud over it 🏠 can indicate bad luck or poverty.

Here is a statement in Kiowa picture writing: The two strong brothers went home because they were afraid of war.

Try to figure out this more complex tale:

One interpretation is: "The grass is dead (there is famine in the land). Come listen to the clouds. In three days there should be rain and plenty of corn to eat."

Here's one I put together:

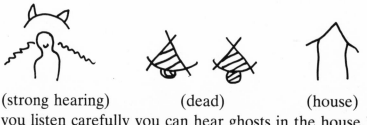

(strong hearing)   (dead)   (house)
"If you listen carefully you can hear ghosts in the house."

I showed these symbols to my son Josh and asked him if he could invent a way of writing. After a few minutes he drew this:

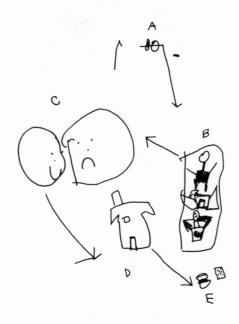

Then he explained to me what it was all about. He said that A meant that first there was a night and then a new day began. The arrow from A to B indicated that he got up in the morning and went to school, which was represented by someone standing up to recite, a playground structure, and someone reading at a desk. He put them all in a box because children do many things at school and he didn't mean just one thing but wanted his symbol to stand for all the things that happen at school. C indicates that sometimes he's happy and sometimes he's sad at school. D is a picture of our house and E some food, meaning that after school he comes home and has a snack.

After doing this Josh told me that he and his friends had some picture writing puzzles they tried to trick each other with and wondered if I'd like to see them. I said yes and here are some of them. What are the following?

1.   <u>MAN</u>
        BOARD

2.   <u>STAND</u>
       I

3. |R|E|A|D|I|N|G|

4.   LEV   EL

5.   DEATH/LIFE

6.   <u>GROUND</u>
      FEET
      FEET
      FEET
      FEET
      FEET
      FEET

7. <u>WEAR</u>
   LONG

8. <u>MIND</u>
   MATTER

9. ECNALG

Answers:

1. man overboard!
2. I understand
3. reading between the lines
4. split level
5. life after death
6. six feet underground
7. long underwear
8. mind over matter
9. a backward glance.

Recently, Mike Sensena and Scott Gardner, readers of *Gamesemag*, a magazine on games I used to edit, sent me some similar puzzlements which they called Wacky Wordles. Here are some of them to figure out. What are the following:

Answers:

1. broken heart
2. sock in the eye
3. sandbox
4. flat tire
5. ring around a rosie
6. Lone Ranger
7. life after death
8. keep it under your hat

9. broken engagement
10. a misunderstanding between friends
11. the worm turns
12. crooked lawyer
13. circles under your eyes
14. right in the middle of everything
15. far away from home
16. downtown
17. one kind thing after another
18. leaving no stone unturned
19. one meal at a time
20. touchdown
21. a broken promise
22. cantaloupe
23. rice
24. cookie

Coming back to the Kiowa writing system, here are some additional pictograms:

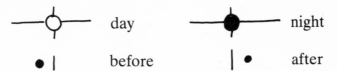

Combining these symbols produces a number of other symbols:

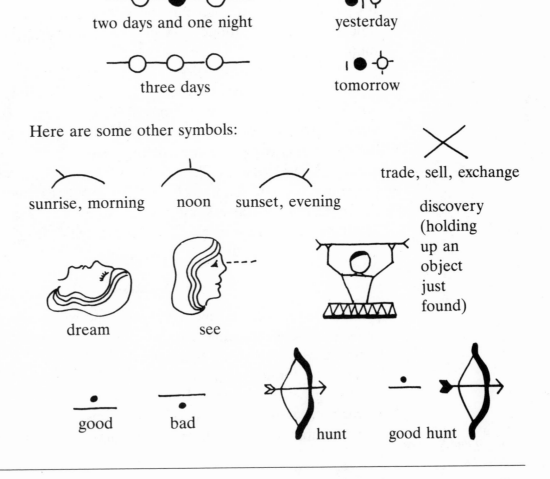

Here are some other symbols:

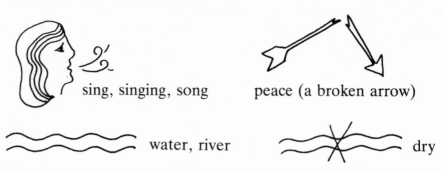

sing, singing, song   peace (a broken arrow)

water, river   dry

Using these symbols, try to develop extended stories.

Hieroglyphics*

The Egyptians expressed themselves in a complex system of picture signs that goes back at least 7000 years. The system, called hieroglyphics, was used in almost unchanged form for close to 5000 years and was abandoned around 100 B.C., toward the end of the rule of the Ptolemies over Egypt. It's possible to see hieroglyphics on statues and mummies and other royal objects that are reproduced in many books, and examples can also be found in museums.

With a little knowledge of some of the glyphs it is possible to get a general sense of what documents in hieroglyphics are about. It is also possible to write your own stories in hieroglyphics. However, without a knowledge of Egyptian it is impossible to get a full sense of a document because many glyphs are used to represent sounds as well as objects or concepts. This would be like having the sign representing an eye sometimes and the sound of the letter *i* at other times.

There are several other things to know about hieroglyphics before looking at some of the signs. Whenever you see a frame around a series of signs that looks like this

called a cartouche, you have a royal name within the frame. Often the name represents someone who is sculpted or painted on the object, or someone who owns or is giving the object.

Another thing to look for is the direction the people and animal signs are facing. As opposed to English there is no single direction that all hieroglyphic writing is oriented. Inscriptions may be written in columns or in horizontal lines, which are sometimes read from left to right and sometimes from right to left. The direction of an inscription is indicated by the position of the signs. When you find the way the men, birds, and animals face, then you read toward them. Thus inscriptions like these are read in the direction of the arrows:

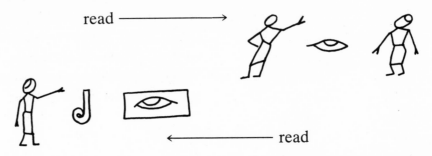

Many signs represent a single object or animal or person. However, these basic signs are varied to represent actions and ideas which cannot be pictured in a simple way. For example, basically the sign for "man" has this structure:

and the sign for "woman" has this structure:

However, they are varied to produce these complex symbols:

to praise

man motioning something to go back, to retreat

a man turning his back, to hide, to conceal

man about to strike with a stick, strength

two women grasping hands, friendship

woman beating a tambourine, to rejoice

to bend, to bow

a pregnant woman, to give birth

Some animal glyphs also take on complex meanings:

lion

the lions of Yesterday and Today

head and neck of a lion, strength

two-fold strength

jackal, wise person

Parts of the body also stand for abstract ideas in a number of hieroglyphic signs:

⏃ not having, to be without, negation

⏁ to give

⏁ to bear, to carry

⏁ bone and flesh, heir, progeny

Here's a short dictionary of hieroglyphics excerpted from E. A. Wallis Budge's book *Egyptian Language* (London: Routledge & Kegan Paul, 1963). The best way to get a sense of the way hieroglyphics works is to try to use these symbols to convey some information or tell a story. Also, go to a museum or look at a book on ancient Egypt and see if you can figure some of it out.

A Short Dictionary of Hieroglyphics

Men

to praise

to be high, to rejoice

man motioning something to go back, to retreat

two men grasping hands, friendship

a man turning his back, to hide, to conceal

man leaning on a staff, aged

man about to strike with a stick, strength

to bind together, to force something together

a baby sucking its finger, child, young person

a child

man supporting the whole sky, to stretch out

a man breaking in his head with an axe or stick, enemy, death, the dead

man washing, clean, pure, priest

submission, inactivity

to praise

to pray, to praise, to adore, to entreat

to write

to fall down

a dead person

to swim

a man swimming, to swim

Women

two women grasping hands, friendship

woman beating a tambourine, to rejoice

to bend, to bow

the goddess Nut, the sky

woman with disheveled hair

a woman seated

a sacred being, sacred statue

a divine or holy female, or statue

a guardian, watchman

a pregnant woman

a pregnant woman, to give birth

to nurse, to suckle a child

to dandle a child in the arms

Parts of the Body

the head, the top of anything

the face, upon

the hair, to want, to lack

a lock of hair

the beard

the right eye, to see, to look after something, to do

the left eye

to see

an eye weeping, to cry

to have a fine appearance

the breast

to embrace

not having, to be without, negation

the breast and arms of a man, the double

hands grasping a sacred staff, something holy

hands grasping a paddle, to transport, to carry away

arms holding shield and club, to fight

to write

hand holding a whip or flail, to be strong, to reign

hand and arm outstretched, to give

to bear, to carry

to give

the two eyes, to see

the right eye of Rā, the Sun

the left eye of Rā, the Moon

the two eyes of Rā

to offer

to offer fruit

an act of homage

to be strong, to show strength

to direct

hand

to receive

to hold in the hand

to clasp, to hold tight in the fist

finger, the number 10,000

to be in the center, to give evidence

thumb

a graving tool

phallus, what is masculine, husband, bull

to beget

male organs

woman, female organ

to go, to walk, to stand

to go backward, to retreat

to flee, to run away

to invade, to attack

to hold, to possess

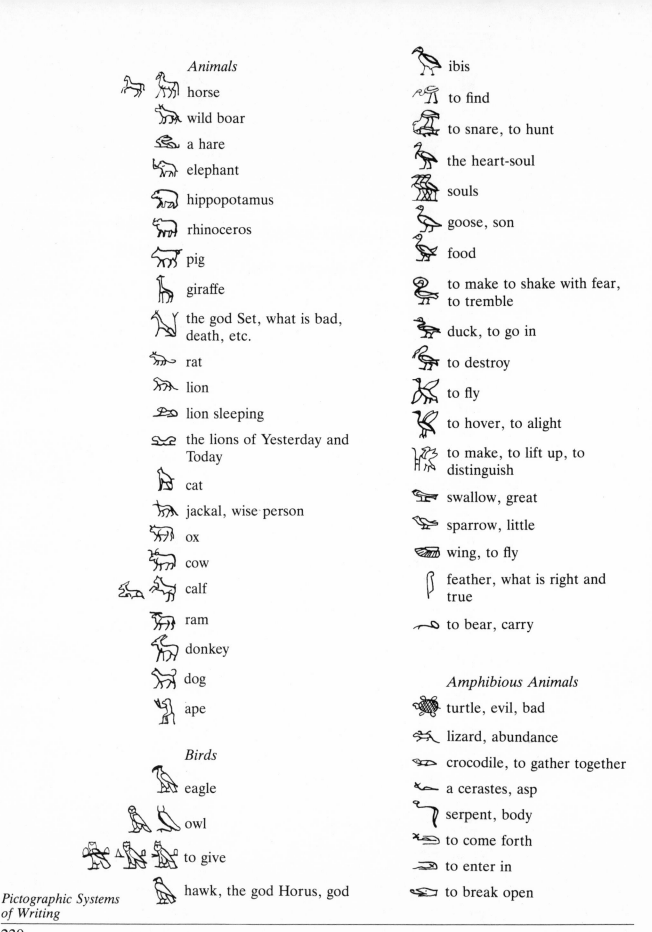

Animals

	horse
	wild boar
	a hare
	elephant
	hippopotamus
	rhinoceros
	pig
	giraffe
	the god Set, what is bad, death, etc.
	rat
	lion
	lion sleeping
	the lions of Yesterday and Today
	cat
	jackal, wise person
	ox
	cow
	calf
	ram
	donkey
	dog
	ape

Birds

	eagle
	owl
	to give
	hawk, the god Horus, god
	ibis
	to find
	to snare, to hunt
	the heart-soul
	souls
	goose, son
	food
	to make to shake with fear, to tremble
	duck, to go in
	to destroy
	to fly
	to hover, to alight
	to make, to lift up, to distinguish
	swallow, great
	sparrow, little
	wing, to fly
	feather, what is right and true
	to bear, carry

Amphibious Animals

	turtle, evil, bad
	lizard, abundance
	crocodile, to gather together
	a cerastes, asp
	serpent, body
	to come forth
	to enter in
	to break open

Fish

dead fish or thing

to transport

fish

Insects

centipede

bee

"King of the South and North"

to roll, to become, to come into being

fly

grasshopper

scorpion

Trees and Plants

tree, what is pleasant

palm tree

acacia

branch of a tree, wood

shoot, young twig, year

eternal year

time

feather

to go

plants growing in a field

an offering

lotus and papyrus flowers growing, field

cluster of flowers or plants

cluster of lotus flowers

young plant, what is green

Ships and Parts of Ships

boat, to sail downstream

loaded boat, to transport

to sail upstream

wind, breeze, air, breath

to stand

helm, rudder

paddle, voice

Heaven, Earth, and Water

what is above, heaven

sky with a star or lamp, night

water falling from the sky, dew, rain

lightning

moon, month

star, star of dawn, hour, to pray

the underworld

land

mountainous land

foreign, barbarian

mountain, wickedness

horizon

water

ditch, watercourse, to love

lake

to go

Buildings

town, city

house, to go out

wall, fort

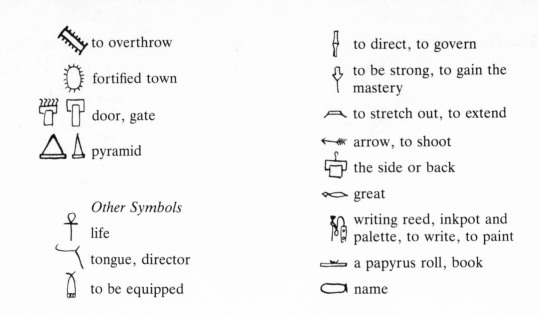

to overthrow

fortified town

door, gate

pyramid

Other Symbols

life

tongue, director

to be equipped

to direct, to govern

to be strong, to gain the mastery

to stretch out, to extend

arrow, to shoot

the side or back

great

writing reed, inkpot and palette, to write, to paint

a papyrus roll, book

name

Some Other Pictographic Systems

The systems presented here are from all over the world and provide an introduction to the many different attempts people have made to record their thoughts and experiences. They can be integrated into ethnic studies programs, presented as a group to show cross-cultural similarities, studied to understand different forms of representation, or simply played with and puzzled over.

The Nsibidi Script

Here is part of a script which is at least a hundred years old. It was used by the Ibo and Efik people in southern Nigeria. See how many stories you can make with these eleven symbols:

(a) a street; (b) money (copper rods bent into semicircles); (c) a quarrel between a married couple (a cushion separates backs turned to each other); (d) passionate love; (e) conflicting evidence (the straight line signifies the true evidence, the crooked one the false); (f) a gourd (as drinking mug); (g) a mirror; (h) trade (a trader loaded with money at a road-fork); (i) a slave; (j) fire; (k) a man in prison.

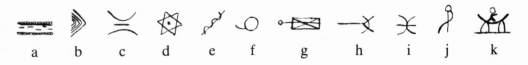

a   b   c   d   e   f   g   h   i   j   k

The Bamum Script

This script is unusual in that it was invented by a single person, King Njoya of Bamum in the Cameroon, around 1903. The signs shown here represented his first attempt to create a written form for his people's language. It is pictographic. After a number of attempts he eventually succeeded in creating a phonic script that could record word for word the Bamum language, which belongs to the southern African Bantu language group. Some of the letter forms he invented are:

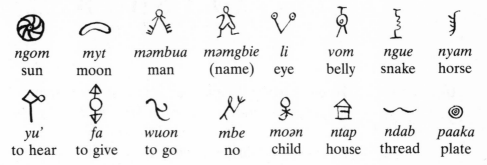

pa-mo̱-m̱
Bamum

Here are some of the signs:

ngom	*myt*	*məmbua*	*məmgbie*	*li*	*vom*	*ngue*	*nyam*
sun	moon	man	(name)	eye	belly	snake	horse

yu'	*fa*	*wuon*	*mbe*	*moən*	*ntap*	*ndab*	*paaka*
to hear	to give	to go	no	child	house	thread	plate

Indian Alphabet

Another individual who invented a writing system was Sequoya, a Cherokee educator for whom the giant sequoia redwoods were named. He reduced his people's language to seventy-eight characters.

A *as in* FATHER

E *as a in* HATE
OR SHORT *as* IN PIT

I *as* I *in* PIQUE
OR SHORT *as in* PIT

O *as in* LOW
SHORT *as in* NOT

U *as* OO *in* FOOT
SHORT *as in* PULL

V SHORT U NAZALIZED

*Some Other
Pictographic Systems*

233

℧ₒ◻₄ ϧ┼Ɛ𝓡 THERE WAS NO SOUND OF
sa s se si sa su sv   P, B, J, R, CH or Z

レWSꞁꞁVⵚ
da ta te te di ti do du dv

ႽꞭLᏟႿℙ
dla tla tlo tli tlo tlu tlv

ᏟVⱳKᏠᏟ~
tsa tse tsi tso tsu tsv

Ᏻᴔ⊙ꝏᏒ
wa we wi wo wu wv

ⱳℬℨⱨᏩℬ
ya ye yi yo yu yv

The entire
language
could be
spoken,
without
closing
the lips
except
for the
sound of "M"

A Zulu Script

Here's a complex problem. This story is written in a Zulu pictographic language described in *Indaba My Children* by Vusamazulu Credo Mutwa (London: Kahn & Averill, 1966), which is an account of Zulu history, legends, customs, and religious beliefs. When you struggle through the story, be patient with the order in which ideas and actions unfold. Pictographic language is not as linear as spoken language and therefore the images of a pictographically presented story often do not parallel the words that would be used to tell it. Furthermore, images are used differently in different languages and Zulu-Bantu constructions are not at all like English. It's a good idea to go through the whole story once quickly and then begin again trying to get a sense of its particular meaning.

we   soul   desire   peace   murderer   chief   your   outside   tribe   our

beast   mountain   skulking   we   oath taken   kill   you   all

emerge   fight   (many) men   rotten   (many) cowards   speak   we

Pictographic Systems of Writing

Here is another story in a slightly different Zulu system of writing:

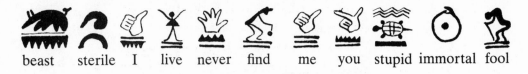

beast   sterile   I   live   never   find   me   you   stupid immortal fool

Here's one interpretation of the stories. For the first:

> We desire peace but you have murdered our chief. You are sulking in the wild mountains and we have taken an oath to kill all of you. We will come with many men. Don't run away like rotten cowards. We have spoken.

The second, shorter story could be interpreted:

> You sterile beast, I am alive and you will never find me, you stupid fool, even if you were immortal and searched forever.

Of course, there are other readings of these stories, and short of knowing what the Zulus intended, no authoritative interpretation.

Symbols and Proverbs

Sometimes pictorial symbols represent more than single objects or concepts. They can stand for proverbs, songs, or stories. These symbols have to be understood and interpreted by the viewer and require a knowledge of the culture and the particular context in which they were created. The range of these symbols is very wide, as the following examples illustrate.

Adinkra Fabric Symbols*

The Ashanti who live in Ghana have fabric symbols that represent proverbs. These proverbs embody central values of Ashanti culture. Each symbol is made into a stamp and fabric is then stamped with different combinations of the symbols. Each bit of Adinkra fabric tells a story and indicates the status and values of the wearers of the cloth. Here are some of the symbols and a sample of Adinkra cloth:

 "Nkyin kyin (ɔhema nkyin-kyin)." Changing one's self; playing many roles.

 Epa (handcuffs). "Onii a n'epa da wo nsa no, ne akowa ne wo." You are the slave of him whose handcuffs you wear.

Aya (the fern). This word also means "I am not afraid of you." A symbol of defiance.

 Dwanimen (ram's horn). "Dwonnin ye asise a ode n'akorana na ennye ne mben." It is the heart and not the horns that leads a ram to bully. (concealment).

 Owuo Atwedie Baako Nfo (obiara bewu). All men shall climb the ladder of death.

 Bi-nka-bi. Obi nka obi (bite not one another). Avoid conflicts. Symbol of unity.

 Akoma (the heart). "Nya akoma" (take heart). Have patience. Symbol of patience and endurance.

 Kramɔ-bɔne amma yanhu kramɔ-pa. We cannot tell a good Mohammedan from a bad one. The fake and the genuine look alike because of hypocrisy.

 "Anibere a enso gya, nka mani abere kɔɔ." Seriousness does not show fiery eyes else you will see my face all red.

 Ese ne tekerɛma (the teeth and tongue). "Wonnwo ba ne se." No child is born with its teeth. We improve and advance.

 Ohene niwa (in the king's eye). The king has lots of eyes and nothing is hidden from him.

 "Akokɔ nan tiaba na enkum ba." The hen treads upon its chicken but it does not kill him.

ADINKRA CLOTH

A Cheyenne Letter*

Picture writing can get very sophisticated and one picture can contain a complicated message. Here, for example, is a very old letter taken from Garrick Mallery's *Picture-Writing of the American Indians* (Washington, D.C., 1893), the Tenth Annual Report of the Bureau of Ethnography, and reprinted in I. J. Gelb's *A Study of Writing* (Chicago: Phoenix Books, 1963). The letter was

sent by mail from a Southern Cheyenne, named Turtle-Following-His-Wife, at the Cheyenne and Arapaho Agency, Indian Territory, to his son, Little-Man, at the Pine Ridge Agency, Dakota. It was drawn on a half-sheet of ordinary writing paper, without a word written, and was enclosed in an envelope, which was addressed to "Little-Man, Cheyenne, Pine Ridge Agency," in the ordinary manner, written by someone at the first-named agency. The letter was evidently understood by Little-Man as he immediately called upon Dr. V. T. McGillycuddy, Indian agent at Pine Ridge Agency, and was aware that the sum of $53 had been placed to his credit for the purpose of enabling him to pay his expenses in going the long journey to his father's home in Indian Territory. Dr. McGilly-cuddy had, by the same mail, received a letter from Agent Dyer, enclosing $53, and explaining the reason for its being sent, which enabled him also to understand the pictographic letter. With the above explana-tion it very clearly shows, over the head of the figure to the left, the turtle following the turtle's wife united with the head of a figure by a line, and over the head of the other figure, also united by a line to it, is a little man. Also over the right arm of the last-mentioned figure is another little man in the act of springing or advancing toward Turtle-Following-His-Wife, from whose mouth proceed two lines, curved or hooked at the end, as if drawing the little figure towards him. It is suggested that the last-mentioned part of the pictograph is the substance of the communication, i.e. "come to me," the larger figures with their name totems being the persons addressed and addressing. Between and above the two large figures are fifty-three round objects intended for dollars. Both the Indian

figures have on breechcloths, corresponding with the information given concerning them, which is that they are Cheyennes.

The letter has a number of interesting elements. It contains

1. A visual representation of names
2. Number symbols
3. A notation indicating movement, or sending a thing from one place to another
4. Cultural identification of the people
5. An indication of who initiated an action and who was on the receiving end, as well as indicators of communication

There are other aspects of the letter, but just using these five a whole system of communication can develop. For example, one could begin by creating:

1. Visual representations of names or pictures that represented something about them, for example,

Jacob	Susan	Erica
a coat of many colors	a one-eyed Susan	a goat (she's a Capricorn)

2. Number symbols. These can be simple alternatives to our numerals (e.g., 1 = x, 2 = Φ, 3 = ө, etc.) or numerals in systems could use these symbols to represent all the numbers (◯ = ☹ and 1 = ☺, so that 5, or 101 in binary = ☹ ☺ ☺).

3. Ways to represent exchange and movement. Here arrows, dotted lines, or double lines can take on interesting meanings; for example,

    going   will go   went

4. Symbols representing cultural indentification. Here one could create and study flags, emblems, coats-of-arms, state and national seal, clothes and fashion.

5. Indications of initiating acts and of communicating. For example, 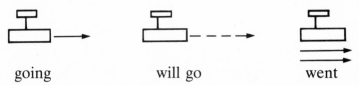 can mean speaking and (((ℰ listening. ᴑ ᷦ→ can

indicate starting a fight and ⌐ can mean ending a fight. Try to make up symbols for actions like these:

whispering
proposing to someone
telling someone you don't like them
asking someone to do you a favor
saying yes, saying no, saying maybe
saying let's stop
        let's start
        let's wait
        let's talk it over

Chinese Character Writing

The oldest and most sophisticated pictorial language developed in China. The system of Chinese character writing is often called ideographic because the pictures express ideas and images as well as represent things. There is nothing that can be expressed in any other writing system that cannot also be represented ideographically. However, ideographs have a strength that our phonic system does not have. Ideographs do not represent sounds. They are not related to a spoken language, and many Chinese who can read the character writing don't understand a word of each other's spoken language. Theoretically one wouldn't need to know a word of spoken Chinese to understand character writing. The price character writing has to pay for this universality is in the number of characters the script encompasses. In the People's Republic of China junior high school students are expected to know at least 1500 characters and sophisticated readers master over 10,000 characters. As awesome as that seems, that is possible because the characters are related to each other and in effect one is mastering a system of related parts and not merely thousands of discrete units.

This section can only provide a superficial introduction to Chinese character writing. However, the following books provide more serious introductions: *How to Understand Chinese Characters,* by Gam Go (San Francisco: Simplex Publications, 1972); *Chinese Writing: An Introduction,* by Diane Wolff (New York: Holt, Rinehart and Winston, 1975); and *You Can Write Chinese,* by Kurt Wiese (New York: Viking Seafarer Books, 1973).

In Chinese character writing the simplest characters are abstract representations of objects, like those in the following list:

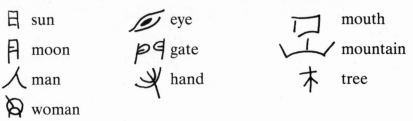

日 sun	⟨eye⟩ eye	口 mouth
月 moon	門 gate	山 mountain
人 man	手 hand	木 tree
女 woman		

Abstract words can in some instances be represented by individual characters:

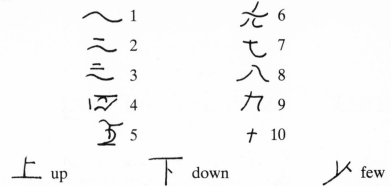

一 1	六 6
二 2	七 7
三 3	八 8
四 4	九 9
五 5	十 10

上 up   下 down   少 few

Meaning can also be conveyed by combining characters, either through joining them into one, more complex character, or by writing them side by side. Thus "man" 人 with his hands outstretched 大 means "big"; when "man with outstretched hands" looks up 天 we get the character for "heaven" or "day." "Two men" 人人 on the "ground" 土 are joined together to make up the character for "sit": 坐

Here are some other combinations:

Three 10s (十 十 十) joined together means "generation," + "ground" 土 makes "world" 世

10 (十) months (口) means ten generations or "ancient" 古

"sun" 日 and "moon" 月 written together mean "bright" 明

"woman" 女 and "child" 子 together mean "love" 好

There are also characters for actions, verbs:

生 to live

用 to use

打 to beat (the characters for "hand" and "nail" written side by side)

Simple sentences are formed as in English by using noun or pronoun characters and then verbs. They can be written from top to bottom or right to left. Thus "The man beats the child" could be written:

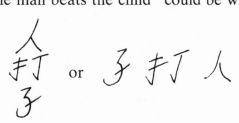

For additional signs I suggest you consult the books mentioned above or one of the guidebooks to the People's Republic of China that have been published since diplomatic relations were established between the United States and the People's Republic. I find that even a superficial exposure to Chinese characters is valuable, for it illustrates that sophisticated abstract writing does not have to be tied to speech.

Picture Sequences and Diagram Stories

Picture sequences tell a story through a series of pictures representing actions. In a way they are the forerunners of comic strips and comic books. The form is very old and no one is sure where it originated or whether it was developed independently in many different places. For example, I. J. Gelb, in his book *A Study of Writing,* gives examples of picture sequences used by Native Alaskans. He explains that Eskimoes use

> drawings to inform their visitors or friends of their departure for a designated purpose. The drawings are depicted upon strips of wood pointing in the direction taken by the departed men and placed in conspicuous places near the doors of their habitations.

> The following is an explanation of the characters in the drawing: a, the speaker, with the right hand indicating himself and with the left pointing in the direction taken; b, holding a boat paddle, going by boat; c, the speaker holding the right hand to the side of the head, to denote sleep, and the left elevated with one finger erect to signify one night; d, a circle with two marks in the middle, signifying an island with huts upon it; e, same as a; f, a circle to denote another island where they touched; g, same as c, with an additional finger elevated, signifying two nights; h, the

speaker, with his harpoon; . . . i, represents a sea-lion which the hunter, j, secured by shooting with bow and arrow; k, the boat with two persons in it, the paddles projecting downward; l, the winter habitation of the speaker.

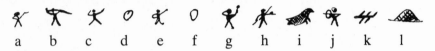

a   b   c   d   e   f   g   h   i   j   k   l

In this second example hunters, who had been unfortunate in their hunt and were suffering from hunger, drew some characters on a piece of wood and placed the lower end of the stick in the ground on the trail where there was the greatest chance of its being discovered by other natives. The stick was inclined toward their shelter. The following are the details of the information contained in the drawing: a, canoe, showing double projections at bow, as well as the two men, owners, in the boat; b, a man with both arms extended signifying nothing, corresponding to the gesture for negation; c, a person with the right hand to the mouth signifying the act of eating, the left hand pointing to the house occupied by the hunters; d, the shelter. The whole thing means that the two men have nothing to eat in the house.

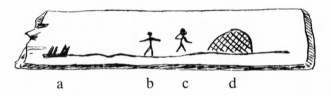

a   b   c   d

These Alaskan signs of departure were taken from Mallery's *Picture-Writing,* p. 353.

Here's an example of a sequence story developed by a six-year-old after seeing these examples:

Sometimes (notice all the hands on the clock)   we go fishing   and catch crabs   and sometimes we catch nothing (the hook is falling off the rod)

Diagram stories are like picture sequences but they use words also. To start a diagram story, draw a circle or oval on a blank sheet of paper, put the name of a place in the oval, and draw an arrow indicating where the next location of the story will be. Then start telling:

Keep adding balloons and arrows as the story develops and try to end up back at the same location you started from. The story can be told or written down. The diagram can also be used to tell any number of stories:

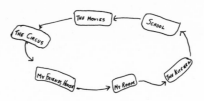

Comic Books*

It's natural to move from picture sequences and diagram stories to comic books, although you don't have to introduce comics to most young people. They are often more knowledgeable than adults about the intricacies and subtleties of comic book design and content.

Comics are not simple structurally. Basically they consist of rectangles that contain characters with bubbles coming from their mouths. But this description is deceptively simple. There are many types of bubbles: the forms of comic book art are quite sophisticated and they make it possible for thoughts, dreams, narrative, and dialogue to be expressed in a single frame. There are smooth bubbles that end in arrows. These represent talk, the arrow pointing to the talker. There are also compound bubbles (called more talk) which make it possible for a single character to say several different things in one frame.

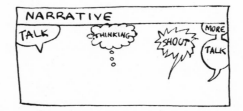

For example, if someone is shot, it is possible by connecting three smooth bubbles to have one character say "There's trouble," "Watch out, you," and "Are you hurt?" all in one box on a page. The joined bubbles represent past, present, and future, whereas the picture has to show one moment. In this case the picture can show a menacing figure, a shot fired, or a body. Although the picture has one temporal dimension the bubbles expand the scene to cover several minutes.

There are dream and thought bubbles too. These are more undulating. There are lots of curves in the bubble, and instead of an arrow going to the speaker, a series of bubbles goes to the speaker indicating that the words are thought but not spoken.

Interesting combinations are possible. It is possible to represent thoughts and words at the same time. For example, if a person hates another but has to seem nice, the dialogue can be represented by this combination of bubbles:

There are three more common comic book forms. One is the spiked bubble that indicates a shout or a denial or a protest. It is like an exclamation point, and usually spiked bubbles are used sparsely to indicate pain, struggle, or serious intent. The other form is the long rectangular shape that appears in almost every frame in comics. It is written by the narrator of the story and carries the movement along from one point to another. There are many different kinds of narrative voices that appear in comic books. Sometimes one of the characters in the story is telling about what happens and the voice is "I." There are other comic books in which the illustrator talks directly to the reader, makes jokes, and comments on the story (as in *Spider Man*). In some comics the narrator is omniscient like the narrator of many novels. He or she can see or know what's happening in many different places and at many different times and has more knowledge of every situation than any of the characters. It's fun to read a batch of comics solely to figure out how they use the narrative voice.

The third form is what could be called the "zap" word. Zap words are words that indicate sounds or actions, and are drawn to look like what they represent. They aren't spoken by the characters and are part of the atmosphere of the world of comics. Here are a few common zaps:

Putting these forms together, you can easily represent a complex action in a single panel:

Below is a comic strip without characters. Try to give it content—and to develop comics of your own using all the forms described here.

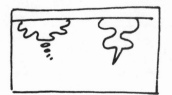

In addition to the comic book forms there are some themes that are common. One of the most popular ones has to do with the origins of superheroes. Concern with origins isn't confined to comic book characters, of course. "Where did I come from and how did I get to be the way I am?" are questions we all ask sometime in our lives. These questions seem to be as old as language. Every mythology begins with accounts of origins—how the earth came to be, why there is order instead of chaos, how people were created, why people walk upright, how language was made, how food and shelter originated. Here, for example, is an Eskimo origin tale:

> There was once a girl who lived in the open desert of white snow. One day she went in a boat with a man who suddenly threw her into the sea. When she tried to hold on to the side of the boat he cut her fingers off so that the boat would not turn over. She sank to the bottom of the sea where she made her home inside a large bubble. Here she became the mother of all life in the sea. The fingers she had lost grew into seals and walruses. And the people of this frozen land now had food to eat. Now they had skins for warmth. Now they had oil for the long nights of winter.

This tale is not as arbitrary as it might seem. The mother of all life in the sea is a person who has been harmed. She lost her fingers, yet they became food for people. What we are and what we eat are not that dissimilar. There is a unity to life that must be respected. The destructive can become creative but we must respect this relationship because those that suffer death nurture us. This simple story embodies a way of looking at people and their relationship to nature.

Comic book superheroes are mythical figures created in our time. The stories of their origins reveal aspects of our culture just as the Eskimo myth displayed some values of that culture. Take Superman, for example. He is an alien, born on the planet Krypton, which was destroyed in an atomic holocaust. He was saved by his parents, sent to earth where he is stronger and purer than the rest of us. The alien Superman becomes our hero and savior. He is not one of us and only presents a human appearance through Clark Kent, his earthly identity. In order to exist on an everyday level he has to disguise himself as one of us.

Wonder Woman is similar. She was born on Paradise Island where no men lived. Her mother was Queen Hippolyte and her original name was Princess Diana. During the Second World War an American pilot, Steve Trevor, crashed on Paradise Island and Princess Diana fell in love with him. Eventually, she had to choose between love of him and loyalty to the Amazons on Paradise Island. One of the early Wonder Woman comics discussed her choice:

> And so Princess Diana, the Wonder Woman, giving up her heritage, and her right to eternal life, leaves Paradise Island to take the man she loves back to America—the land she learns to love and protect, and adopts as her own!

Again, an alien comes to rescue us. This time her motive is love. For Superman the motive was to prevent the earth from destroying itself the way Krypton did.

The Hulk is a more recent superhero, and the story of his origin reverses that of Superman and Wonder Woman. He was born a human, Bruce Banner, who became a famous nuclear physicist. In experimenting with physical forces beyond his control, Dr. Banner found himself transformed into the Hulk—a superhuman although subintelligent force. Bruce Banner and the Hulk are a contemporary version of Dr. Jeckyll and Mr. Hyde. It is never clear however whether the Hulk is a positive or a negative force. When science gets the upper hand is it a positive or negative force? That is the problem posed by the Hulk.

The Hulk reminds me of the Golem, a figure in Yiddish mythology. The Golem is compressed out of the letters of the Hebrew alphabet and is a giant force similar to the Hulk. The Golem has an aleph (the first letter of the Hebrew alphabet) imprinted on its head. When the Golem is called forth (by a rabbi or mystic who can unleash the power of the alphabet) it can be used to destroy evil. However, once it gets its job done it keeps on destroying what is around it until someone erases the aleph from its head. As a force the Golem can be used for good purposes, but it is itself neither good nor evil. Like most force its effectiveness depends on how it is controlled.

Mythology is open-ended. We can all create our own villains and superheroes. One way to involve young people in writing and in making comic books is to ask them to create their own superheroes. Usually first efforts will imitate what is already in the comics or on TV. That is where origins can help people develop and clarify their own creations. After making up a superhero, it makes sense to create adventures.

However, writing, creating comic books, or making up fables and proverbs shouldn't be looked on as solely the province of artists or young people. As adults we can all stand to play a bit with language, to step out of our usual modes of functioning, and let ourselves draw and write for the pleasure these activities can provide for us and our friends.

Sources for Additional Word Puzzlements

Some Ongoing Sources of Word Games and Play with Words

Word Ways: The Journal of Recreational Linguistics is the journal of logology, the study of words. It is for people interested in word puzzles and other aspects of recreations with words. The writing in this journal is delightful, although some articles are quite detailed and somewhat technical. Anyone serious about language games should find this enjoyable. Subscriptions: $8.00 per year. Available from: Faith W. Eckler, Spring Valley Road, Morristown, NJ 07960.

Games is a new American magazine that tries to cover as much ground as *Games and Puzzles,* an English puzzle magazine that has unfortunately just ceased publication, but is written for a much more popular audience. The casual game player is more likely to be interested in this. For information, write: Allen Bragdon Publishers, 220 East 73rd Street, New York, NY 10021.

Games with Words

An Almanac of Words at Play, by Willard R. Espy (New York: Clarkson N. Potter, 1975). This book is organized as a calendar with word games for every day of the year. The games are a bit archaically presented, but they include palindromes, acrostics, higgledy-piggledies, anagrams, etc. A good volume to have and peruse when you're looking for new ideas.

The Magic of Lewis Carroll, edited by John Fisher (New York: Simon and Schuster, 1973). This is a collection of the essays and games invented by Lewis Carroll and is a must for the gamester as much to see how Carroll's mind worked as to find games to use.

Codes, Ciphers and Secret Writing, by Martin Gardner (New York: Archway Paperbacks, 1974). This small book is the clearest presentation of codes that I've seen. It is full of simple and complex codes with delightful historical notes and anecdotes thrown in. At 75¢, it is a special bargain and would make a good textbook for third grade on, as well as a valuable resource for teachers.

The Codebreakers, by David Kahn (New York: Macmillan, 1967). This book lives up to its jacket blurb which says that it is "the first comprehensive history of secret communications from ancient times to the threshold of outer space." I've often thought that a whole year's curriculum could be built out of the material in this book.

The Lore and Language of Schoolchildren (London: Oxford Paperbacks, 1967) and *Children's Games in Street and Playground* (London: Oxford, 1969), by Iona and Peter Opie, are classics. These books are full of riddles, games, songs, chants, insults, teases, jokes. There are hundreds of variants, and thousands of examples of the language of English children, which turn out not to be that different from our children or other children of the world. The Opies' analysis is as interesting as their examples are exhilarating—a must.

One Potato, Two Potato: The Secret Education of American Children, by Mary and Herbert Knapp (New York: W. W. Norton & Co., 1976). This delightful and rich book is in some ways the American equivalent of the Opies' work. It deals with the rich language and law of children in the United States, and is full of examples. However, it also speculates on the importance of such material in children's lives and is concerned with issues like sex stereotypes, power, prestige, racial roles. It is also full of games that aren't verbal. A rich source book for teachers and a delight for anyone who can still remember what childhood was like.

Games and Songs of American Children, collected and compared by William Wells Newell (New York: Dover Books #T354). This is a reprint of a nineteenth-century collection of early American children's games and songs. The language of most of these is fascinating, showing obvious roots in Scottish and Irish and early English.

Jump-Rope Rhymes: A Dictionary, edited by Roger D. Abrahams (Austin: University of Texas Press, 1969). This book is just what the title implies, a collection of over 600 jump-rope rhymes. There is enough material here to make a dozen basal readers, and to make children attend to their own rhymes to go along with games.

Step It Down, by Bessie Jones and Bess Lomax Hawes (New York: Harper and Row, 1972), is full of games, plays, songs, and stories from the Afro-American heritage. This is one of the richest and most useful books I know. The stories, tales, dances, and games here can't be found anywhere else, and Bessie Jones's descriptions of how they can be played (and were played over the generations) make marvelous reading for children as well as for adults.

Africa Counts, by Claudia Zaslavsky (Boston: Prindle, Weber, and Schmidt, 1973), is an account of the mathematical contributions of many African peoples in the context of their social and economic development. The book has sections on children's games, chants, and rhymes, and is useful to broaden one's perception of the range of children's lore.

Games at the Cedilla, or The Cedilla Takes Off, by George Brecht and Robert Filliou (New York: Something Else Press, 1967), is packed with madcap games and collages which are part of what the authors call "aesthetic research." The book is full of short events that involve random, or at least unexpected, juxtapositions. I use the material and have been able to adjust it to create games and improvisation that interest students from kindergarten through senior high school.

Thank You for the Giant Sea Tortoise, edited by Mary Ann Madden (New York: Lancer Books, 1971), contains dozens of examples of the *New York* magazine competitions, some of which were mentioned in chapter 4. These competitions were done by adults but they are just as delightful for young people.

Comic Alphabets, by Eric Partridge (New York: Hobbs Dorman, 1961), is the best if not the only book on the history and development of comic alphabets. Partridge writes the book in an antic style appropriate to his theme, and presents dozens of delightful and zany alphabets.

100 19th Century Rhyming Alphabets, in English, from the library of Ruth M. Baldwin (Carbondale: Southern Illinois University Press, 1972), is worth looking at. The alphabets in the book are very diverse, and are full of ideas that can be used for making alphabet books with children.

The books mentioned above by Iona and Peter Opie and Mary and Herbert Knapp are also useful sources of children's games, riddles, jokes, and word tricks that involve silliness and nonsense.

Symbol Systems

A Study of Writing, by I. J. Gelb (Chicago: Phoenix Books, 1963), is a systematic presentation of the history and evolution of writing. This book is well written and provides the basic background a teacher should have in order to teach about writing systems. Although it is possible to use the material presented in this catalog without such a background, it would be better to have the historical and cultural perspective presented here.

Sign, Symbol, and Script, by Hans Jensen (New York: G. P. Putnam, 1969), is a more elaborate presentation of the development of writing than Gelb's book. I find it useful for the wealth of visual material it contains, and although it is more expensive than Gelb's book, there is more to be found here that can be worked into the curriculum.

There are a number of books about the writing systems of specific peoples. Here are some of the best of them:

Indian Picture Writing, written and illustrated by Robert Hofsinde (Gray-Wolf) (New York: Wm. Morrow, Morrow Junior Books, 1959).

Shaking the Pumpkin: The Traditional Poetry of the Indian North Americas, edited with commentaries by Jerome Rothenberg (New York: Anchor Books, 1972).

Egyptian Language: Easy Lessons in Egyptian Hieroglyphics, by E. A. Wallis Budge (London: Routledge & Kegan Paul, 1963).

You Can Write Chinese, by Kurt Wiese (New York: Viking Seafarer Books, 1973).

Chinese Writing, by Diane Wolff, with calligraphy by Jeanette Chien (New York: Holt, Rinehart and Winston, 1975).

There are a number of sources for the history and nature of comic-book art. Here are three to begin with:

The Comics: An Illustrated History of Comic Strip Art, by Jerry Robinson (New York: Berkeley Winhover Books, 1974).

Secret Origins of the Superheroes, introduction by Carmine Infantino, text edited by Dennis O'Neil (New York: Warner Books, 1976).

Origins of Marvel Comics, by Stan Lee (New York: Simon and Schuster, 1974).

Teaching Suggestions

The suggestions in this appendix are directly related to specific sections of the book. However, there are some general ways in which the book can be used. The structure of the book parallels the structure of many reading programs. It begins with play with alphabets and sound combinations, goes through parts of speech, phrases, and sentences, to complex meaning and symbol systems.

Puzzlements in these sections can be used to introduce students to new concepts in reading or writing. They can also provide practice in skills that students already have. If a particular game or puzzle isn't referred to in these teaching suggestions, it isn't because it can't be used in the classroom. Rather, it's that its use seems obvious and I thought it best to leave the particulars of applying it to individual teachers. Several other general teaching suggestions are:

1. Even though the material in the book moves roughly from phonics to meaning, almost all the material in the book can be used at any grade level. Comic alphabets can be as interesting to high school students as to first-graders. The same is true of crossword puzzles, codes, etc. It is simply a question of adjusting the level of sophistication and the content to your students.

2. Because of the structure of the book, the games and exercises can easily be tied to behavioral objectives if that happens to be a requirement or quirk of your teaching situation.

3. It might be interesting to engage in solving a problem or writing fables or proverbs or riddles with your students. It will make it easier to sustain a tone of nonjudgmental play since your results are not likely to be much better than those of your pupils in many of these exercises.

4. Encourage your students to make up as many puzzlements as possible, to change the rules of games and see what happens, to feel free to make mistakes and explore language. The material in the book is meant to be used playfully and not turned into a series of testing situations.

Warm-Up Games

Warm-up exercises are a good way to begin class in the morning or to introduce language arts. Throughout the book there are simple exercises (many simpler than in this section) that can take up five or ten minutes of class time to reinforce particular skills and provide occasion for students to practice what they've just learned. For the most part, interesting games and puzzles do not explicitly teach skills, although skills can be learned through play. However, they do provide an opportunity for students to *utilize* and *solidify* skills that they have acquired. These games also provide *occasions* to teach skills prior to playing a game that requires them, since students are often more patient about learning what they need to know in order to play than in learning from workbooks or lectures.

Warm-up exercises can be used with the whole class or with groups. They can be posted on the board or somewhere in the room for students to do at the beginning of class or during some short time during the day. These short problems can also be done in groups or as an alternative to more traditional homework.

Some Comic Alphabets

Comic alphabets provide a good example of a form of writing that can be adopted for students in all grades. Kindergarteners and first-graders can make up rhymes, dictate their alphabets, and use them as reading texts. Story and phonetic alphabets will challenge high school students. It is a matter of adopting the form to one's students. When I was teaching a combined kindergarten/first-grade class I introduced the alphabet through comic alphabets. Each day we took a different letter and made up a series of couplets or rhymed sentences for that letter. The students then illustrated the rhymes, and the illustrations, the rhymes, and the letter (written about eight inches high in lower- and uppercase) were posted. Some of these couplets were:

> E is for that skinny elf
> who only thinks about his self.
>
> E is for everyone
> in this class—we have lots of fun.
>
> M is for mustard
> and not for custard.
>
> M is for the mouse
> that lives under my house.

Many of the students read the rhymes to each other during free time or just in passing. The alphabet and most of the simple sounds represented by the letters were learned informally by all but a few students, to whom I then gave some other letter games.

With junior high and high school students, alphabets dealing with mystery, romance, horror, and adventure work well. For example, here are a few beginnings that can get a class composing a comic alphabet:

> A is for Allan
> B is for Beth
> C is for cool, which they were

D is for dead, which they became
E is for (etc.)

A is for auto
B is for boat
C is for Carl
D is for the deal he made to get them both
E is for (etc.)

In addition to the alphabets mentioned in this section, here are a few other alphabets students might develop and illustrate:

monster alphabets
animal alphabets (or, as they're called, alphabestiaries)
superhero alphabets
car alphabets (A is for Alpha Romeo)
sports and sports hero alphabets
musical alphabets (using names of groups, songs, singers, etc.)

Combinations

A version which I've used in first, second, and third grade is to ask children to write out their names on three-by-five index cards, with one letter on each card. Then they are to try to move the cards around to make up new words with any number of those letters. Each time they get a word, they copy it on a separate sheet of paper.

After a bit of practice there are several variations that can be introduced:

1. Pick a friend and put the letters of both your names together. How many words can you come up with?
2. Now ask your students to put the letters in their names together. See if sentences can be made from those letters.
3. Here's a more complex one. You can add one more letter—any letter—to the letters in your name. Then how many more words can you make up? Why did you choose the letter you did? Can you choose a letter which will yield no extra words?

The question about choosing a letter that will yield no additional words brings up an important issue: Which words are to be accepted as legitimate in the game? Are abbreviations and names to be allowed? Slang? These questions have no set answer. It's possible to pick a dictionary and use that as the source of legitimacy, or to take a vote about marginal words. The more discussion about rules and language, the better. Rather than set up all the conditions for a game, I prefer to let the players make many choices about the rules they care to play under, and have them feel free to change rules if they make the game boring or confusing.

Palindromes and Semordnilaps

In a number of stories the main character's name is a semordnilap, the reverse of which describes some characteristics of the character. For example, Tobor (the mechanical marvel on the old "Captain Video" TV show) would be a robot's name, Regna the name of a mean and angry person, and Nuf a clown's name. This technique occasionally comes in handy when students are writing and having a hard time creating or naming a character.

Palindromes and semordnilaps are anomalies, forms that are interesting to know about and play with a bit. They might even be used to point out to some students the nature of reading reversals.

Reversals are all semordnilaps. Such words as *saw-was, not-ton,* and *on-no* could be called semordnilap pairs in the spirit of Lewis Carroll. Sometimes pointing out that fact in a playful way helps children who make frequent reversals understand what they're doing and get control over it. I've seen it happen with a number of my students, and with my son Joshua as well.

Simple Word and Letter Grids

FILLING IN SIMPLE GRIDS

I've found that after students get the knack of filling in these simple grids they can easily make up their own grid puzzles. A group of fourth-graders I'm working with made up a small booklet of simple three-letter grids which they called:

C A N   Y O U   W I N   ?

Each page of the booklet had three-letter word grids and simple definitions of the words. The students printed up the booklet using Ditto masters and stapled it together. They used red paper for the cover "to make it look more professional," as one of the students said.

Some of their definitions were:

Don't eat like a ☐☐☐

Put it on your head ☐☐☐

Don't ☐☐☐ me

Water comes out of my ☐☐☐

(Notice that most of the grids have more than one solution. For example, PIG and HOG will both do for the first, BUG and DOG will make sense for the third, and JUG, POT, and TAP all work for the last.)

The students took copies of the booklet to second- and third-grade classes and explained the puzzles to the students. They then sold them for five cents each. After selling out, one of the students suggested that they make up some more complex puzzle booklets and try to sell them to the school as language workbooks. There certainly is no reason why students can't become an ongoing resource for curriculum material in the schools.

These word games and many other games with language have another basic advantage: they allow students to practice skills and be inventive at the same time. There is no single correct way to fill out a grid or create a sentence from words in a grid. There are also different ways to reach the same solution. These conditions provide the opportunity to discuss with the class how different people came to their solutions, and consequently to compare thinking strategies. For example, in the following grid

one of my students began by filling in the corners and then looking for vowels to add in order to generate words:

In this case the student discovered that a single vowel, *O*, would solve the grid. Another student began with the vowels in the middle position and then experimented with consonants in order to complete the words:

A third student began with whole words and worked her way around the grid:

We discussed these strategies, not looking for the best way to solve a problem so much as to help everyone develop a whole repertoire of problem-solving strategies.

INVENTING NEW PUZZLES

Many of the games and puzzles in this section could more accurately be described as game and puzzle forms. The grids, for example, are just forms which can be used for many different puzzles. For example, there are dozens of ways to fill in even a simple form like

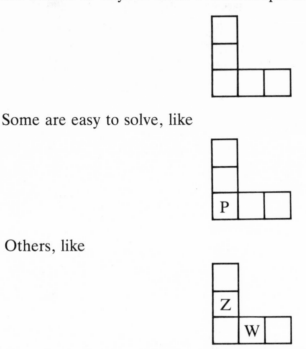

Some are easy to solve, like

Others, like

might not even be possible. Students can create and duplicate their own versions of puzzles and games after they have played a bit. They can do a number of things with these versions:

Run puzzle contests in the school.

Package the games and sell them to make money for a class project.

Teach games and set puzzles for other classes, and especially introduce simple puzzles and games to younger children.

Write, print, sell, and distribute a monthly games and puzzles magazine. The magazine can be distributed in local stores, sold door to door, or just distributed within the school.

Individual students can do booklets of their creations, and can write instructions and strategy books.

PUZZLE OF THE WEEK

Every week a particularly difficult puzzle can be posted in the class which individuals or groups of students can solve at their leisure. The solutions should be written out if possible, and at the end of each semester a small book of difficult puzzles, with solutions, can be published. If more than one solution to a problem is given, publish both and ask students to write down how they got the solution as well as the answer. The ability to develop strategies to solve problems is one of the most valuable skills taught by games and puzzles.

ANALYZING SOLUTIONS

Word combinations and constructions provide students with the opportunity to look at words thoughtfully and to think how they are put together. Because this is done in the context of play it is possible to make discoveries and acquire skills without the pressure that is felt when an exercise is graded. In games and puzzles if you don't win or figure out the right answer it is always possible to play again or try a new approach to the problem. In fact, the analysis of losing strategies and wrong solutions to a puzzle is an important educational tool. I remember a simple instance where a second-grade class was asked to see how many words they could make out of the letters of MEAT. One girl couldn't get any words other than A, AT, and EAT out of MEAT. I asked what she was doing and she explained that she was looking at MEAT for words and then underlining them. She had this on her paper:

MEAT

By drawing those lines and looking for whole words she overlooked combinations such as MAT, MET, and TEAM. I suggested that she figure out a way to avoid looking for words that were contained in order in the original word. Her solution was to scramble up the original word so she wouldn't be limited by the original order of the letters. She wrote down:

E M A T

and began to work on the problem again.

This illustrates an important aspect of word combinations and constructions. They require thought and help students develop problem-solving skills. Analyzing correct solutions is as important as analyzing incorrect ones. What is important is to give students the opportunities to experience different ways of thinking and to help them understand ways of going about solving problems.

ENJOYING THE GAME, MASTERING THE PUZZLE

Enjoyment and mastery are the main reasons for playing games and solving puzzles. Certainly some games teach specific skills.

It is possible, for example, to talk about the way E is sometimes silent in English after students have filled in the grid with different words. An analysis of the students' results could lead to a generalization about the final E. However, a good puzzle or game is interesting after the skills it helps teach are acquired. It's important not to reduce games and puzzles to vehicles for something else. Certainly they are helpful on occasion for other educational reasons. But if there is no time to play or ponder without some exterior motive, the student risks losing the ability to seek out, invent, play, and think through games and puzzles, and to enjoy using the mind and the imagination.

Transformations

Here are a number of exercises using word and letter transformations that can be used to help develop what could be called phonic flexibility—the ability to distinguish quickly and with ease words that differ only slightly.

1. Consider the vowels (A, E, I, O, U, Y). Given a list of three-letter words, perform the following transformation: $T \wedge$ (vowels, 0,0,0), i.e., substitute all the other vowels for the vowels in the given word. Which word or words transform to the most other words?

Example:		HAT	LET	CAT	FOR
Substitute	A	—	LAT	—	FAR
	E	HET	—	CET	FER
	I	HIT	LIT	CIT	FIR
	O	HOT	LOT	COT	—
	U	HUT	LUT	CUT	FUR
	Y	HYT	LYT	CYT	FYT
Number of words made:		HAT	LET	CAT	FOR
		3	2	2	3

This exercise can be made more interesting if you use a dictionary and allow any word that appears in the dictionary to count. I've found that the addition of the dictionary makes the challenge more interesting for older students, and adds to their vocabulary. Whenever a new word is discovered it can be added to the class spelling or vocabulary. For example, I came upon the following discoveries while looking up all the combinations I wasn't sure of on the above list:

FER—an obsolete form for the words "fire,"
    "far," and "fear"
LAT—an obscure form of "let"

Here are two four-letter words and their vowel substitutions:

	MUST	LEFT
A	MAST	LAFT
E	MEST	—
I	MIST	LIFT
O	MOST	LOFT
U	—	LUFT
Y	MYST	LYFT

Number of words before using dictionary:

3	2

Number of words after using dictionary:

(*mest*—early form of "mast")	(*laft*—early form of "left")
4	3

Using the dictionary in this way has raised some interesting questions. As one third-grader pointed out, the existence of all those obsolete forms implied that spelling was different in the past and possibly even that it might be different in the future. I used this occasion to bring in some old English poems as well as Renaissance and Scottish verse to let the class see how English was written hundreds of years ago. It's also possible in this context to study the history of standardized spelling and its growth out of the development of the printing industry. One good source for information on this is *The Coming of the Book,* by Lucien Febvre and Henri-Jean Martin (New York: Schocken Books, Verso Books, 1978).

2. It is also possible to make consonant and blend transformations. For example, make a list of consonants and blends, then substitute them for the first letter in a number of words and see how many new words result. The dictionary can also be used here.

Consonant/blends	MOST	BAND	PART
L	LOST	LAND	LART
W	WOST	WAND	WART
M	—	MAND	MART
R	ROST	RAND	RART
T	TOST	TAND	TART
S	SOST	SAND	SART
SM	SMOST	SMAND	SMART
SP	SPOST	SPAND	SPART
PR	PROST	PRAND	PRART
ST	STOST	STAND	START
FL	FLOST	FLAND	FLART

Note that this kind of exercise gives students practice reading combinations that are not words as well as words. In that way it strengthens phonic fluency and helps students learn to sound out combinations of letters they've never seen before.

4. Take a series of three-letter words and *add* a consonant to the beginning (or end) of the word. Again, how many new words does it create? Then subtract the first letter from words and see how many words result. These exercises are variants of other games and puzzles in this section. They can be used, however, as practice without in any way having to bring up the subject of word transformations or introducing the abstract notation. Like most material in this book they can be separated from the context in which they are presented here and articulated into just about any classroom program.

DRILL

Many of the games and puzzles in this section involve phonic skills. They can easily be worked into reading programs at different grade levels and, I believe, can provide an adequate substitute for drill. However, there is reluctance on the part of many school people to consider replacing drill with word play, perhaps because play and learning are considered opposites. Certainly not all learning is play and not all play is learning. Still, there are many forms of play in which skills are practiced and solidified, which is the intent of drill. There are also bonuses if one plays with words. Through letter and word play students not only learn how letters go together to form words, but also learn about the flexibility of our written code, about sound variation and shifts of meaning, and about techniques for problem solving. If as a teacher you are required to produce behavioral objectives in order to justify your work, take those written in any text for phonic drill and use them to justify word games. I've found that just about any drill exercises can be replaced by games without any modification of the so-called objectives—and with considerable enlivening of the classroom.

Some Simple Constructions

The simple game described here can be used to introduce nouns, verbs, adjectives, and adverbs as concepts that will help students play the game. After they have practiced the game for a while, the concepts can be generalized to apply to language in general. There are times, as in this case, where playing the game first, and then dealing with the significance of the concepts used in the games afterward, is a useful teaching strategy.

In the rest of this chapter there are other games and language exercises that can be used to introduce the parts of speech. There's no single best way to introduce the ideas, and from my perspective it makes sense to try a variety of approaches, especially since playing with the same concepts in different ways gives students the opportunity to internalize the concepts and apply them with ease.

Creating New Words

It's a good idea to introduce the creation of new words and definitions through examining recent additions to the dictionary. Most dictionaries have up-to-date supplements giving their new listings. These provide an insight into things happening in the world and make interesting reading as social documentaries. Sharing these new words and definitions with your students will provide them with ideas that can be incorporated into their definitions as well as with areas of experience like science, human relations, politics, etc., to develop new words for. As students create definitions and words emerge, it is worth discussing them with the class, making up imaginary stories about how the words were coined, and giving sentences that use them. Exercises like these provide occasion for interesting noncompetitive class discussions where students have opportunities to test out their own ideas and ingenuity without worrying about being graded.

Crossword Puzzles and Thematic Word Squares

If you're working with young children it probably would make sense to begin with a much simpler puzzle than the one developed in this section, and a theme children respond to easily. Some themes I've used are toys, games, pets, and feelings. Here are some lists these themes have generated:

Toys	Pets	Feelings
ball	goldfish	love
doll	frog	like
bat	dog—poodle	hate
car	shepherd	angry
Hot Wheels	golden retriever	happy
GI Joe	cat	hip
Barbie	rat	hep
checkers	hamster	tired
Sorry	mouse	energetic
glove	snake	sad
		envy
		mad

In order to make up a puzzle using these words it's sometimes necessary to add small filler words like *at, am, of, or,* etc., so the grid doesn't look too empty. Here's a simple five-by-five puzzle using the feeling words: *like, love, sad, mad,* and the fillers *to, ho, pm, is.* The word *hep* has also been added since it fits nicely into the grid and relates to feelings.

```
    ┌───┬───┬───┬───┬───┐
    │███│ T │███│ H │ O │
    ├───┼───┼───┼───┼───┤
    │ L │ O │ V │ E │███│
    ├───┼───┼───┼───┼───┤
    │ I │███│ P │ M │   │
    ├───┼───┼───┼───┼───┤
    │ K │███│ I │███│ A │
    ├───┼───┼───┼───┼───┤
    │ E │███│ S │ A │ D │
    └───┴───┴───┴───┴───┘
```

The filler words can be defined to work into the theme in many cases. For example, in this puzzle here are some definitions that involve feelings:

> *pm*: I feel tired after 11 __?__.
> *ho*: laughter
> *is*: She ____ sad.

How Do I Love You?

Most phrases begin with words like "to," "from," "of," "with," "through," "at." It might help students if a few sample phrases were put on the board and played with. For example, beginning with:

to the moon   with all my heart
at last   from here to Chicago

students can develop variations that get increasingly complex:

to the moon
to the dark side of the moon
to the lunar crater
to the moon's surface
to the faces of the moon
to the left eyeball of the man in the moon.

Here's another variant: Who could say?

I love you with all my heart
          with all my stomach
          with all my hair
          with all my fingers
          with my big toe
                etc.

Sentence Grids and Magic Sentence Grids

Making up magic sentence grids provides exercises in sentence structure and in shifts of meaning. It can be done in groups as well as by individuals, and grids as large as eight-by-eight can be attempted. You can even put up a big eight-by-eight grid on the wall and put a nail at the top of each square. Then, using perforated index cards with single words written on them, you can experiment with making magic sentence squares of any dimension up to eight-by-eight.

Good News/ Bad News

There are many different ways to fit in an exercise like Good News/Bad News. It can be used as an individual writing exercise or as a group lesson with all the students in the class taking turns making up an item. The exercise can also be varied so that after trying Good News/Bad News variants like the following can be attempted:

1. Bad News/Good News: This has an opposite tone to it and poses different problems. Here are some examples:

Bad News: I just got pushed off the roof.
Good News: I landed in a haystack.

Bad News: I lost my mail yesterday.
Good News: My worst enemy sent me a time bomb which was in yesterday's mail.

Bad News: We couldn't sell the first copy of your book.
Good News: We sold all the other 999,999.

2. It's Hopeless/So What

It's hopeless, I can't fly.
So what, I'll take an airplane.
It's hopeless, the record player won't work.
So what, I can sing.

Preliminary Distortion

There are many school texts (especially basal readers) that are boring. And yet for many teachers these are the only books available. Instead of throwing these books out, I found that they can be used as a basis for developing parodies and systematically distorting or changing their meaning. Even *Dick and Jane* can be a starting point for the development of interesting parodies. Here's a version of a Level 1 *Dick and Jane* reader done by my daughters Antonia and Erica:

This is Dick.
Dick's mother left home.
Dick's father left home.
Dick's mother will not come back.
Dick's father may come back.
Poor Dick.

Hands

This little essay on "hand" can be used to introduce students to figurative language. After reading the story, students can "try their hands" at making up similar mythic tales about the extensions of words like "eye," "mouth," "ears," etc. A way to begin would be to list figures of speech using the word, and then make up a story using those words. For example, here's a list of "mouth" words and phrases:

> loudmouth
> mouthing off
> foul-mouthed
> born with a silver spoon in one's mouth
> melt in one's mouth
> take the bread out of one's mouth
> shoot off one's mouth
> look a gift horse in the mouth
> put one's foot in one's mouth
> leave a bad taste in one's mouth
> live from hand to mouth

Riddles

I love to put these early riddles on the chalkboard in their old spellings and ask students to read them. They provide a glimpse of how much spelling has changed over the past 400 years and provide an occasion to discuss the need for standardized spelling. Most students (and many teachers as well) think of spellings as a universal, when actually uniform spellings for words developed along with the printing industry. The reason for uniform spelling wasn't some linguistic or intellectual rightness but the desire to distribute books as widely as possible, and therefore get people speaking many different dialects of a language to become accustomed to reading a single text. Standard spelling was part of an attempt to centralize printing rather than have regions print books in their own dialects. Language wars still exist in parts of Europe where people refuse to give up their regional identity and resist attempts to speak and read the language of the dominant group (not to mention the French-English language struggle in Canada). It's important for students to understand that uniform spelling is a consequence of economic and political decisions and not a universal unalterable given.

We have recently seen a good example of this in the change in the English spelling of Chinese words which was decreed by the government of the People's Republic of China. These changes would have made little difference in spelling in the United States had not diplomatic relations recently been established between the People's Republic and the U.S.

Here are some selections from the *San Francisco Chronicle* of March 5, 1979, which provide an excellent curriculum unit on spelling as a human creation:

New Chinese Spellings—It Isn't "Peking" Anymore
Beginning today, the *San Francisco Chronicle* is adopting a new system of

spelling for names of people and places in China.

Called "Pinyin," the system has been put into effect by the Chinese government to standardize the Romanization of Chinese names in English, French, German, Spanish and other languages.

Since January 1, China has been using Pinyin in its news dispatches abroad and in its dealings with foreigners. The new system has now been adopted by the U.S. State Department, the United Nations and, in modified form, by nearly all major Western news agencies.

Under the new system, China's capital, "Peking," becomes "Beijing," a spelling that more accurately reflects the standard Chinese pronunciation (Bay Jing).

"Peking," according to some reference books, was the spelling adopted by the Chinese post office in the 19th century for international use.

"Beijing" means "northern capital," and Chiang Kai-shek's Nationalist Chinese government, which had its capital elsewhere, sidelined the name in 1928 in favor of "Peiping" (pronounced Bay Ping). The Communists restored the traditional "Beijing" when they came to power in 1949, but in the political climate of the time, "Peiping" lingered for years in some Western publications before giving way to "Peking."

Shanghai's spelling does not change because it is the same in both systems, but Canton becomes Guangzhou, and Tientsin becomes Tianjin.

The name of China's premier and party chairman will be written Hua Guofeng instead of Hua Kuofeng (the new system eliminates the hyphens between the two given names), and the vice premier who dominated the news a few weeks ago as Teng Hsiao-ping becomes Deng Xiaoping.

Names of historical figures such as Confucious, Sun Yat-sen and Chiang Kai-shek will be written in their familiar forms, but Pinyin will be used for the late Chairman Mao Zedong (Mao Tse-tung) and the late Premier Zhou Enlai (Chou Enlai). The old spellings will be printed in parentheses for a time until the new spellings become well known.

Part of the problem with foreign spellings of Chinese words stems from the nature of Chinese writing, which uses one or more characters to represent a person, place or thing. The character, or ideogram, conveys the meaning, but not a particular sound, as an alphabetical writing system does. In fact, Chinese in different parts of China may pronounce characters differently if they speak different dialects.

Pinyin, which means spelling or transcription, is based on standard Mandarin as pronounced around Beijing.

Fables

Fable writing is a good way to have students produce short works that can be read aloud and revised in a single class session. I've found that a good way to introduce students to fables is to begin with a list of morals (which are proverbs). One way to begin is to list clichéd proverbs and ask students to vary them:

A stitch in time saves nine.
A stitch in time saves my old pants.

Too many cooks spoil the broth.
One cook is never enough for a banquet.

Then fables can be written that end with the morals generated. One teacher I worked with at Teachers and Writers Collaborative, Lila Eberman, used this technique as part of her approach to fable writing. Here are notes on her two introductory lessons that she made for the Collaborative:

Two Lessons Introducing a Unit on the Fable
(Taught at Benjamin Franklin High School to two tenth-grade classes of children in the College Bound program. There are 17 pupils in each class.)

I decided to begin the unit by giving for homework an assignment to copy down everything the students saw written on walls, sidewalks, subway posters, on their way home from school that day. Both classes responded by laughing:

"Everything?"
"You don't mind foul words?"
"There's a *lot* of poets on my block!"
"Where should I look when I read them?"
  (aloud in class the next day)
"Your mind's goin' to conk out."

One boy remarked that he knew that there was a name for these writings but couldn't remember what it was. I told the class it was "graffiti" and wrote the word on the board. The boy then said that he thought that there was a man doing a book on graffiti—was this for that book? I told him that it wasn't, but that we were going to use the graffiti for a lesson. The general feeling among the students was that it was an unusual homework assignment, but they were enthusiastic about doing it.

Lesson 1
    The aim of this first lesson was to get across the idea of people expressing thoughts and feelings through writing. First there was a recitation of the graffiti they had seen. All were anxious to read what they had copied down—but they did not want to read the most vulgar. We then discussed the reasons that people write on walls, the general conclusion being that the writers wanted to reach a wide audience. We made a frequency chart describing the subject matter of the writing:

Love messages (real and puppy love)/insults (to the reader and others)/bragging/humor/politics/foul language/sex/hatred/the truth about people/identification of territory

As to the type of language used—the pupils said that slang or "hip" language was used because everyone understands it. After the discussion, I told them that they could go over to the blackboards and write whatever they wanted. One class jumped right up, but the other class was slightly shy and didn't begin until I had personally given each student a piece of chalk. They all enjoyed themselves finally, laughing, talking, and reading one another's graffiti. Here are some of the results:

Your mother plays drums
With the midnight bums

Your father is a nice lady

False teeth are what's happening

Your father works in the
marqueta

Your mother sells shopping
bags in Spanish Macy's

Your mother plays shortstop
for the hunchback dodgers

Edwin dont wash He crusty

Irving is a whiteman

The junkies are coming

Your mother wears Bozo
getaways

Edwin eats chitlens

Junky go home

Larry is a hippy

Edward takes LSD

Hitler and Charlie Chan
were brothers

All of these turned out to be in the category of insults, but the humor and imagery are quite imaginative. One pupil remarked that the writings reminded him of buttons he's seen around.

After they sat down, I showed them the covers given out by the Teachers and Writers Collaborative behind which they were to keep their writing. On the front is a photo of a written and drawn-over wall. I suggested that if they wanted to, they could turn the sheet over and make their own wall and use *it* for the cover. I was then asked whether we could have a paper put up on the bulletin board on which the students could write. I agreed that it was a good idea.

After some thought I decided that this lesson, although it bore little relevance to fable writing, was a good one in which to present the idea that original or creative writing by "ordinary" people—young people especially—is fun and interesting to do and to read. In this, I feel, is the value of a lesson of this type.

Lesson 2

In this lesson I wanted to introduce fable writing to the class. I put on the board "All that glitters is not gold" (because it was the first one I thought of) and began by asking the class what kind of statement this was. They said that it was a proverb or saying or moral, which was defined by the pupils as something that tells you about life so that you learn something, so that you don't make the same mistake. It tries to teach you a lesson.

The students gave examples of other proverbs that they knew and we listed them on the board and discussed each one. They came up with the most common—Don't put all your eggs. . . . Don't count your chickens. . . . You scratch my back. . . . etc. One student contributed an original:

"Do unto others' mothers before others' mothers do unto you." One boy remarked that these sayings were not always true—for instance, regarding "counting chickens," he always does chores for his mother and he figures out beforehand how much money he'll earn and how he is going to spend the money—and he is usually right.

I then asked the students to choose a proverb and make up a story to illustrate it. After writing, they read the stories aloud and handed them in. Because the class meets for a double period (about 90 minutes), the pupils were able to complete the assignment and read their fables during the course of one class meeting. Even though the choice of proverbs was fairly small (8–10) there was a lot of interest in writing and in listening to each other's fables.

Of course, there are many different ways to approach the teaching of fables. Elna Wertzel, a sixth-grade teacher who also worked with the Collaborative, plunged directly into reading different variations of the same fable to her class. Here's her diary, as well as samples of some of her students' writing:

Notes on Fable Lesson #1

The purpose of this first lesson was to concentrate on stories which end with a moral, or as I called it, a "message."

I wanted to emphasize that the messages did not have to conform to "good thought" or "good behavior" usually demanded of children. Therefore I told the following three stories.

Story I (in summary)—Peter Rabbit goes out to play. His mother says, "Don't go in Mr. McGregor's cabbage patch." He plays around and is finally tempted into the cabbage patch. He enjoys it, eats cabbages, and falls asleep. Mr. McGregor captures him. At the last moment he escapes.

I asked the class what message we could add as a last line on this story. Many hands went up. Everyone seemed pleased to feel that he knew the message.

The Messages:
1. Now listen you guys, don't go outside without your mother and father.
2. When your mother says don't go in the cabbage patch, don't go in the cabbage patch—and don't you forget it.
3. Stay out of cabbage patches.
4. Keep out of other people's property.
5. Don't go where your mother says not to.

Story II Peter Rabbit—same beginning as above. Once again Peter Rabbit is tempted to go into the cabbage patch. He plays around, eats cabbages, and begins to feel sleepy. Then he says, "Boy, I'm not going to be a dumb bunny and fall asleep in the cabbage patch!" So he sneaks out again, sleeps somewhere else, and finally goes home. "What have you been doing?" asks his mother. "Oh, nothing," he replies.

I asked the class what message we could add on as a last line. The children were somewhat confused, as the usual moral was not so clear to them.

Someone said, "You shouldn't tell lies to your mother." I asked if that was what the story taught us. She said no.

Several other children wanted to add on to the story so that something bad would happen to Peter Rabbit so that we could then have the ending, "You shouldn't tell lies to your mother."

I told them to try to stick to the story just as I had told it. Was there any message in that story? Two children volunteered,

1. Be smart enough not to stay in the cabbage patch.
2. Be smart enough not to fall asleep in the cabbage patch.

When I waited after those two, one child said plaintively, "We can't think of any more."

I said all right, we could go on to the third and last story. Then I mentioned that I thought the story said the opposite of what some of them had been trying to say. I thought it said something like this: "It's OK to do what your mother tells you not to, as long as you don't get caught."

They looked at me in mystification.

Story III—Same beginning as above. Once in the cabbage patch, Peter Rabbit finds a treasure chest full of gold, takes it home, tells his mother where he found it, buys her a new dress, the family goes to Coney Island and has a ball. As they are going to bed, Mother Rabbit says, "Isn't our Peter a wonderful little rabbit!"

This time there were a lot of hands with messages.

1. Finders keepers.
2. What people lose, you find, you keep.
3. Sometimes doing what your mother tells you not to do is OK because you might find money.

I asked the class if they would like to try to write stories with a message. They were eager. I asked if many wanted to use a fairytale person and they did. So we listed some familiar names on the board —Cinderella, Three Bears, Rapunzel, etc. I said they could make their character do anything at all. If it helped them, they could pick a message from those we had listed on the board. A couple of boys did not want to use fairytale characters and I urged them to make up any character at all that they wanted to.

Two of the papers follow with the student's uncorrected spelling:

Juan Bobo

One day Juan Bobo was looking for a job and he found one. His job was peeling banabas and they told him to peel the bananas and throw the cakasas away but then the bananas away the took the cacaras and them they hit him and threw him out of his job then he went to his mother house his mother was going out to the movies and he said o.k. and his mother told him when the baby cries give him milk and when the pig cry

took put him out side and she went, he sat down and them the baby cry
he forgot when they told him and put a injection and keeled the baby he
told the slep but the baby was dead. And them the pig cry he forgot that
she siad that the said o.k. pig I'll send you to your mother and you know
what, he put all the gold purse on the pig and sent him a lone to the
movie and he fell in a mud and was very dirty and when she came threw
him out of the window and he went to a orange tree and ate 30 oranges
and them ate 25 nuts, 30 pears and bananas and he drink whiskey and got
so drunk, he climb a tree. The tree was about 300 feet and he touch he
was in a swing and jumped and killed himself.

So remember, don't eat to much.

The Three Bears

Once there were three bears, Papa Bear and Mama Bear and Baby. And
mama did a soup.

Pap Bears soup to hot and Baby Bear was hot to, so Papa Bear and
Mama Bear and Baby Bear went out for a walk. While the three bears
was out for a walk a girl came to their house, the name of the girl was
Goldilock and she tasted Papa Bear's soup and it was too hot, she tasted
Mama Bear's soup, and it was to hot, so she tasted Baby Bear's soup and
it was just right. And then she fell sleepy and up to bed and she try papa's
bed and she said, "It was to hard, and she tried mama's bed and it was to
soft, and then she tried baby bear's bed and she said that bed was just
right. And then while Goldilocks was sleeping, the three bears went on
their way to eat their lunch. And when they got home, Papa Bear said,
"Somebody was eating my soup, so what said Mama Bear somebody was
eating my soup and somebody was eating my soup to and they heard a
noise in their bedroom and they ran up and saw Goldilocks, and she was
sleeping in Baby Bears's bed, when she saw the bears, she got out of bed
and ran down the stairs as fast as she could.

Boys and girls, never go to someone's house without permission.

Fable Lesson #2

After the first lesson I wanted to get the children away from messages
which they knew to be all right, safe, what mothers and teachers had
been telling them all their lives. And I wanted to lead them into more
original stories.

Formally, I wanted to concentrate next on the idea that a moral can
be symbolic, not necessarily literal, to prepare them to hear some fables
read to them.

The visit of the fireman to the school was too good an opportunity to
pass up, and so that same day, after seeing the fire prevention movie, I
asked them to write a story with the moral "Don't Play with Fire." This
was of course a literal message. The stories follow:

I am a little boy. I play with fire. I love fire, do you? No you can get
burned. I still like fire. One day I will set the park on fire and burn a bird
and I did set the park on fire and burn a bird but I could not get out of the
park in time so I got burned and got killed.

So don't play with fire.

This is what Happened in my Block

I went to my friend's house and I came in. She was playing with matches and I told her to put them away and she did and I was going and then she took them and took a newspaper and the paper was on fire and she was laughing and the whole house was on fire and she tried to open the door. The door was locked and she opened the door and she ran she went to my house and she said My house is on fire. And I told her don't ever play with matches and she said I will never play with matches and then her mother came in. What are you doing here? And she said There is a fire in the house and her mother said And who did the fire? and she said I did it.

Don't never play with matches.
Don't play with fire.

Fable Lesson #3

After the class had read the "Don't Play with Fire" stories to each other, I asked them if fire was all bad. They decided no, that it had some good uses. We listed the good and bad qualities of fire:

good	bad
to cook	burn people
to keep warm	burn houses
to make steam	smoke suffocates
	destroys forests

Then I asked what other things they could think of which could be both good and bad. "Knife" and "gun" were named right away. The others named follow:

rifle	lion	boat
screwdriver	dog	submarine
hammer	leopard	spaceship
pen	porcupine	rocket
car	cat	brother
bus	elephant	mother
dynamite	robot	father
firecrackers	baseball & bat	teacher
torch	horse	sister
airplane	truck	

The children were interested all this time and it took about half an hour to compile this list. As we went through the people listed at the end I assured them that as a teacher I knew I had a good side and bad side, and that sometimes I was angry and spoke like fire. I said I imagined their parents were the same. I asked if there were any other people we hadn't mentioned who could be both good and bad. After going through uncles and nieces, and other distant relatives, someone jumped up and said "Us!" With that the lesson ended.

Unfortunately it was two days before we got back to this lesson, so a lot of the impetus was gone. However, I asked them to think back to our discussion, think how the things on the list could symbolically "burn" the way fire can burn you. Then I asked them to pick one thing from the list and make up a story in which someone gets "burned" symbolically. The moral was to be "don't play with fire" as a symbol. Real fire was not to be used in the stories.

As an example, I suggested a mouse who played around with a sleeping cat until the cat woke up and ate him. I asked what was the fire in the story—they got the idea. Some of the stories follow:

Once upon a time there was a mouse named Felix. He came out of a wall. He liked to play with Lion. He lived in the jungle. One day he was walking in the jungle. The Lion was asleep. The mouse came to him and pulled his nose and it went honk-honk and he awoke and he caught him. And the Lion said I will let you go but don't do it again. And the next day he thought he was brave and did it again and the Lion ate him up.

Moral: Don't play with fire.

Once upon a time there was a greedy germ that drink ink out of pens. He drank ink out of ten of my pens. Now I had a new pen and I put something in the ink that would kill him but it made him drink more of my ink. He like to squeeze into the pens to drink the ink. I bought a little pen. He squeezed in it and drank the ink and could not get out of the pen. He lived on ink but he could not get no more ink and he died.

Moral: Don't play with fire.

One day my father was in the street getting some sunshine so then came a man and said to my father Hey you. You want to fight? And my father said Why? And man said because I want to fight, that's all. And the man said if you fight with me sonny my man will kill you like a cat. You know, I'm coming tomorrow if you don't have ten dollars tomorrow morning at seven o'clock my man and me will kill you.

So my father didn't answer yes or no to the man. My father followed the man. The man went to his cave and my father found out the man was a crook so my father got a gun and went to his cave at 12 evening, when the man was alone. And my father told him HELLO Ramon I know you are a crook but now I'm going to kill you and I'm going to call the police right now after I kill you. And Ramon the crook said Please don't kill me. I don't want to die so young and my father said You're not so young you had 40 years BANG BANG Goodby Ramon remember don't play with fire.

Fable Lesson #4

At this point I still wanted to get into more personal subject matter, and decided to go into animal projections. After that, I thought the children would be ready to hear some Aesop and other animal fables, with a feeling for the characteristics of the animals and for the symbolism of the morals.

Introduction to animal stories

Teacher: Yesterday I heard one child in the class call someone else a rabbit, and that child called the first child a little mouse. (Giggles) That seemed to make both children very angry. (Giggles, finger pointing) Are there any other animal names that you know which make people angry?

Child:	Chicken!
Teacher:	What does it mean?
Child:	You're *afraid*.
Child:	Goat!
Teacher:	What does it mean?
Child:	That he eats *tin cans*, and don't get no food in his home.
Child:	Pig!
Teacher:	What does it mean?
Child:	He eats too much.
Child:	Hog!
Teacher:	What does it mean?
Child:	Like he makes a belch.
Child:	Rat!
Teacher:	What does it mean?
Child:	He eats too much.
Teacher:	Is that what rat means?
Several children:	Yes!
Child:	Skunk!
Teacher:	What does it mean?
Child:	He stinks.
Child:	(Whispering) Jackass.
Teacher:	Yes, jackass (in loud voice) (Giggles, embarrassment) What does jackass mean?
Child:	He's dumb.
Child:	Cat!
Teacher:	What does it mean?
Child:	That's Felix (boy in room). Felix the cat.
Teacher:	They don't all have to be insults. Are there some that you would like to be called?
Child:	Tiger!
Teacher:	What does it mean?
Child:	That he's the toughest guy on the block.
Child:	Bird!
Teacher:	What does it mean?
Child:	Like Bird Man. That's a guy on television.

Teacher: Now everybody is going to become one animal. You can pick any animal at all in the whole world. You're going to write a story as though you were that animal, and you had always been that animal.

Begin your story "I am . . ." and tell something about yourself. Then tell an adventure you had. You can start the second part something like this: "One day . . ."

I did not ask for fables or morals, but two children added on morals anyway. In several other connections the children started sticking morals onto things they were writing. One of these was a project in which everyone in the class wrote a letter to whomever had been stealing pens, pencils, and money in the classroom. Johnny wrote:

Dear Unknown Person:
    Do not steal no more because that is very bad and God sins you and you get hit. And you know that you took pencils and pens so give up.
    Don't steal fire.

Bouncing-ball Rhymes and Games

These games and others in these chapters have passed from one generation of children to another. However, I've observed recently that children play many fewer song and poem games. There seems to be a greater discontinuity between children of different ages than there was when I grew up in the 1940s. Perhaps it is due to TV, or to the number of manufactured toys and games children have. Or it might be that the streets are meaner in the city and the opportunity for casual play practically nonexistent in the suburbs. In any case it would be a great impoverishment of children's lives if play with rhymes and songs were lost. In addition to the fun they provide, they stretch the mind and imagination, extend verbal facility, and give every child an opportunity to invent his or her own verses and chant them in public without inhibition. For these reasons it makes sense to introduce them into the classroom, to collect rhymes and tape songs, to play the games with the students, and to encourage them to play them with each other and invent their own variations. In the following sections I'll present some variations created in class as well as those that arose in the context of spontaneous play.

Jump-rope Rhymes

There is a dictionary of *Jump-Rope Rhymes* edited by Roger D. Abrahams (Austin: University of Texas Press, 1969) that gives 619 jump-rope rhymes, all arranged alphabetically. The book is a decent source of rhymes. Another way to collect rhymes is to ask your friends, your students, your parents, and your students' parents and grandparents for jump-rope rhymes they know. Just about everybody has some to swap and an anthology of jump-rope rhymes is easy to print up and use as a reading text. (The word anthology is derived from the Greek *anthos*, "flower," and *legein*, "to gather" or "to pick up," and means a gathering or bouquet of flowers, something you might want to share with your students when introducing the idea of putting an anthology together.)

It's fun to create and use jump-rope rhymes as well as swap and record them. A simple way to start is to make up a few couplets that lead to counting and suggest that your students elaborate on them. Here are a few that were made up by some young people:

I went downtown to buy a coat
But I got bit by a goat
How many times did it bite?
1, 2, 3, . . .

Batman tried to beat my butt
But I just beat him up
How many times did I hit him?
1, 2, 3, . . .

Memory-response Games

This game helps develop thinking about images, and builds a facility with the use of adjectives. It's possible to restrict the rules so that the images aren't strictly arbitrary and nonsense. One way to do this is to make it possible for a player to challenge the image maker to give some generally reasonable explication of any image used.

Cipher Systems

Keys are crucial when introducing secret codes to students. If you teach codes and give the impression that you can decipher all the codes you teach, the power of passing secret messages is taken away from students. However, without the key it's impossible to know which cipher system is being used, and therefore impossible (of course, with a computer and sophisticated mathematical techniques you might succeed) to decipher a message. Two students can decide on a key and pass messages that others can't decipher even if they have a general sense of the kind of cipher systems that might be used.

Simple Substitution Codes

Remember that with the Alberti disk you can change the outer disk in any way you want—put symbols on it, or use dots and dashes or numbers. Giving students a blank outer disk to fill in is an easy way to encourage them to make up an original code.

Binary Ciphers

Several other ways of using the binary cipher are: (1) have students use other pairs of symbols to dress up the cipher. Here are a few pairs students have used:

This can even be abbreviated, as one student did, to

(2) use a series of five lights and switches to send messages using the binary cipher:

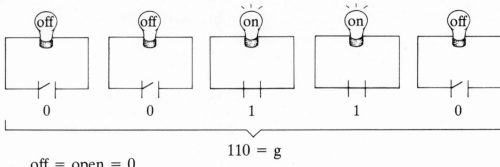

$$110 = g$$

off = open = 0
on = closed = 1

Codes

As a final exercise with codes, students could find out about the following:

> color-coding of electrical wiring
> coding of products in the supermarkets
> codes or computer languages and how they are developed
> ZIP Codes and area codes, and how they are developed
> parking lot codes, seating codes in stadiums
> legal codes, and how they resemble secret codes

There is also a simple guessing game using partial codes that you can play with students. The object of the game is to figure out the meaning of the following equations:

$$1. \ S + M + T + W + T + F + S = W$$
$$2. \ R + O + Y + G + B + I + V = R$$
$$3. \ M + NH + V + M + RI + C = NE$$
$$4. \ 3J + 2A = FH$$
$$5. \ JL + PM + GH + RS = B$$
$$6. \ S + S + G + H + D + D + B = 7D$$

Answers:

6. 7D = The 7 Dwarfs
5. B = Beetles (letters are initials)
4. FH = full house (3 Jacks and 2 Aces)
3. NE = New England (letters are the states)
2. R = rainbow (letters are the primary colors)
1. W = week (letters are the days)

Students can also make up their own equations and set them as puzzles for the class.

Hieroglyphics

In conjunction with learning a bit about hieroglyphics it's possible to make up new pictographic systems for recording ideas and stories. Here are three stories told in symbols from writing systems invented by elementary school students who studied a bit of hieroglyphics:

1.

What   do   you   mean   I'm   fat?   Look   at   you.

2.

Respect   northern   California   wildlife.

3.

I   am sad   in   war   because people die.

Adinkra Fabric Symbols

A poster containing over fifty Adinkra symbols and the proverbs they represent is available from the Coastal Ridge Center, P.O. Box 243, Point Arena, CA 95468, for $3.00.

Several teachers have used the posters to stimulate their students to come up with sayings of their own and turn them into visual images which were cut into linoleum blocks and used as fabric stamps. Here are two of the results:

1. Always think before you open a door.

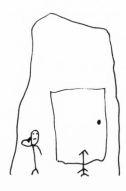

2. When you're fighting, watch out because someone may hit you from behind.

A Cheyenne Letter

It's interesting to ask children to draw a picture that tells the story of one of their favorite songs. Often the songs have themes that can be represented in one visual image and it's a lot of fun trying to capture that image. Here are a few we've managed to collect:

Working at the car wash   Shake, shake, shake your boodie

Comic Books

It is possible to develop tales of the origins of mythical figures thought up in class. Where did they come from? How did they get their powers? Do they have connections with their old lives? All these questions help create characters in depth and make future adventure stories more than imitations of the latest TV serial.

There are other uses of origin themes. Young children enjoy making up wild explanations for things when given the opportunity. Here are a few specific types of tales that lead to interesting writing and drawing:

1. "Why are . . . ?" tales, i.e., why are owls creatures of the night? Why are there stars? Why are there so many animals? Why is there night and day? Why does it rain?

2. "Why is there . . . ?" tales, i.e., why is there hair? Why is there love? Hate? Laughter? Tears?

3. "Why do . . . ?" tales, i.e., why do people live in the air and fish in the water? Why do animals let themselves be tamed by people? Why do

people stop growing? Why do living things die?

4. "Why don't . . . ?" stories, i.e., why don't animals talk? Why don't people fly? Why don't trees walk? Why don't stones cry?

Some other things to discuss in connection with creating comics are:

secret identities
the development of families for the characters
love interests
the setting for the story in time and space
superpowers: how they are used and how they are limited
designing costumes
making weak points in all the characters so there is some tension in the
    story
supervillains—developing worthy opponents
developing allies, people to work with, groups like the League of
    Justice and the Blackhawks
developing a "to be continued" story that maintains interest from
    episode to episode

Acknowledgments

Iona and Peter Opie. *The Oxford Nursery Rhyme Book,* assembled by Iona and Peter Opie. © Iona and Peter Opie, 1955. Reprinted by permission of Oxford University Press.

Howard W. Bergerson. *Palindromes and Anagrams.* Copyright © by Dover Publications, Inc., New York, 1973. Used by permission of the publisher.

John Fisher. *The Magic of Lewis Carroll.* Copyright © 1973 by John Fisher. Reprinted by permission of Simon & Schuster, a Division of Gulf & Western Corporation.

Dmitri Borgman. From *Language on Vacation* by Dmitri Borgman. Copyright © 1965 by Dmitri A. Borgman. Reprinted by permission of Charles Scribner's Sons.

Jacob S. Orleans and Selma R. Orleans. *Pencil Puzzles,* copyright © 1974 by Jacob S. Orleans and Selma R. Orleans. Reprinted by permission of Grosset & Dunlap, Inc.

Mad Libs #1. Used by permission of Price/Stern/Sloan Publishers, Inc., Los Angeles (publishers).

Joan McCreary. By permission of Gamesemag and the Center for Open Learning and Teaching, Berkeley, Calif.

Mike Sensena and Scott Garner. By permission of Gamesmag and the Center for Open Learning and Teaching, Berkeley, Calif.

Iona and Peter Opie. From *The Lore and Language of Schoolchildren.* © Iona and Peter Opie, 1959. Reprinted by permission of Oxford University Press.

Tom Wilson. Ziggy.

Eugene P. Northrop. *Riddles in Mathematics: A Book of Paradoxes.* Copyright © 1944 by Eugene P. Northrop. Published by D. Van Nostrand Company, Inc., New York. Used by permission of Mrs. Eugene P. Northrop.

Mary Ann Madden. *Thank You for the Giant Sea Tortoise,* edited by Mary Ann Madden. Copyright © by Mary Ann Madden, 1971. Published by Lancer Books, New York. Used by permission of Mary Ann Madden.

David Le Count. "A Selected Table of Contents to an Imaginative Journal," used by permission of David Le Count.

Allen Ginsberg. "What sphinx of cement 'to' imagination," from *Howl, Part II.* Copyright © 1956, 1959, by Allen Ginsberg. Reprinted by permission of City Lights Books.

Wallace Stevens. *The Collected Poems of Wallace Stevens.* Copyright © 1954, Alfred A. Knopf, Inc. (publisher).

Emily Dickinson. *The Complete Poems of Emily Dickinson,* edited by Thomas H. Johnson. Permission to reprint Poem #254 given by Little, Brown and Company. Copyright © by Thomas H. Johnson, 1960.

Sarah Cleghorn. From *Portraits and Protests* by Sarah Cleghorn, published by Holt, Rinehart and Winston.

Langston Hughes. "A Dream Deferred" from *The Panther and The Lash.* Copyright © 1959 by Langston Hughes. Reprinted by permission of Harold Ober Associates, Incorporated. Published by Alfred A. Knopf, Inc.

Wystan Hugh Auden. "The Unknown Citizen" from *W. H. Auden: Collected Poems,* edited by Mendelson. Copyright © 1976 Mendelson. Reprinted by permission of Random House, Inc.

Harold Courlander. Material from *A Treasury of African Folklore.* Copyright © 1975 by Harold Courlander. Used by permission of Crown Publishers, Inc., New York (publishers).

M. J. Herskovits and F. S. Herskovits. Material from *Dahomean Narrative.* Used by permission of Northwestern University Press (publisher).

Stith Thompson. Material from *The Folktale.* Copyright © 1946 by Stith Thompson. Published by Holt, Rinehart and Winston, New York. Used by permission of the publisher.

Peter Farb. *Word Play: What Happens When People Talk.* Copyright © 1974 by Peter Farb. Permission to use excerpt from book given by Alfred A. Knopf, Inc. (publisher).

A. H. M. Kirk-Greene. Material from *Hausa Ba Dabo Ba Ne.* Copyright © A. H. M. Kirk-Greene, 1966. Reprinted by permission of Oxford University Press, Ibadan.

Isaac O. Delano. Material from *Owe L'Esin Oro—Yoruba Proverbs*. Copyright © Isaac O. Delano, 1966. Reprinted by permission of Oxford University Press, Ibadan.

Hanan J. Ayalti. Excerpts from *Yiddish Proverbs,* edited by Hanan J. Ayalti. Copyright © 1949, renewed © 1976, by Schocken Books, Inc. Reprinted by permission of Schocken Books, Inc.

James Thurber. "The Rabbits Who Caused All the Trouble" from *Fables for Our Time.* Copyright © 1940, 1952 by James Thurber. Copyright © 1968 by Helen Thurber. Published by Harper and Row. Originally printed in *The New Yorker*.

Len Jenkin. "*Birds, Beasts and Bat.*" Reprinted with permission of Len Jenkin and the Teachers & Writers Collaborative, New York.

Grace Paley. "The Sad Story about the Six Boys About to be Drafted in Brooklyn." Used by permission of Grace Paley.

Claudia Zaslavsky. Material from *Africa Counts*. Copyright © 1973 by Claudia Zaslavsky. Reprinted by permission of Prindle, Weber, & Schmidt (publishers).

William Wells Newell. *Games and Songs of American Children,* collected and compared by William Wells Newell. Copyright © 1963. Published by Dover Publications, Inc., New York.

Jesse Stuart. *The Thread That Runs So True*. Copyright © 1949, 1970 by Jesse Stuart. Reprinted by permission of Charles Scribner's Sons.

Esther Nelson. Material from *Dancing Games*. Copyright © 1973 by Esther Nelson. Used by permission of Sterling Publishing Co., Inc. (publishers).

Richard Chase. *Singing Games and Playparty Games,* compiled by Richard Chase. Copyright © 1967 Richard Chase. Dover Publications, Inc., New York.

I. J. Gelb. Reprinted from *A Study of Writing* by permission of the University of Chicago Press. Copyright 1952 in the International Copyright Union. All rights reserved. Published 1952. Second Edition 1963. First Phoenix Impression 1963. Printed in the United States of America.

Tom B. Underwood. *The Story of the Cherokee People*. Copyright © 1961 by Tom B. Underwood. Published by Cherokee Publications. Reprinted by permission of Tom B. Underwood.

Garrick Mallery. *Picture-Writing of the American Indians*. Published by Dover Publications, Inc. "Two Lessons Introducing a Unit on the Fable," used by permission of the Teachers and Writers Collaborative, New York.

The Oxford University Press for permission to reprint material from *The Shorter Oxford English Dictionary*.

Word Ways and Maxey Brooke for permission to reprint "A Complex of Compounds" by Maxey Brooke. Copyright © 1978 by Word Ways.

Word Ways and A. Ross Eckler and Dover Publications, Inc., for permission to reprint "Mary Had a Lipogram" by A. Ross Eckler. Copyright © 1969 by *Word Ways*. Reprinted in *Word Recreations* by Dover Publications, Inc. Copyright © 1979 by Dover Publications, Inc.

Word Ways for permission to reprint "Super Titles" by Temple G. Porter. Copyright © 1968 by *Word Ways*.

Harper & Row, Publishers, Inc., for permission to reprint excerpts from an article by Charles Frances Potter appearing in *Funk & Wagnalls Standard Dictionary of Folklore, Mythology, and Legend* (copyright 1972).

The Chronicle Publishing Company for permission to reprint "New Chinese Spellings—It Isn't 'Peking' Anymore." © San Francisco Chronicle, 1979.

Index

Abrahams, Roger D., 250, 276
additions, 46–48
  defined, 40
Adinkra fabric symbols, 235–236, 279–280
Aesop, 166
Africa Counts (Zaslavsky), 183, 250
alazon, 123
Alberti disk, 205, 277
Alice in Wonderland (Carroll), 102
Almanac of Words at Play, An (Espy), 249
alphabet, Indian, 233
alphabets:
  Caesar's, 205
  cipher, 203–206
  see also comic alphabets
Altschuler, Ira, 196
anagram, derivation of, 24
anagrams, 24–28
  antigram type of, 27–28
  of names, 26–27
  word vs. phrase, 26
anthology, derivation of, 276
Arnold, Benedict, 214–215
A-to-M and N-to-Z words, 4
A to Z words, 3
Auden, W. H., 120, 121, 138–139
Ayalti, Haman J., 165

bad mixers, 20
Bamum Script, 233
Bergerson, Howard, 26
Bird in Hand Is Worth Two in the Bus,
  A, 106–107
Blake, William, 120
Borgmann, Dmitri, 27, 48–49
bouncing-ball rhymes and games, 180–181, 276
Brecht, George, 250
Brooke, Maxley, 58
Brown, Theresa, 174
Budge, E. A. Wallis, 228
building words, 6
buried words, 21–23

Caesar, Julius, 205
Carew, Thomas, 120
Carroll, Lewis, 249
  anagrams created by, 26
  ciphers invented by, 211–212
  doublets developed by, 44–45
  paradox created by, 105
  riddles written by, 158–160
  semordnilaps named by, 24

cartoons, paradoxes in, 103
Chain of Death (Grant), 208
Chappell, L. W., 148
Chase, Richard, 188
Che Che Koole, 187–188
Chemasit, 195–196
Cheyenne letter, 237–239, 280
Children's Games in Street and Play-ground (Opie), 250
Chinese character writing, 239–241
Churchill, Winston, 216
ciphers, 203–214, 277–278
  binary, 210–211, 277–278
  Carroll's, 211–212
  codes vs., 204
  Shadow, 207–208
  transposition, 213–214
  triangle, 208–209
Cleghorn, Sarah, 138
Codebreakers, The (Kahn), 203, 216, 249
codes, 214–218, 277–278
  backward substitution, 203, 204
  basic vocabulary used for, 203–204
  ciphers vs., 204
  development of, 217–218
  grid, 206–207
  key-word substitution, 206
  single-shift, 204–205
  in World War II, 216
Codes, Ciphers and Secret Writing (Gardner), 208, 249
combinations, 20–40, 255
  anagrams as, 24–36
  buried words as, 21–22
  catchy, 83–86
  defined, 20
  grids as, 28–36
  mazes as, 36–40
  palindromes as, 23–24
  word interlocks as, 22–23
comic alphabets, 15–20, 254–255
  Nelson's, 15–16
  phonetic, 18–20
  puns in, 18–20
  rhymed, 15–16
  story, 16–18
  Swift's, 18
Comic Alphabets (Partridge), 251
comic books, 243–248, 280–281
  superheroes in, 246–247
compounding words, 58–61
constructions, simple, 55–56, 262–263
Corlander, Harold, 146, 156
crossword puzzles, 73–83, 263–264

cryptanalysis, defined, 203
Culin, Stewart, 197

Dahomean Narrative (Herskovits), 147
dancing games, 185–194
  in Appalachia, 185–187
  in Ghana, 187–188
Dancing Games (Nelson), 187
definitions, games with, 65–66
Delano, Isaac O., 165
deletions, 48–50
  defined, 41
diagram stories, 241–243
Dickinson, Emily, 135–136
dictionary game, 114
distortion, preliminary, 95–96
Donne, John, 122
doublets, 44–45
  see also transpositions

Eckler, A. Ross, 22, 61–63
Egyptian Language (Budge), 228
eiron, 123–124
Espy, Willard R., 249
euphemisms, 68–71

fables, 166–175, 267–276
Fables for Our Time (Thurber), 170
Farb, Peter, 151
figures of speech, 117–141
  see also specific figures of speech
Filliou, Robert, 250
Fisher, John, 44, 249
Fish Fry, 75
folklore, 148–149
Folktale, The (Thompson), 149
Foster, Franklin, 171
Fowler, H. W., 68
From Poland, With Love, 106

Games, 83, 249
games, warm-up, 3–12, 253–254
Games and Puzzles, 22, 83, 249
Games and Songs of American Children (Newell), 184, 250
Games at the Cedilla (Brecht and Filliou), 250–251
Gamesmag, 224
Games of the North American Indians (Culin), 197
Gardner, Martin, 208, 249
Garner, Scott, 96
Gea, Donald, 174
Gelb, I. J., 237, 241, 251
Ginsberg, Allen, 123